HOW TO DEVELOP SELF-ESTEEM IN YOUR CHILD:
6 Vital Ingredients

OTHER WORKS BY BETTIE B. YOUNGS

BOOKS

Stress in Children, Avon Books, 1985

Helping Your Teenager Deal with Stress, Tarcher/St. Martin's Press, 1986

A Stress Management Guide for Young People, Learning Tools, 1986

Problem Solving Skills for Children, Learning Tools, 1990

Achievement, Happiness, Popularity and Success: A Self-Esteem Book for Young People, Phoenix Foundation, 1988

Is Your Net-Working? A Complete Guide to Building Contacts and Career Visibility, John Wiley & Sons, 1989

Friendship Is Forever, Isn't It?, Learning Tools, 1990

Goal Setting Skills for Young Adults, Learning Tools, 1990

Getting Back Together: Creating a New Relationship with Your Partner and Making It Last, Bob Adams, Inc., 1990

AUDIOCASSETTES

The Six Vital Components of Self-Esteem and How to Develop Them in Your Child, Sybervision, 1990

Helping Children Manage Anxiety, Pressure, and Stress, Sybervision, 1991

Developing Responsibility in Children, Sybervision, 1991

Helping Your Teenager Deal with Stress, Learning Tools, 1987

How to Raise Happy, Healthy, Self-Confident Children, Nightengale/ Conant, 1990

HOW TO DEVELOP SELF-ESTEEM IN YOUR CHILD:
6 Vital Ingredients

(Formerly titled *The 6 Vital Ingredients of Self-Esteem and How to Develop Them in Your Child*)

Bettie B. Youngs, Ph.D., Ed.D.

Fawcett Columbine • New York

A Fawcett Columbine Book
Published by Ballantine Books

This edition published by arrangement with Rawson
Associates, an imprint of Macmillan Publishing Company.

Library of Congress Catalog Card Number: 92-90389

ISBN: 0-449-90687-6

Cover design by Sheryl Kagen
Cover photo by Ken Randall

Manufactured in the United States of America
First Ballantine Books Edition: January 1993

10 9 8 7 6

To my mom and dad,
Arlene and Everett Burres—
and my sisters and brothers,
Judy, Mark, Kevin, Tim,
and Laurie—and, of course,
my beloved daughter Jennifer

CONTENTS

3

SAFETY: DOES YOUR CHILD REALLY FEEL SAFE AT HOME?   30

4

PHYSICAL SAFETY: DOES YOUR CHILD FEEL SAFE AT SCHOOL?   47

5

SAFETY: SAFEGUARDING YOUR CHILDREN FROM ALCOHOL AND DRUGS

6

EMOTIONAL SECURITY: BUILDING YOUR CHILD'S EMOTIONAL SENSE OF SELF

7

EMOTIONAL SECURITY: WHAT YOU SHOULD KNOW ABOUT YOUR CHILD'S FEARS

8

EMOTIONAL SECURITY: CAN YOUR CHILD COUNT ON YOU?

9

EMOTIONAL SECURITY: SKILLS FOR EMOTIONAL WELL-BEING   *124*

10

"WHO AM I?": HELPING YOUR CHILD ANSWER THE QUESTION   *144*

11

FEELING SPECIAL: YOUR CHILD'S SEARCH FOR SELF

12

AFFILIATION: THE BELONGINGNESS NEEDS

13

BELONGINGNESS: HELPING YOUR CHILD MAKE AND SUSTAIN FRIENDSHIPS

14

COMPETENCE: HELPING YOUR CHILD FEEL CAPABLE

15

COMPETENCE: UNDERSTANDING YOUR CHILD'S WORLD OF WORK

16

COMPETENCE: SKILLS FOR HELPING YOUR CHILD FEEL CAPABLE

17

MISSION: HELPING YOUR CHILD DEVELOP A SENSE OF IT

18

GETTING THERE: HELPING YOUR CHILD SET AND ACHIEVE (WORTHWHILE) GOALS

19

HOW DO YOU FEEL ABOUT BEING A PARENT?

ACKNOWLEDGMENTS

I respectfully recognize the work of colleagues Robert Ball, Nathaniel Branden, Jack Canfield, Stephen Covey, Connie Dembrowsky, Gail Dusa, LeRoy Foster, Egil Hjertaker, Hanoch McCarty, Robert Muller, Bob Reasoner, Brad Winch, the late great humanitarians Virginia Satir and Carl Rogers, and the many others whose beliefs, work, and dedicated research in the field of self-esteem have helped to raise our consciousness of what it means to be human. The importance of their contributions in this, our life's journey, is enormous. Their role modeling of self-efficacy and self-esteem is exemplified in their own lives and amplified in the way they respect and esteem others.

Writing this book has come at a time when I faced a most difficult challenge, forcing me to examine the very core of my own self-esteem, most especially in the area of affiliation—the belongingness needs. As I searched inwardly for the lessons and teachings I thought I was to learn, friends circled around to envelop me and provided a shield of strength and a source of love that was both nourishing and heartwarming; the kindness and depth of friendship they brought were like nothing I had ever known before. What began as a time of pain was transformed into an illuminating and glorious time of faith, friends, and frolic. It could not have been more timely.

Space doesn't permit me to mention all who deserve to be included, but among those who offered care and rooted for my well-being were Jaime and Sam Ramey, whose heartfelt support was cherished throughout—no finer friends exist. To the special friendship and strength of Rick Torres, whom I admire immensely. To friends of integrity, Dianne and Ure Kretowicz, Sharon Mulligan, Jim Gordon, Vic and Bev Risling, Greg and Julia Kubicek, Dale Halaway, Brian Klemmer, Fran and Peter Bilicki, Sr., Jeff Mangum, Jim Berson, Stephen Fox, Tommy Dobran, and Geoff Mann, who offered encouragement and provided perspective. To Day and Lee at Lion-in-the-Sun, who showered my home with the most gorgeous flowers in the world. To precious and life-giving moments shared with Laura Stacey and newborn Christine. To friends like Joanie Marx, Mary Louise Martin, Barbara Retsky, Steve Smith, Andrew Miller, Susanna Palomares, John Wingo, Sharon and Jerry Wrobel, Robin Blanc, Helice Bridges, Dave Leadingham, and Lynn Campbell, who all insisted that I make time for them and didn't let me give excuses—I appreciate that. To a great friend, Mel Davis, and the can-do efforts of Jim Doan, Toni Fulciniti, and Joel Maiman—all exuded grace under pressure. To Peter Pavone, period! To Tommy Groff, Bill De Leeuw, and Paul Thoryk, whose mission was to make me have fun throughout it all—and who, with their shenanigans and the dancing we did till dawn, succeeded!

Love to two special soulmates: My lifelong friend and companion, Dic Youngs, who has always encouraged and believed in me and provided emotional support along the way. He is the father of our darling daughter Jennifer, whose life and love have taught me the most about self-esteem: She has always had a direct line to my heart and soul. I am a better person because Dic and Jennifer have been an interdependent part of my life. They are a vital source of inspiration.

Special thanks to super agents Julie Castiglia and Bill Gladstone at Waterside and to my publisher, Eleanor Rawson, whose loving encouragement and tough professionalism on this work made it both meaningful and joyful.

I lovingly acknowledge my parents, Everett and Arlene Burres, and my five brothers and sisters, to whom this book is dedicated. Their sense of fairness, strength of character, time-honored values, and unconditional caring and loving have always been a powerful force in my life, wherever I am on the globe, making it clear that the heart of a healthy family always moves to reclaim its own.

And to Roger Norman, whose playful heart, sense of humor, and endearing love helped me rediscover the child within and, best of all, was my playmate.

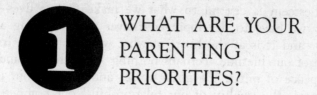

WHAT ARE YOUR PARENTING PRIORITIES?

○ THE CARE AND NURTURING OF SELF-ESTEEM IS SERIOUS STUFF

Self-esteem. The word is used a lot these days, but what does it really mean?

- What detracts from or enhances self-esteem?
- How is self-esteem developed in childhood years?
- How is self-esteem enhanced or eroded in the home?
- What specific actions do we as parents take, what language do we use, that encourage positive self-esteem in our children?
- What is the relationship between self-esteem and motivation?
- How does the possession of high self-esteem relate to setting and achieving goals?
- What is the contribution of self-esteem to our developing a sense of responsibility for our own well-being and, on a larger scale, social responsibility?
- Why does a positive self-esteem engender inner happiness and contribute to attracting healthy relationships?
- How does self-esteem help us to live out our full potential, to become "fully functioning persons," as Carl Rogers would say, or to become what Abraham Maslow, the famous psychologist from Brandeis University, called the "self-actualizing person" and "the fully human person"?

1

Self-esteem is central to what we make of our lives—the loyalty we have to developing ourselves and to caring about others, and it is at the heart of what we will achieve in the course of our lifetime. Perhaps nothing affects health and energy, peace of mind, the goals we set and achieve, our inner happiness, the quality of our relationships, our competence, performance, and productivity, quite as much as the health of our self-esteem.

Because self-esteem is so important to human endeavor, we need to know how we can best use our parenting time to help our children develop a sense of self that will yield inner strength and motivation, create a desire to achieve and excel, and unleash the potential that will help our children create for themselves a rewarding and purposeful life. This is one of the most important roles of parenting.

Self-esteem affects everything we do and say, because our behavior is consistent with the inner picture we hold of ourselves. This is true for children as well as for adults. Your child's actions will stem from his inner picture of himself and will influence the way he treats himself and others, as well as how much he loves and respects you. It will affect his school performance, determine how capable and competent he will become, and how much he is liked and accepted by others and shows acceptance in return.

Everyone Needs to Be Valued

For nearly twenty-five years I've worked with and counseled both adults and children. From the classroom to the boardroom, many of these individuals were looking for a greater sense of satisfaction in what they were doing and, in particular, a greater sense of being—of "personhood." They wanted to make a difference but weren't sure whether they were doing anything meaningful with their time and talent. Or they were in relationships (whether at work or in family life) unworthy of their joy, attention, and life energy—where reciprocity of love and caring were missing. Some didn't care for or love themselves.

All people want and need to matter. All of us need to know that we are using our time—the substance of our life—for something special. That's as true for children as it is for adults. When we don't feel valued (by ourselves or others), we are saddened. Without value, we feel out of alignment. The result is that the esteem we hold for our own value is lessened. Low self-esteem is pain registering at a very significant level. This feeling is a red flag—it indicates that it's time for human repair.

How are humans best repaired? I've been involved with both youth and adults—as an educator, administrator, and university professor, and as a consultant to business, education, and industry for more than two decades. I've observed and been a part of counseling, education, and training trends to improve the climate (environment) of schools and business organizations, as well as efforts to improve both personal and professional effectiveness—in other words, to help others learn how to achieve greater personal empowerment so that value and commitment could take place.

My work has involved writing a number of books for parents and youth and for professionals working with youth. Initially I focused on stress and pressure and its impact on achievement. My book *Stress in Children: How to Recognize, Avoid, and Overcome It*, for example, provided counsel on how to lessen the effects of stress and their toll on our children. I deliberately aimed my work at parents rather than at the educational community because of the powerful influence we as parents have on the lives of our children. It has become increasingly clear to me over the decades that the one vital ingredient that holds the key to unlocking potential and achievement and minimizing the ravages of stress (for both adults and children) is positive self-value—a healthy self-esteem.

The best chance a child has of securing a level of high self-esteem is to have parents who possess it, model it, and want to instill it in their children. If parents rear their children with love and respect, allow them to experience consistent and benevolent acceptance, give them the supporting structure of appropriate rules and reasonable expectations, if they don't assail them with contradictions, don't resort to ridicule, humiliation, or physical abuse as a means of controlling them, and help them believe in their abilities and goodness—then children have a chance of internalizing those attitudes and thereby acquiring the foundation for healthy self-esteem.

It's an awesome responsibility. How can you help your child feel loved and be loving, develop warm and mutually satisfying relationships, achieve, and excel? What can you do to safeguard your child's physical safety and emotional security? How can you best use your parenting time to help your child develop a sense of self that will yield inner strength and motivation, unleash potential, develop effective life skills, and choose a rewarding and purposeful life?

That's why I've written this book for you, the parent: to help you examine self-esteem—to help you understand what it is and isn't and why and how it influences our lives in such a powerful way; to delineate for you the six facets that make up this personal view of self; and, more specifically, to help you develop self-esteem in that most cherished person in your life, your child.

○ BEING AN EFFECTIVE PARENT IS TOUGHER TODAY

Parenting is more difficult today than ever before. There are so many things to distract us from caring for our children—demanding work loads, hurried lifestyles, competition for our children's time (school and homework, friends, television, social and sports activities)—that it's sometimes easy to become overwhelmed and get discouraged wondering if we can do it all. We really can't, not in the key years of parenting, at least.

Aside from the new adult lifestyle and career opportunities (and parenthood expectations), childhood faces its own set of changes. More exposure to television, violence, sexual exploitation, more association with many more children (themselves in need of a more healthy and whole sense of self), and the availability of drugs, all have changed the nature of rearing children. We must decide how we'll meet the needs of our children, and the demands of parenthood, in a way that nurtures us both.

How Do Some Parents Get So Disconnected?

We're always hearing about how to make time, save time, take time, and manage time, but there never seems to be enough time. The lack of time we spend with our children is one of the biggest complaints I hear from children of all ages, especially teens. That's because children equate our time with how much we love them.

The amount of quality time parents fail to spend with their children should be a national concern. Not spending enough focused time with our children is reflected in the alarming incidence of delinquent behaviors seen in children today. Last year over a million children ran away from home. Some said their parents wouldn't notice. Sadly, many said their parents didn't care. That was hard to believe, yet when 34 percent of these children were located by child-find agencies, who attempted to return them to their homes, many parents refused to take them back in. Not to be wanted physically or emotionally is a terrible feeling. The response to parental indifference is anger, and today there are many angry children—both out there and in our homes.

What Children *Really* Want from Their Parents

Have you ever wondered what children really want and need from us? I've asked the question to young people across the country. Here's what they list in order of importance.

- I want my parents to think I'm somebody special.
- I want my parents to be warm and friendly to me, just as they are to those who phone or come to the door.

- I want my parents to be more concerned about me.
- I want my parents to know the "me that nobody knows."
- I want to talk to my parents about what's important to me (and have those views be valued).
- I want to go to school with kids I relate to. (Children see parents as controlling this by setting up their home in a certain neighborhood.)
- I want to be part of a happy family.
- I want my parents to "lighten up."
- I want my parents to learn more about my feelings and emotions.
- I want to live in a world at peace. (Children see parents as controlling this through acts such as voting.)

What is very obvious about this list is that its focus is primarily on internal needs, and not just on getting or having things. In a recent workshop I conducted for parents and teens in Boston, a sixteen-year-old boy said it best: "My dad is always telling me what he does for me," he said in a tone riddled with sarcasm. "I wish he'd do less *for* me and more *with* me." The other youths in the room clapped and cheered because he had said what they too felt.

"Yeah, tell me about it!" said James, a fourteen-year-old sitting several seats behind him. "I asked my dad if we could go to the batting cages on Saturday and he said he didn't have the time. But when his buddy from work called and asked him to go golfing, he was gone in a heartbeat!"

What children want—and need—are attention, acceptance, and active parenting from us. Think about the young child who says, "Watch me, Mommy! Watch me, Mommy!" or "Watch me, Daddy! Watch me, Daddy!" No matter what your child's age, he wants you to notice. Lorraine, a thirty-eight-year-old friend of mine, said to me yesterday, "I sent my mother a newspaper article written about an award I had recently won. I called to see if she had received it. She did, but rather than recognize my winning the award, she talked about other things.

I felt so let down." Children want to be important to us! And they want to know just how important we think they are to us.

Unfortunately, many parents become frustrated and uninterested in caretaking chores as their children get older (or even when they are very young). Some parents substitute money and things in place of time and attention. Many lose faith that they even make a difference in their child's life. Still others become easily intimidated and back down or act with aggression when their children begin testing the boundaries of the rules put in place to protect them.

Children will get your attention—one way or the other. We need to pay attention. The sad and bothersome numbers of young people today who are destructive to themselves and others are a mirror of the attention many youngsters are not getting. Paying attention means we have to value our children as much as the other things we find important. It also means that just as we protect our children physically, we must do our part to develop their emotional health as well.

○ SELF-ESTEEM—A DEFINITION

Perhaps you've heard the term **self-esteem** defined as "how much you like yourself." Well, yes, but self-esteem is much, much more than that. Self-esteem is a composite picture of perceived self-value. It's the disposition to experience yourself as worthy of happiness, health and wellness, respect, friendship, love, achievement, and success. Each of us wants to know that we are able to cope with the challenges of life. We search for the boundaries of our being, hoping of course to find none.

Author and psychologist Nathaniel Branden, the father of modern self-esteem therapy, sees self-esteem as the integrated sum of self-efficacy and self-respect. **Self-efficacy** means confidence in your ability to think and in the processes by which you judge, choose, and decide. It's knowing and understanding your interests and needs. It incorporates self-trust and self-reliance. The experience of self-efficacy generates the sense of control over your life, the sense of being at the vital center of your existence—as contrasted with being a passive spectator and a victim of events. **Self-respect** means assurance of your values. It's an affirmative attitude toward the right to live and be happy, toward freedom to assert your thoughts, wants, needs, and joys. The experience of self-respect allows for mutual regard of others and makes possible a nonneurotic sense of fellowship with them.

Self-efficacy and self-respect are the dual pillars of healthy self-esteem. If either one is absent, self-esteem is impaired, says Branden.

"Consider that if an individual felt inadequate to face the challenges of life, if an individual lacked fundamental self-respect, confidence in his or her mind, we would recognize the presence of self-esteem deficiency, no matter what other assets he or she possessed. Or if an individual lacked a basic sense of self-respect, felt unworthy, or undeserving of the love or respect of others, unentitled to happiness, fearful of asserting thoughts, wants, or needs—again we would recognize a self-esteem deficiency, no matter what other positive attributes he or she exhibited."

THE SIX VITAL INGREDIENTS OF SELF-ESTEEM

The extent to which we feel that worthwhile practices are not only appropriate, but deserved is based on how we are faring in six very important and specific areas:

Physical Safety: the freedom from physical harm
Emotional Security: the absence of intimidation and fear
Identity: the "Who-am-I?" question
Affiliation: our sense of belongingness
Competence: how capable we feel
Mission: what we believe is the purpose of our lives

○ HOW WILL YOU KEEP YOUR CHILD SAFE FROM LOW SELF-ESTEEM?

For many years researchers have been looking at the influence parents exert over children. They've generally focused on such factors as genetic inheritance and health, personality characteristics, cultural conditioning, and the opportunities that parents make available for their children—such as intellectual stimulation, enrichment activities, and the choice of school environments. Today we're probing deeper and acknowledging that the relationships we form with our children are, in fact, as vital a contribution in detracting from or empowering their lives as these other influences. In the long run, it's what we do and say to children about themselves that quite often is the deciding factor in their acceptance of personal and social responsibility.

Like you, I'm a parent. It's by far the most challenging (and the most satisfying) role in my life. My daughter is very dear to me. When my daughter was little, I worried that she would pull a pan of hot water from the stove onto her head, stick a finger into a light socket, or be treated badly by another child. My concerns haven't changed too much over the years. Now that she's sixteen, I worry that she will leave a burner on in the house (or an iron or hot rollers) or that she (or another driver) will exercise poor judgment while she's in a two-ton car, or that she will be emotionally devastated in a relationship. How then will I protect my daughter and keep her safe, as well as guard her from the emotional strains that could change her life in a negative way?

It begins by acknowledging her as a most important priority in my life and then paying attention to her needs and the values she is assimilating. With your own child, these come from you.

What Are Your Highest Values?

A common practice in helping organizations look at what they're about, to find out what they're really in the business of doing, even how to conduct business on a day-to-day basis, is to help them identify and prioritize their highest values. "What exactly are your values here," we ask. We cull the list, prioritize it, and then look at the top five values. We do this because a company's mission—its work—is about its values. Priorities stem from the rank order of these values. What a company and its people should be doing is based on what they stand for. Most everything falls into place from that point on—what mission and goals the organization must imbue, what leadership skills are needed, what assigned roles need to be delineated, the competencies needed from the work force.

Bringing our values into focus shows us where to spend our energy, and therefore helps us to be purposeful. Like companies, parents must prioritize the many choices we have from which to choose. That, more than anything else, is what being effective is all about. It's focusing on what's really important and doing it well.

Think about your highest values. What are they? What areas of your life are the most important to you? List six, in their order of importance to you. Do this now.

What did you list as the most important value? Is your top priority also the most meaningful to you? Perhaps peace of mind, spirituality, family, purposeful work, friendships, your health and well-being, and happiness were among your top priorities. Did you rank your children as number one? Most people do. But are you living your values—are you "walking your talk"? Aligning our actions with what we say is important to us isn't always easy, but it helps if we look to our highest values.

We All Need Occasional Repairs

This book is about nurturing self-esteem in children, but many of us may need to look at the condition of our own self-esteem as well. We can begin by examining the esteem that emanates from living a life characterized by purposeful values. The price is very high when we don't. Drug involvement and other destructive behaviors don't happen just to other people's children.

Once, or so it seemed, only certain children were at risk for becoming involved in destructive behaviors. Not so today. When parents aren't paying attention to the emotional life as well as the physical whereabouts of a child, that child is at risk. Drug involvement, dropping out of school, youth pregnancies, and little attention to character building and the importance of ethics can change the course of a young person's life in a seriously negative way.

It's Never Too Late to Be a Good Parent

Don't be discouraged if you feel that you aren't the best parent now. It's never too late to begin. But do begin now! The stages of childhood pass all too quickly. Whether you're at the stage of checking in on your newborn—still in awe as you watch your baby sleeping—patching up scraped knees, or helping with algebra homework, the next phase of your child's development is right around the corner. Don't miss your role in it. Many parents wish they had been more active in their children's childhood, wish they hadn't let so many things go unattended, nor allowed so many things to happen by chance. Not taking the time or giving enough attention to their children is one of the greatest sorrows expressed by parents who missed a child's growing years. Yet for parents who truly experienced this challenging role in a purposeful way, it was the most joyful and rewarding period of their lifetime. Parenting needn't be chancy but, rather, deliberate and thus much more joyful. That's what it's all about.

○ IT'S UP TO YOU!

You can't just assume that your child will automatically develop a sound sense of self. Can't schools and teachers help? Yes, but while most educators want to guide, nurture, and shape the hearts and minds of youth, their primary role is to teach academic skills in preparing children for the next grade level, for college, trade schools, or the job market. Unfortunately, educators can't give our children all the time they need nor teach in-depth personal skills that develop a child's emotional life. Who, then, will tend to your child's self-esteem in a way that will allow him to care for his physical and emotional self, to be fair with his friends, to choose purposeful work based on inner aspirations and innate gifts, to choose a life partner who won't mistreat him emotionally or physically? To be personally and socially responsible? You. Children live up to the dreams and aspirations of their parents. Are you dreaming big enough? Seeing your child as a winner helps you convince him that he's a winner, that he can do whatever he puts his mind to, and that he has to participate in the plan for becoming all that he is capable of being.

2 HOW CAN SELF-ESTEEM POSSIBLY BE THAT IMPORTANT?

○ THE ALL-IMPORTANT SELF-ESTEEM

Outer actions are motivated by the inner sense of self. Because your actions are a reflection of the way you view yourself, it's fairly easy for others to discern what *you* think of *you*.

Far from making you conceited or self-centered, a healthy self-esteem gives you a realistic awareness of yourself and of your abilities and needs. With an all-encompassing respect for yourself, you are unwilling to allow others to devalue your worth, nor will you let them deprive you of all your needs. You don't squander your talents and aptitudes, be it through procrastination, substance abuse, or other means. You care about your well-being: You protect your inner spiritual essence—your core. You bring dignity and sustenance to your relationships, and your work contributions reveal the value of service to others.

The Six Facets of Self-Esteem

A sense of physical safety.   A child who feels physically safe isn't fearful of being harmed or hurt. Because he feels safe, he learns to be open and to trust others. He freely exercises a curious nature (that contributes to learning). He moves about with a sense of healthy assuredness. His body posture displays

13

confidence. His tone of voice is hearty and he'll maintain eye contact when he's talking with you.

A sense of emotional security.   A child develops a high level of emotional security when he knows he won't be put down, or made to feel less worthy, or be beaten up emotionally with sarcasm or other hurtful words. Because he feels emotionally secure, he learns to be caring and compassionate with himself and others. He becomes trustworthy. He feels secure in sharing his opinions and ideas. He is respectful and considerate. He is outgoing and friendly. He'll come to you for hugs of affection on his own. He'll reach out to touch; he'll enjoy being close to you. He'll like to snuggle.

A sense of identity.   A child with self-knowledge develops a healthy sense of individuality. He knows himself. He's friends with the face in the mirror. He's able to "knock, and find somebody (himself) home." He believes in his worth as a human being. He believes he is worthy of praise, and he feels secure in praising and complimenting others. Feeling secure with himself, he is open and caring toward others. He takes responsibility for his actions and will own up to them.

A sense of belonging.   A child who feels accepted by and connected to others feels liked, appreciated, and respected. He learns to seek out and maintain friendships. He is able to cooperate and share. While maintaining a sense of independence, he learns *inter*dependence—a healthy perception of interrelatedness.

A sense of competence.   When a youngster feels that he is good at some things, he's willing to learn how to do other things. Because he feels capable, he is willing to persevere rather than give up when things become difficult. He is not only aware of his strengths, but he is also able to accept the areas where he's less able and can do so without developing "victim" behavior. Because he tries, he experiences the successes that encourage him to try new things. He is self-empowered through realistic and achievable goals and, therefore, has initiative.

A sense of mission. A child with a strong sense of mission feels life has meaning. Because he has a sense of direction, he not only sets goals, but he also follows through on achieving them. When faced with obstacles, he creates alternatives that work. He has an inner knowledge, and an inner peace. He is intuitive. He laughs easily. He is joyful.

○ ASSESSING YOUR CHILD'S SELF-ESTEEM

As adults, you and I are responsible for how we care for ourselves and how we allow others to treat us. Children, however, are mostly recipients of what adults bring about for them. Throughout the years of childhood, the six powerful ingredients of self-esteem are largely initiated for children by us. I'll be talking about what each of these ingredients means to your child (and what you can do to empower your child in each area) in later chapters.

What daily activities affect self-esteem? How can you as a caring and loving parent see the effects of self-esteem? You'll want to help your child understand that while he can't always control what happens, he can control his reactions and not let events lessen his self-esteem. The goal is to help your child see (1) how the events of his days add to or detract from his self-esteem and (2) how the events of his day are less important than his responses to these events. In other words, his responses are in his control. It's up to him. *How* he responds affects his self-esteem by sending messages of being capable (or not) of managing his day-to-day life.

As you read the brief vignettes below, think about your child, and see if you can determine how he is affected by certain events (some within his control, some wholly outside of it) and how these can affect his self-esteem. I've provided a couple of stories here, but the best ones are those that happen daily in the life of your child.

Following each story you'll find a chart to copy to help your child see the effects of Gail's and Rick's (or his own) self-esteem. It's a good idea to design and have your child duplicate a number of these charts regularly. The goal is to help your child think about how the things that happen each day can make him feel good about himself or can depress him without his even knowing they are doing so.

Read the following scenarios and then put a + (plus sign) next to any statement that you think would enhance self-esteem, a − (minus sign) next to one that you think would lower self-esteem, and a 0 (zero) by one that would seem to have little or no effect on your child's sense of self. There are no right or wrong answers, and there is no best score. The idea is to show you how events, both major and minor, can change how your child views himself and can affect his sense of comfort with the person he is.

Seven-Year-Old Gail

A. Gail wakes up to your giving her a hug and kiss and telling her, "Wake up, wake up, my lovely daughter. Wash that sunny face and let me smile at it over cereal and milk."

B. As Gail brushes her hair, she knocks over the bottle of shampoo on the countertop and spills it. She tries to mop it up but makes a complete mess.

C. On the school bus, Gail's best friend sits with another girl and giggles, giving Gail looks and whispering to the other girl.

D. Gail tries to ignore her friend's giggling and reads a little more in her book. She gets involved in the story and hardly notices when the bus stops.

E. During lunch, Dick, the little boy Gail thinks is the cutest in the class, teases her about her sweater, telling her that the orange color makes her look like a pumpkin.

F. In math class, Gail gets back a paper with a $B+$ grade. The teacher has written, "You could have gotten an A if you didn't make so many careless mistakes. Slow down!"

G. Gail gets caught whispering during science class. The teacher reminds her not to talk but is nice about it.

H. You are supposed to pick up Gail after school and you are about fifteen minutes late. She is the only child standing there waiting by the time you rush up.

I. That night, you praise Gail's sister for doing the dishes without having to be told, but you forget to mention that you've looked at Gail's $A+$ English paper.

Mark how each event affected Gail's day.

	Low self-esteem 1 2 3 4	No effect 5 6	High self-esteem 7 8 9 10
Event A			
Event B			
Event C			
Event D			
Event E			
Event F			
Event G			
Event H			
Event I			

Sixteen-Year-Old Rick

A. Rick wakes up to the clock radio playing the song he and his girlfriend think of as their song. He remembers how he and Melanie danced to it at Homecoming.

B. Rick looks in the mirror and discovers a pimple right on his cheek. He washes his face hard and that seems to make it worse.

C. Rick walks to school, commenting for the hundredth time as he leaves home that all of his friends have cars and can drive. He ignores you as you remind him that you live only a block from school.

D. Rick runs into his friend Bob, who teases him about his pimple.

E. During lunch, Melanie says hardly anything to Rick, talking with her girlfriends instead.

F. In algebra class, Rick gets called to the board to work a problem. He does it correctly and gets a high-five from his friend Nick when he goes back to his seat.

G. Rick gets praised by the Spanish teacher but then teased by the other kids about being the teacher's pet.

H. At soccer practice after school, Rich finds out that his best friend is going to summer camp and won't be around to hang out with all summer.

I. That night, Rick and his buddy, Nick, spend two hours on the telephone, doing their homework together and talking.

Mark how each event affected Rick's day.

	Low self-esteem 1 2 3 4	No effect 5 6	High self-esteem 7 8 9 10
Event A			
Event B			
Event C			
Event D			
Event E			
Event F			
Event G			
Event H			
Event I			

As you can see, there are all sorts of things that happen to your child during the day that affect how he views himself. For example, when a child is teased, how does he interpret that? We tell our children that "they only tease you because they like you," but do they believe us? When a friend teases your son about a pimple, is that different from when others tease him about being a teacher's pet?

Every Child Needs a Healthy Self-Esteem

Everyone has a need to feel unafraid, secure, connected, capable, and competent in the world. Children have an especially strong need to feel these things with their parents and others who are important to them. All children need a sense of worth and a feeling of being okay in situations that are new and

perhaps frightening to them as they learn, grow, and change—
the elements of the childhood years.

That's true for high-IQ children and low-IQ children, for
mentally disabled children and gifted children, for athletic children and physically disabled children, for poor students and
good students, for the child you like, and, most especially, for
the child you find it difficult to like.

Your child's behavior is a direct result of his feelings of worth
and value. That's why behavior is such a tell-tale sign of how
your child feels about himself. Bad behavior is often a sign that
something is wrong. School dropouts, early pregnancy, drug
abuse, and other destructive behaviors, for the most part, have a
lot to do with a child's self-esteem. Just as does school performance. I have never heard of a child who was asked to leave a
school because he was incapable of learning. A dropout is a
child who sees little purpose to his life, has a difficult time
relating school success to the outside world, and sees few reasons
to attempt to improve himself. He also has difficulty developing
warm relationships with peers and teachers—the support system
that makes school a fun and endurable place. His negative
behaviors and feelings are almost certainly a direct result of his
negative sense of himself.

Characteristics of High-Self-Esteem Children

What separates high-self-esteem children from low-self-
esteem children is a can-do attitude. By focusing on their
strengths and achievements, high-self-esteem children accept
mistakes and weaknesses without undue self-devaluation. Like
adults, when children have a reserve of positive experiences to
call on during the tough times, they're better able to persist on
their chosen course. Motivation and productivity skyrocket
when these children reach their goals. They don't depend solely
on others for approval and are able to say to themselves, "I did
it!" "I did a good job!" "I can do even better!" "That was great!"
"That was fun!"

The value of building self-esteem in children is much the same as Nathaniel Branden describes it in adults (in an address given at a conference in Oslo, Norway, in August 1990).

- The higher children's self-esteem, the better equipped they are to cope with adversity in their educational, personal, and social lives; the better able they are to pick themselves up after a fall; the more energy they have to begin anew.
- The higher children's self-esteem, the more ambitious they tend to be, especially in terms of what they hope to experience in life—emotionally, academically, creatively, spiritually, and in achieving fitness and well-being. The lower their self-esteem, the less they will aspire to, and the less likely they are to achieve. Either path tends to be self-reinforcing and self-perpetuating.
- The higher children's self-esteem, the more inclined they will be now, and later in life, to develop enriching relationships.
- The higher children's self-esteem, the better able they are to attract others who enjoy their lives. Children with low self-esteem seek other low-self-esteem children who think poorly of themselves.
- The higher children's self-esteem, the more secure they are in confronting obstacles, fears, and interpersonal conflicts rather than avoiding them—to solve problems instead of worrying over them. Low-self-esteem children see problems as grounds for quitting and often say to themselves, "I give up." Instead of comparing their achievements with their own goals and potential, they compare themselves with others and wait for others to create their "successes."
- The higher children's self-esteem, the better able they are to find ways to get along well with others and then respond positively to them. They strive to be useful, helpful, purposeful, and responsible.
- The higher children's self-esteem, the better able they are to find compassion for themselves and to be compassionate with others. Compassion exposes self-worth: They have discovered the treasured value of their personhood.

- The higher children's self-esteem, the more secure, decisive, friendly, trusting, cheerful, and optimistic they are. Look closely and you'll also discover that they are motivated or empowered. That's because they recognize their own worth and achievements without a constant need for approval from the outside. This does not mean that they don't need others but, rather, that they are interdependent (vs. dependent) on others. Low-self-esteem children are usually described as moody, aloof, fearful, aimless, negative, and indecisive. Look closely and you'll note that these children need constant reinforcement from others and use attention-getting antics to meet their needs of self-worth.
- The higher children's self-esteem, the more responsibility and control they will take over their actions. This is important, not only because children who monitor their own actions are responsible, but also because these children are more willing to accept challenges and extend their boundaries because they have experienced previous successes. Recognition of personal strengths and capabilities serves as a powerful coping and buffer strategy for overcoming obstacles, and it helps compensate for weaknesses and setbacks. Obviously, these children have met with their share of failure, but they focus on the good stuff—the positive experiences.
- The higher children's self-esteem, the better they are equipped to cope with life's adversities.

How Do Children Learn to Be Motivated?

From these four areas: *physical safety* (a child who feels safe at home, at school, and in his everyday environment); *emotional security* (a child who feels emotionally trusting knows he won't be put down or ridiculed); *identity* (a child with self-acceptance feels comfortable with himself); and *belongingness* (a child who feels that he is wanted and that he belongs). These images of himself are gleaned primarily through your child's relationship with you and others with whom he spends considerable time. His self-concept is a product of not only what he tells himself, but of the messages others give him about his worth as a person. Besides what others tell him, he can see how important he is by our actions toward him. This demonstrates how we value him— the actions-speak-louder-than-words concept.

Because the first four components are for the most part (especially in the first sixteen years of his life) initiated and directed by you and other adults, we're largely responsible for the degree to which he is motivated.

In the other two areas—*competence* (a child who feels capable and that he is good at some things) and *a sense of mission* (a feeling that life has meaning, that there are things worth doing)—your child's self-esteem is no longer solely dependent on the forces of others. These last two components expand your child's sense of self and set his empowerment cycle spinning in a forward motion:

- He now acts on his own sense of what's important and what's not.
- Because he feels capable, he's willing to get involved.
- Setting goals and achieving them is his goal.
- His life has meaning and direction.
- Because he consistently sets goals for himself, a cycle of success is created.

All of this adds up to an internalized validation that "I'm a worthwhile and can-do individual."

High-Self-Esteem Children Do Better in School

There are a lot of payoffs in school for high-self-esteem children. A child who considers himself capable of learning is willing to put in the effort of studying and to overcome frustrations when something doesn't come easily. A child with low self-esteem is defeated before he begins. He assumes that he's not intelligent enough to master the rigors of learning, and he gives up at the first obstacle. For example, a high-self-esteem child is willing to stand up for what he considers his right. I saw proof of this again just this week when my daughter's friend, Debra, got a B− on a paper she turned in for her history class. Debra felt that she deserved a better grade and presented her case to the teacher. The teacher took the time to sit down with her and explain in detail exactly where he thought the paper was weak. He also listened closely to her argument. The result was that Debra got a B, a slightly higher grade, but even more important, she got extra attention from the teacher and felt good knowing that she had the courage to stick up for what she felt she had earned. And you can bet that because she has now presented herself in that way to her teacher, she's going to win his respect, consideration, and attention on future assignments. Furthermore, that additional attention will correlate in greater learning and will result in another measure of success, adding once more to her positive sense of self.

It's doubtful that a child with low self-esteem would take on this challenge. He would shrug and say, "I got this grade because the teacher doesn't like me." He would feel powerless to effect any other outcome. With each downbeat experience, he would become less willing to attempt standing his ground when deserved or when necessary to get his needs met.

Notice the behavior cycles created here: A child with strong self-esteem performs actions that allow her self-esteem to be strengthened even more in adverse situations. A child with low self-esteem doesn't perform such actions and, as a result, has her self-esteem lowered even more in similar situations.

How your child manages his day-to-day life gives you clues as to how well he is doing overall. That's why you want to know how well your child is doing in his relationships at home (and this includes a parent from whom he may be separated) and at school with his teachers and coaches, as well as with his peers and friends.

Do You Have a High-Self-Esteem Child?

How can you tell whether your child has a healthy sense of self or is suffering from low self-esteem? You can't always assume that the child who is quiet and somewhat shy has a low self-esteem, while the outgoing, rambunctious child has a high self-esteem. There's more to it than that. Below are some guidelines to help you make an assessment of your child's self-esteem.

Willingness to participate. Children with high self-esteem are willing, even eager, to join in, to feel secure in their ability to succeed, or at least to have fun trying. When your child is invited to participate in an activity or group, how does he respond? For example, does your child want to try out for a team or want to belong to an organization or club (such as school intramurals or a library or book club); does he want to participate in school activities (such as the debate team, the photography club, or pep squad); does he eagerly look forward to the fun of being together with friends at school outings (such as attending special events or sports functions); when asked to join a particular group of classmates for a project, or even a discussion, does your child willingly do so? Does he think of all the fun he'll have, or is he reluctant to participate in just about everything?

Children with a healthy self-esteem are likely to participate joyfully in a number and range of experiences, feeling that they have something to offer. They aren't bogged down with the notion that they have to excel at everything in order to participate; they don't worry that others will poke fun at them if they are good at it. They have a curiosity, a desire to experiment, and a natural willingness to be with others.

Willingness to share. Most children enjoy talking about themselves and their interests. We call this *self-disclosure.* Children with self-knowledge and an appreciation of themselves are not shy about passing along compliments or the praise others

have given them. This sharing is healthy and normal in children: Talking about their successes doesn't necessarily denote an
unhealthy ego. It indicates a sense of comfort with and acceptance of oneself. Best of all, children who are able to talk about
the compliments that others have given them are willing to
compliment and praise others.

**Ability to accept advice without viewing it as crit-
icism.**   When children have high self-esteem, they are able to
accept advice without viewing it as criticism. Even constructive
criticism is received with an attitude of acceptance. Such children are willing to admit when they are wrong or have made a
mistake. Low-self-esteem children, on the other hand, view all
advice as criticism and take criticism as a form of rejection. Due
to this fear of rejection, they will resist admitting when they are
wrong or have made a mistake.

Comfortable when alone with themselves.   Children with a
healthy self-esteem are happy with their own company: They
don't have to be surrounded by others every minute. Nor do they
have to "find themselves" or be defined through others. While
there exists a normal desire to be one of the crowd (peer
acceptance is an important issue for all children), they can be
with others without an excessive dependence on the opinions of
others.

Commitment to achieving.   Children with a healthy self-
esteem want to do well and aren't intimidated by tackling the
challenge of understanding something they don't yet understand
(such as learning). These children will generally compete with
themselves rather than with others. They talk about what they
can do, and even good-natured teasing ("I can run faster than
you can!" "I bet I can beat you do . . .") is done with a light-
hearted spirit. Throughout it all, they are comfortable with
themselves and aren't desperate to be better than absolutely
everyone else. Children with low self-esteem feel that they are

failures anytime someone is able to do something better than they are.

The signs indicating low self-esteem are not always obvious. They may take diametrically opposite forms, manifesting themselves in behavioral problems demanding constant attention or in complete withdrawal. Below are a few of the more general warning signs that can alert you to problems your child is having with his sense of self.

Negative behavior. A naughty child, one who intentionally repeats behavior you have told him is unacceptable, may be showing you how little he respects himself. He is constantly seeking criticism from you to convince himself that the picture he has of himself really is unlovable.

Constant self-belittling. Children who always make "I can't" or "I'm not" (such as "I'm not smart enough!") statements, or other self-defeating remarks that contribute to their feeling unworthy, have low opinions of themselves. All children are going to make comments of this sort on occasion; it's time for concern when these self put-downs become a frequent part of their communications.

Admiration without emulation. Children want to be like those they look up to. If your child talks about his heroes or friends but never makes an attempt to be like them, it might be because he feels he can never be as good as those heroes or friends are. For example, a girl might copy an admired friend's hairstyle. If she has a healthy sense of self-esteem, she will do so from a feeling that she has the capability to accomplish what she wants and a willingness to try something new. If she constantly says things such as, "Everybody likes Amanda but nobody likes me. No one ever likes me," she lacks the self-confidence and self-esteem to risk those behaviors necessary in making and sustaining friendships.

Lack of caring about attention from you.   All children want their parents to notice their accomplishments. Even teens who think that we, as adults, are hopelessly outdated and that they are fatally misunderstood will occasionally seek our approval in a casual, off-handed way. It's time for concern when your child no longer seeks your approval, no longer bothers trying to get your attention (because he feels he isn't worthy), or when he doesn't care about your feelings toward him.

Excessive criticism of others.   When children almost constantly criticize you and others, it indicates they have a lack of confidence in themselves and feel that in order to build themselves up, they must belittle those around them. This is their way (though they may not be conscious of it) of trying to feel superior—their way to escape their feelings of inferiority.

Excessive concern with the attention and opinions of friends.   Children who make the opinions and attention of friends of tantamount importance are rarely able to assert their judgment when faced with the disapproval of their peers, because they don't trust their own sense of ideas and thoughts. They take on the thoughts, values, and actions of others, even when they know in their hearts that those actions are contrary to what they want, to what they have been taught, are wrong, and can land them in trouble.

○ IT'S UP TO YOU!

What you believe about your child's worth becomes a self-fulfilling prophecy. In other words, children become what you believe they will become. As parents, we want to build positive self-esteem in our children so that they can see themselves as the winners we know them to be.

Secure, decisive, friendly, trusting, cheerful, optimistic, and purposeful: What parent wouldn't want a child to possess these attributes—the benefits of high self-esteem?

Your child needs you. Helping your child develop a healthy self-esteem is by no means an overnight accomplishment. It's triggered by the caretaking actions of responsible parents and by active parenting.

3

SAFETY: DOES YOUR CHILD REALLY FEEL SAFE AT HOME?

I've just boarded a flight for New York City. "Welcome aboard," says the flight attendant. "Your safety is our number-one priority." Safety—it's our first sense of moving about our world with freedom, in the absence of fear. Physical safety is the first in the hierarchy of the six building blocks of developing self-esteem. Its importance lies in the fact that we feel we are in control of our own self within our environment—we have mastery over our being.

An inner feeling of outer safety is a prerequisite to helping your child progress to other areas. Physical safety is so crucial that without it, the development of a strong and healthy self-esteem is severely limited. Only when your child feels physically safe will he move beyond fear and be willing to explore his day-to-day challenges with a naturally curious nature.

There's a difference between the safety measures you put in place to protect your child and his feelings of safety. A child who feels physically safe isn't fearful of being hurt in any way. When you protect your child and show concern when he is fearful, he learns to trust. He develops a sense of assuredness that there are people he can count on. When a child is fearful, he distrusts others and shies away from them. Being insecure, he is uncomfortable in many situations, especially in new ones. He becomes defensive and is quick to judge others. Over time, he becomes a very angry child.

We live in a world where the absence of physical safety affects the lives of many children—sexual abuse, physical assault, starvation, homelessness, physical neglect and so on. That so many of our children should be afflicted with these conditions is not only embarrassing, but cruel and inexcusable. In the absence of fulfillment of the most basic human needs, should the lessening of caring, looking out for and helping others, the apathy and general decay of motivation in the schoolplace, and the violence we see children inflict on other children come as a surprise to us?

○ SAFETY BEGINS AT HOME

Last year more than 43 percent of school-children came home to an empty house—the latch-key children. Nearly two-thirds of these children said they were afraid to be there while their parents were away. Of the children who came home to caretakers other than their parents, 17 percent expressed a deep fear of the person put in charge to protect them. Most surprising of all, 12 percent of all children feared one or both of their biological parents, and more than half said they were fearful of a step-parent.

Parents and Children Have Different Perceptions of Safety

Sometimes, the best-meaning parents can do things to ensure their children's safety that the children perceive as cold and frightening. Lisa was a beautiful nine-year-old girl, small for her age. Her teacher noticed that Lisa seemed fearful all the time, timid at being around other children, especially those taller and bigger than herself. The teacher commented on this to Lisa's mother, only to hear that "Lisa is a sensitive child." The teacher pressed further, emphasizing that Lisa had trouble concentrating and didn't make friends easily. She reiterated that Lisa seemed constantly frightened and insecure.

Lisa's mother became defensive, bristling at the idea that her daughter might be feeling insecure about something. She told the teacher that Lisa had child care from a highly reputable agency that prided itself on professional, efficient help. Every day after school Lisa would be cared for by one of these professionals. Unfortunately, the staff turnover was high—so high that Lisa was unable to remain with any one person long enough to form a bond. She found herself constantly surrounded by large adults. What the adults considered professional, Lisa found cold, uncaring, and "angry at me." She became afraid of anyone "big" and fearful of forming a bond with them.

Sometimes, it is not the strangers but the parents themselves who make the children insecure. Four-year-old Tony spent his weekends with his father. Concerned that his ex-wife was coddling their son and not providing the firm discipline that he felt a small child needed, Tony's father felt compelled to provide a stern hand. He frequently slapped and spanked his son, often for minor infractions. Tony didn't understand the love behind the discipline and felt only hurt and afraid. He was confused. He saw that his father was basically a good-natured, easy-going man, but to Tony he was frightening. What his father perceived as discipline, Tony saw as rejection. He carried this over to his time with his mother, rejecting her new boyfriend, who bore a slight resemblance to the boy's father.

Your child must see his homeplace as a nonthreatening environment. That means he must feel safe with his parents (and others who live there) and feel safe in his home. Finding out how safe your child feels is important to you because without a feeling of safety, your child becomes a victim to fear. Would you stay in a job if you were afraid there? Would you shop at a center where you were afraid to walk to or from your car unaccompanied? Probably not. But many children today feel fearful and, what's more, are feeling alone in those fears. Take the time to view your child's sense of safety through his lens.

Like Lisa and Tony's parents, you might be surprised to learn how your child feels about safety in his home. What you're looking for is your child's response, how he feels. When these questions are asked of parents and their children, the children's responses are often quite different from the responses parents give. Ask yourself these questions:

- Does my child feel we live in a safe neighborhood? Why or why not?
- Are there neighbors my child feels comfortable about asking for help if I'm not here?
- How safe is our home?
- Are there places in our home that are frightening to my child?
- How much time does my child spend alone at home?
- Does my child know what to do, whom to call, and where to go in case of an emergency, if I am not there? Have we discussed (for small children) using the telephone? Is it where he can reach it?
- Does my child look forward to coming home; is he eager to spend time at home, or does he try to stay away as much as possible?
- Does my child feel that family members (and others, such as lovers, live-in help, or people providing yard-care service) are nonthreatening, encouraging and positive people?
- Does my child seem comfortable to stay home with siblings or the other parent, or is he really upset when I'm not around?
- Does my child show fear of anyone associated with our home: parents, siblings, other relatives, lovers, roommates, or people who service our home or yard?
- Is my child proud to bring friends home, to show off his home and especially his room?
- Does my child (especially a teenager) feel that this is "my home," not just "my parents' home?"
- Does my child fear being alone?
- Is my child afraid of me?
- What is my philosophy of discipline? Do I spank or hit? Is my discipline fair or harsh?

- Who disciplines my child besides me? What is their approach to discipline?
- What are my child's fears?

The more you learn about your child's feelings, the more you will be able to help him view the house as a safe haven, a warm and comforting place.

Sexual Abuse Is Cruel and Inexcusable

Being sexually victimized takes an enormous toll on the value children place on their worth. Children who fall victim to sexual abuse suffer physical hurt and psychic pain that can last a lifetime. It can also result in their hurting others. Research shows that sexually abused victims often repeat the cycle with their children.

If a child is being sexually abused in your home, do not let it continue. If you are sexually involved with your child, get help immediately for coming to terms with it. There are community centers for helping you learn how to overcome these destructive actions toward your child and to help you discover healthy ways to care for yourself. If your parenting partner is molesting a child and you're afraid to do something for fear of retaliation, get assistance. Call your local information hotline for service agencies in your community. Many of these are offered without cost to you. Make an appointment with a child-, family-, or marriage therapist in your community to talk about what you can do to change the situation. The Suggested Reading section at the back of this book lists some references and support services as a way of beginning. Other sources to call upon are the counseling services located at the central administrative center in your local school district. Ask for sources of assistance to parents and their children (many of these services are provided at no cost or minimal cost).

○ HOW DO YOU DISCIPLINE YOUR CHILD?

All of us are afraid to be hurt by someone who is bigger and more powerful than we are. And that's what physical punishment represents to children. Punishment is about teaching children that there are consequences for not keeping rules—it's not about being hurt. What philosophy guides your teaching your child about good behavior? How do you decide on fair and appropriate consequences for inappropriate behavior? Do you react to your child's behavior based on how you're feeling at the moment, or do you have guidelines for your actions? Do you have a consistent approach to helping your child learn to monitor his behavior?

Managing Yourself First

Lilly, the parent of two very active six-year-old twins, attended a parenting workshop conducted in Colorado. She told a story about her sons, who shared a room and frequently squabbled over sharing toys and turf. There were constant shouts to Mom to come and settle their disputes. As their demands began wearing on her, she found herself storming into their room to "clean house" as she called it. "I would shout and spank and leave their room feeling awful. My sons would be crying and hurt, and I would get even more frustrated. I'd hit them again, feeling even more terrible." She hung her head in shame as she described her actions.

We talked about her philosophy toward discipline. "What do you want your sons to learn?" I asked. "What are your intentions when you head to their room? What do you really want to accomplish when you go there?" I wanted her to see the connection between her behavior and teaching her sons to manage their behavior.

That idea made her look at the situation differently. She decided that what she really wanted her boys to learn was how to manage their behavior. But first she needed to model good behavior, so they could learn from it and act accordingly. She had to be able to manage herself. Her first decision was to decide that she wasn't going to take the boys' bad behavior personally. That is, she decided she wasn't going to get snagged into their fighting and shouting. She had to stay in control in order to help them learn a different way—namely, to stop fighting and behave themselves!

The next time they called her to referee a squabble, she walked calmly to their room and helped them settle a dispute. Twenty minutes later, she did the same. An hour later, she was summoned again. This time, she fell back into her old routine of shouting and spanking.

We looked for a way to help her consistently reinforce what she wanted for her sons. To help her do this, Lilly put up a large sign on the boys' door that read, "My sons are learning how to manage their behavior. Don't blow it!" That was a very important guidepost for Lilly, because as she approached the boys' room—sometimes at the end of her patience—the sign was her signal of the value she held for helping her sons learn appropriate actions.

As Lilly began to consistently implement her philosophy of discipline, she started to view her sons differently. Rather than seeing two terrible kids, she saw two little boys who needed and wanted her help in managing their behavior. She was then able to help them learn to share toys and to respect one another.

I talk with Lilly now and then, and she often tells me how this one act was a real breakthrough idea in her whole approach to parenting. "Parenting is so much more joyful," she said, and eagerly talked about her sons. Talking about the exciting things going on in their lives had now replaced the disgruntled feelings she had once had about their behavior.

What Is Your Philosophy of Discipline?

Just as Lilly learned, at the heart of all parenting activity is an attitude that governs our actions toward our children. This attitude also contributes to how competent we feel in our role as parents—thereby adding to or subtracting from our self-esteem. And that's why taking the time to ponder and formulate the philosophy that governs what you want is so important. *You* choose your philosophy of discipline.

Parenting, by its very nature, is a series of learning-by-doing experiences. Winging it is not very beneficial. Parenting requires thought, not just action. It requires deliberation, not just doing. In other words, we need to think about what we are doing, recognize and understand the underlying motivation of our parenting actions—the way we do what we do—and know how we will go about guiding and nurturing our children.

Can you identify your philosophy of discipline? Do you manage on the basis of crises, moods, quick fixes, and instant gratification—or is it thought out and based around the values you want to instill in your children? Write it down now. Then look it over. Ask yourself these questions:

- How does my parenting philosophy govern my actions?
- How did it come about?
- How did I formulate it?
- Was it deliberate, or did it just sort of happen?
- Am I pleased with it?
- How is my child faring under my guidance?
- What am I trying to teach my child by my approach to disciplining him?
- Do I admire my parenting style?
- Would I like to have me for a parent?
- What is the parenting philosophy of friends whose children appear happy and well-adjusted?

Is Your Philosophy the One You Want?

By writing out your philosophy, you give expression to the values you want to bring about in your children. You're not being driven by the moment but, rather, by what you're trying to do. In the last chapter of this book I'll help you examine both an individual parenting philosophy and a family mission, and you'll see how to align your philosophy of discipline to be consistent with your values. You may want to refer to Chapter 19 now. You might also want to review Chapter 1, where you listed and examined the highest values you hold for your children to determine if they are being expressed and reinforced by your actions.

As children learn, grow, and change in each new phase of childhood, we must help them surmount the challenges along the way. Guiding and disciplining is how we steer our children in ways we want them to go. There are ground rules to consider for keeping children's self-esteem intact while they learn appropriate behavior.

Punishment should be fair, in proportion to the offense, and without recrimination. Children should always see the possibility and the necessity of making a fresh start. Decide on reasonable, clear rules and enforce them consistently. Make only those rules that you believe to be truly important to which your child can adhere, and that you intend to enforce. If your child breaks a rule, the consequences should be certain, prompt, and related directly to the offense. And remember, punishment has impact because of its certainty, not because of its severity.

Example: Seventeen-year-old Gena and her best friend left school at lunchtime—without permission and without telling anyone—to have a hamburger at a local fast-food restaurant. They got carried away ogling the cute guy behind the counter and became late for their next period class. They decided that because they were late anyway, they wouldn't go back to school but would just drive around until it was time to go home.

The school, alarmed at Gena's absence, called her mother. When Gena came home, her mother heard the story from her. Without fighting, calling names, or turning her daughter off by becoming dramatic ("Do you know what your life would be like if you didn't get your high school diploma?"), she fit the punishment to the crime. For the next week, she drove Gena to school. "We agreed when you got the car that you would use it in a responsible manner. Driving off campus without permission and cutting classes and driving around all afternoon are not responsible actions. I will take you to school and pick you up after school. At the end of the week, if you feel you can behave responsibly again, your driving privileges will be restored."

Example: Three-year-old Donny leaves his toy truck in the middle of the hall. His mother says, "Donny, what is the rule for your toys? You know that you are to put them back in the box after you are done with them. I'm going to put your truck up here on the shelf for today; you can't play with it anymore. You must remember to follow the rules. I will give your truck back to you tomorrow."

Notice how well Donny's mom fit the punishment to the crime. She didn't scream about Donny being irresponsible or overdramatize a small incident. She reminded Donny of the rule, had him recite it with her, and put the toy away immediately. She withdrew the exact toy that had been left out, not all the toys. By doing so, she made the cause and effect clear to Donny immediately. She also provided reassurance that the truck would eventually be returned and, that once atoned for, the crime would be forgotten.

Example: Your sister and her four-year-old daughter, Heather, are visiting. Heather and your son, Blaine, are eyeing each other on the carpet. When Heather reaches over to pick up Blaine's ball, he screams and grabs it back. The same thing happens when she tries to pick up his stuffed animal. Soon Blaine is sitting on his pile of toys, glaring at Heather as if to dare her to touch his treasures. While you and your sister are amused, you know that you must give your son a lesson in sharing.

Because Blaine is obviously reluctant to give up the power which his toys represent, you can allow him a different type of power. Select three toys and ask, "Honey, which of these toys do you want Heather to play with while she's here? They're your toys, so you get to choose." Note that you are reassuring him that the toys are his and that he will get them back. He might be afraid that Heather wants to abscond with them. You are giving him the power of choice and the ability to act like a good guy with no cost to him.

Once he has made the selection, praise him strongly. "Blaine, you are so good. It is very nice of you to let Heather play with one of your toys. When we are at her house, I'm sure she'll let you play with one of hers." You are now showing Blaine that he gets three benefits from sharing: (1) he gets the power to make a choice; (2) he gets praise and attention from you; (3) he gets something in return in the future.

Example: Seventeen-year-old Dennis feels overwhelmed by the expectations that his parents and teachers have of him academically. He has always done well, but this year calculus has him completely bewildered. Even after extra tutoring and personal attention from the teacher, he seems unable to cope. Rather than focusing on this one weakness, emphasize how well he is doing in his other classes. "Dennis, I'm so impressed at how well you are doing in Spanish. Do languages come easily to you, or do you have to work at them? Have you thought about a career in which you could use your facility for languages?" Discuss a few areas in which he can make a good career for himself without ever having to think about calculus again.

Get help during a crisis.   If you're going through a trauma (such as a separation, divorce, or job chaos) and worry about the effects on your child, get assistance. You may want to become part of a support group. Positive approaches to dealing with your child while your resilience is low are a sign of health and increase your self-esteem. When you nourish your child's self-esteem, you'll best help him through the tough times; your child will be able to weather some crises—yours and his—without suffering long-term consequences.

Example: Six-year-old Jamie is having temper tantrums—long, screaming ones that leave both of you exhausted. While your friends are counseling you to "give him a good swat and show him who's boss; he'll stop crying soon enough!" you choose to sit down and talk with him. The conversation might go something like this:

"Jamie, I bet you are feeling that you can't really do anything right now to make things the way they used to be. I know that you want Mommy and Daddy to get back together, but even though you are a very good boy and we both love you very much, that is not going to happen. I saw how you cleaned up your room, and I have noticed how nice you have been to your sister. I appreciate that, and I love you even more for it. I told Daddy how good you've been and he loves you extra special too. But Daddy and I are not going to be able to live together anymore, no matter how good you are. I know that's a scary feeling. That's okay. Sometimes it's okay to be scared. If you saw something scary and weren't scared, it would be silly. I'm a little scared too. That's natural. We can't always control things. Remember when you had the mumps? We both wanted them to go away because you felt so bad and grumpy. But no matter what we did, no matter how hard we wished, we couldn't control them. We had to go to the doctor and get help. This is like that. I'm going to a counselor to get help with my fear. Maybe we can have you come along too. What do you say?"

Example: You have just lost your job and, as a single parent, are very concerned about making ends meet. You sit down with your fourteen-year-old daughter, Marsha, and have a talk about not spending money as rapidly as you used to. Unfortunately, Marsha is now very scared and is talking wildly about dropping out of school and getting a job to help out. You are already feeling somewhat panicked, but you have to be strong to keep your daughter from becoming hysterical. It's time to talk about all the help that is available, both financial and emotional. Marsha is worried that her friends will find out if you have to get support payments from the government and is embarrassed and ashamed. Sit down and talk with her about the taxes you have paid, and that now is your time to get some of that back, or that you'll be looking for extra work to manage through this time. Generate alternatives that show effective ways to cope with the crisis at hand.

Encourage your child to talk about when he is afraid. Sharing and understanding will encourage your child to tell you when he is afraid—and why. Ask your child how he feels when he has done wrong. If he begins discussing how afraid he is, it might be because he is overly concerned about your discipline. Is it too harsh? It's normal for a child to be concerned about a spanking or a grounding, but if he is honestly frightened of telling you of a wrong, it might be time for you to reexamine your style of disciplining. Your goal is to provide discipline as a foundation, something that shows your child that there are secure boundaries within which he may feel protected. This security—sense of safety—enhances self-esteem. Low self-esteem occurs when the child is so fearful about discipline that he convinces himself that he must be bad to need such awful treatment. Talk about his concerns. A child who keeps his fears bottled up becomes filled with stress and anxiety.

Example: Nine-year-old Mark was doing wheelies on his skateboard in the driveway. He lost control and sent the board shooting into the side of his father's car, leaving a small dent and a sizeable scratch. He immediately panicked, running over to the house of Gene, his best friend, and refusing to come home. At dinner time, his parents began to get worried and called around. Gene's parents, unaware that Mark was cowering in their garage, told Mark's folks they hadn't seen him. Mark finally got home around dark, and didn't talk about where he had been. No one had noticed the scratched car yet, nor was it discovered by the time Mark went to school the next morning. He came home from school to hear his father swearing about some moron who dented his car in the parking lot. Mark didn't say anything.

Over the next few weeks, Mark became more and more clumsy, breaking dishes when washing them, knocking over a knick-knack in the living room, and chipping the bathroom mirror. His parents spanked him after each infraction. Soon, Mark was misbehaving in school. His teachers tried talking to him and finally sent him to the principal's office. It seemed that Mark only got attention when he was misbehaving.

Mark's behavior became worse and worse, and he became more and more withdrawn. Finally, a school counselor sat him down and got the whole story. His parents had a conference with the counselor as well. They came to see that Mark was so afraid of the discipline that he could not open up and be a healthy, normal nine-year-old. He saw himself as an ogre, a careless clown who merited only punishment. His parents were horrified to learn of Mark's insecurity. The story does have a happy ending. They had a long talk with Mark and told him that they disapproved only of his actions, not of him. They set down rules (something they had never done specifically before) and defined consequences for those rules.

Disciplined Parenting

Parents and their children are generally about twenty years apart in age and light-years apart in experience and reasoning ability. They also have different ideas, expectations, beliefs, and values about themselves, each other, and what they want. For example, children are not born knowing that it isn't all right to write on walls and will only learn to express their artistic talents if their parents consistently teach them where they can write. Children do not see their tantrums as a problem—they simply have not yet learned more appropriate or self-controlled ways of seeking satisfaction. Is it any wonder that parenting children is naturally full of conflicts?

Are you aware of your tolerance for teaching your child appropriate ways to respond? Do you separate your child from his behavior when you deal with misbehavior problems? Calling a child lazy because he doesn't make his bed or pick up after himself will do little to get him to make his bed or pick up after himself. About the only effect that name-calling will have on your child may be to contribute to an unhealthy self-image and possibly to become a self-fulfilling prophecy.

It's best for your child's self-esteem if you concentrate on specific, constructive ways of changing behavior, such as explaining specifically what to do and how to do it, and then assisting with those tasks until your child understands the standards for them. In their excellent book, *Discipline Without Shouting or Spanking*, authors Jerry Wyckoff and Barbara Unell provide a summary of effective disciplined parenting. These principles are based on more than twenty years of behavioral research proving that it's important for practical as well as philosophical reasons to separate children from their behavior when you deal with misbehavior problems. Their recommendations follow.

The ABCs of Disciplined Parenting

Decide on the specific behavior you would like to change. If you deal in specifics rather than abstractions, you will manage better. Don't just tell your child to be neat; explain what you want him to do (to do his math homework; to make his bed and hang up his clothes; to pick up his blocks before he goes out to play, etc.).

Tell your child exactly what you want him to do and show him how to do it. If you want your child to stop whining when he wants something, tell him how to ask you for it. "Jason, when you want a glass of milk, say 'Mommy, may I have more milk?'" Physically guiding your children through the desired action helps them understand exactly what you want them to do. If you want him to make the bed in a certain way, for example, show him step by step and then make a point of coming into his room for several days (or longer) to assist if he still doesn't have it right.

Praise your child's behavior.   Don't praise the child, but do praise what the child is doing. Say, "It's good you're sitting quietly," rather than "You are a good boy for sitting quietly." Focus your praise or disapproval on your child's behavior because that is what you are interested in controlling.

Continue the praise as long as the new behavior needs that support.   Praising all the correct things that your children do reminds them of your expectations and continues to hold your own model of good behavior before them. The best way is to exemplify what you want your child to do. Praise continues to restate the correct way of doing things.

Try to avoid power struggles with your children.   Using a technique like Beat-the-Clock when you want your children to get ready for bed faster, for example, will help reduce parent-child conflict because you transfer the authority to a neutral figure, the kitchen timer.

Supervise your children.   This is not to say parents must be with their children every minute of every day, but it does mean that children need fairly constant supervision. If parents are there while children are playing, they can help their children learn good play habits; if you're around while homework is being done, you can monitor study habits. If you aren't paying close attention, many behavior errors will go uncorrected.

Avoid being a historian.   Leave bad behavior to history and don't keep bringing it up. If a child makes an error, constantly reminding him of his error will only lead to resentment and increase the likelihood of bad behavior. What is done is done. Working toward a better future makes more sense than dwelling on history. Reminding your children of the errors they make only holds their errors as examples of what not to do, but doesn't show them what to do. If reminding children about their errors does anything, it acts as practice in making errors.

○ IT'S UP TO YOU!

The British have an expression, "As safe as houses." They use it to indicate something that is completely secure. "Is my car going to be all right parked here overnight?" "Sure, lady, it's as safe as houses." The expression builds on the feeling that we all have of home as a haven from worries and fears.

You want your children to have that same feeling. You want them to think of their home as a place where they are welcomed, cherished, respected, and loved. You want them to think of home as the one place they can be assured of their safety. This feeling isn't automatic. We as adults often lose sight of how large and overwhelming a house or roomy apartment can be to a child. Even a teenager can think of a house as threatening if it signifies only fighting and lecturing. As a loving parent, it's your job to see that you understand your children's fears and address them in order to make home truly the one place where the heart is.

4 PHYSICAL SAFETY: DOES YOUR CHILD FEEL SAFE AT SCHOOL?

The length of time adults will stay in a job is determined first and foremost by whether or not the person considers it to be a safe and orderly environment. This perception of safety also affects the level of performance and productivity, the trust an employee has in fellow workers, and how much they will respect and support their supervisors. Individuals who do not feel safe while at work are more prone to depression and mood swings, to have the highest absenteeism rate, and to file a great many more insurance claims than do their co-workers, and they are more likely to cope with pressure by using drugs or alcohol.

O CHILDREN GO TO WORK EACH DAY, TOO

Children, like adults, go to work each day. School is your child's workplace. Your work environment and your child's workplace are surprisingly similar. Children must confront people, projects, and pressures. Learning is tough stuff, and the atmosphere is often one of competition and challenge.

Your child will spend a great deal of time in the school environment over the course of a thirteen-year career. You should know about his safety there. School isn't always the fun and easy experience we might like to believe it is. Chapter 15 is devoted to helping your child manage that workplace; for now, let's look at the nature of school safety.

○ WHY CHILDREN FEAR GOING TO SCHOOL

Many children are fearful while they are at school or in school-related functions. Children are most distressed when they fear another student, when school activities are not well supervised, and when they either hear about an incident of violence or are themselves the victim of violence. It's not uncommon for your children to fear the unknown disciplinary techniques that a teacher may use "if I'm not good." Even older, timid, or shy children can be fearful of a teacher and of classmates. These fears have repercussions. Countless parents have told me about their children who, after being enrolled in school, began stuttering, bedwetting, nail biting, thumb sucking, having nightmares, or complain of headaches and stomach aches. These stress responses are (physical) manifestations of being (emotionally) fearful.

Trinh, a slender, self-effacing, quiet seventh-grade boy, became frightened of going to school. Morning after morning, he would make up transparent excuses of having headaches, backaches, or toothaches—anything to get out of class. Since he had always liked school before and was constantly involved with school activities, his parents were concerned. They found out finally from a long talk (which he made them promise never to repeat to anyone else) that the problem was not academics and grades as they had thought, but the last concern they ever would have suspected: physical security. Trinh was being bullied.

Two large eighth-grade boys came up to Trinh one day, pushed him into a locker, shoved him around, and demanded his lunch money. They threatened to beat him up unless he gave them all his money that day, and a dollar every day from then on. They told him where to meet them and to give them the money wrapped in a piece of notebook paper. Trinh handed over his money the first time and tried to ignore them the next day. They once again singled him out, slammed him around, and threatened him. He began giving them money every day. He was afraid to tell anyone, as they had yelled at him that if anyone found out, they would "hurt you bad." He didn't know that the same boys were doing the same thing to several other students in his class. Everyone was too afraid to talk, and the bullies prospered.

Girls are not immune from fears for their physical safety either. Darlene, a popular cheerleader, demanded that Karen, a bright but timid classmate, do her science homework for her each night. When Karen protested, Darlene said that not only would she spread bad rumors about "what you do with boys," but she would also hurt Karen physically. Karen was terrified. When she told her best friend, Leanne, what Darlene was doing, Leanne confronted Darlene. Darlene "accidentally" slipped and knocked Leanne down in the shower after gym one day. Because Darlene was so popular, no one believed Leanne when she said that Darlene had done it on purpose. Leanne acquired a reputation as a liar and someone jealous of Darlene's popularity; Karen kept on doing the science homework.

These things can happen to very small children too. Fourth-grader Sam innocently walked into the school restroom one afternoon, interrupting some sixth-grade boys who were smoking. Shoving him up against the wall, they threatened to burn him with the cigarette. When he began crying, they made fun of him and shoved him down to the floor. Although Sam promised not to tell anyone of the incident, the older boys made a point of glaring at him whenever they came across him at recess or in the cafeteria. Sam was terrified and had trouble concentrating for weeks.

When we send our children to school, we don't imagine the things that can happen to them. We think that they are safe and protected. This is not always true. Not all schools provide the safe environment in which we would like our children to spend large amounts of time. Sadly, student violence escalates every year. Common incidents include verbal and physical threats, assaults, injury, theft, arson, and vandalism. According to a safe-school study, the scope of criminal activity in America's secondary schools is alarming. The study reported that in a typical month 282,000 students were physically attacked; 112,000 students were robbed by someone using weapons or threats; 2.4 million students had personal property stolen; 800,000 students stayed home from school because they were afraid to attend; 2,400 fires were set in schools; and 1,000 teachers were assaulted seriously enough to require medical attention. Is it any wonder so many children are frightened?

Does Your Child Eagerly Look Forward to School?

It isn't always violence that creates an atmosphere of fear in school. Jean was a happy third-grader, enjoying school, chattering every day about what was going to happen the next day. One week she stopped talking about school. Soon she began complaining of being tired and saying that she didn't like school. Concerned, her parents talked to Jean's teacher. They found out that Jean was being teased by two girls in her class who pinched her all the time. Jean had started it, teasing the girls who wore green on Thursday ("That means you're a nerd! *Nerd! NERD!*") Jean pinched the girls once, and they never let her forget it. They pinched her back—hard—every chance they got. Jean complained to the teacher, who told the other girls to stop the pinching. Instead, they pinched harder and got some of the other kids to join in. Even those kids in the class who liked Jean began pinching her—just because it was the thing to do. The teacher tried to stop the pinching, but it went on out of her sight most of the time. Jean began to fear going to class.

An unsafe school environment is damaging to your child. In addition to the obvious seriousness of being a victim of a crime, all students are indirectly but seriously affected by the threat of physical or emotional harm in the schoolplace.

When children view the school as a hostile environment, they are likely to dislike the school, teachers, and fellow students. Students who are afraid at school are more likely to rate themselves as below-average students and actually do receive lower grades. Fear reduces their ability to concentrate on schoolwork and creates an atmosphere of mistrust. It undermines morale and teaches that the staff is not in control—that student disorder is more powerful than the adult call for order. Students who are attacked without provocation, or who do not know their assailants—and the majority of assaults are of this type—experience the greatest prolonged levels of anxiety, stress, and depression.

Children who have been victims of attack, robbery, or verbal abuse often admit that they are afraid on the way to and from school and while they are actually in school. If their uneasiness becomes intolerable, they will stay away from school altogether. (Currently, more than a million children drop out of school each year, and the figure continues to increase.)

Many students are unable to strike back when they become the targets of violence or hostility. These children are most susceptible to stress-related illness because they have an impaired ability to deal effectively with fear or anger. Instead, they internalize their fear or rage. Remember, children don't receive training to prepare them for the threat of violence and abuse in school, and many are ill-equipped to confront the dangers they find there.

Making Sure Your Child Feels Safe at School

Your child's school safety is your concern. Making sure he goes to school is not enough. Here's what you can do:

Be aware. Be aware of your child's fears and anxieties about his physical safety. Don't underestimate or ignore the fears your child may be experiencing; the expectation of a stressful event can be every bit as potent as the event itself. Adolescents, like young children, need to feel that they can turn to trusted adults for help when it's needed. This reduces the feelings of helplessness. Teach your children what to do, what to say, and where to turn for help should they encounter situations that cause fear while at school.

The areas in the schoolplace that account for some of the biggest fears include

- *The restrooms.* Children fear encountering other students there who will "rough them up" in order to make them harbor secrets (from the school staff or other students) about using drugs or smoking.
- *The bus.* Children fear rowdy, aggressive, and verbally abusive students who force them to leave a favored seat or rough them up just for the fun of it.
- *The empty hallway.* Children fear encountering the school "tough guys" while they are walking alone.
- *The lunch room.* Children fear being shoved, poked, or being pushed out of place in line or having food thrown at them by another student.
- *The unsupervised classroom or hallway.* Children fear getting into a fight with another student and being hurt or embarrassed in front of other students.
- *The principal's office.* All children, even the tough guys, fear going to the office when discipline is the issue.

Don't hesitate to intervene.   Children who want the attention and admiration of older children may become willing victims, often giving up money or objects in exchange for group friendship. Don't let your child struggle in an unhealthy environment without intervening. Many fathers tell me that they think their children (especially sons) should be left alone to solve their own problems because it builds character. That's simply not the case. It's more likely to lead to feelings of abandonment, fear, depression, and mistrust.

Take your child seriously.   Though an incident may not seem serious to you, it's your child's perception that counts. Hear him out, and then decide how to help. For example, many children today watch a lot of television, including the news. They cannot avoid hearing stories of child molesters. We parents talk seriously to them about avoiding strangers and reporting suspicious activities to teachers and parents, but then how seriously do we take them when they do so?

I still consider myself very lucky that I took my daughter seriously when she, as a sixth-grader, told me of seeing a strange person driving by the school and staring at her. After the third time she told me, I decided to drive my daughter to school rather than let her walk the three-and-a-half blocks on her own. Within a week, my ten-day-old car disappeared from my assigned parking space at the university where I taught. At first I made no connection, thinking I had just been an unfortunate victim of the very frequent crime of car theft. But a few days later, when the car was found by the police, it contained a log detailing both my daughter's and my activities. Someone had been watching and noting everything we did. A professional theft ring had been planning to take my car and keeping track of our activities to make their job easier. My very alert daughter had noticed herself being watched. It was only a car that was taken, thank God.

Older students are sometimes reluctant to talk about their fears and suspicions, feeling that they will look silly or paranoid. Yet because they are older and more perceptive, they, too, should be listened to carefully. They have a good sense of what is wrong.

Bonnie, a freshman in high school, noticed a carload of older boys cruising the junior high every day after school. At first she thought they were the boyfriends or brothers of some of the kids, but no one seemed to know who they were. Some of her friends thought they were cool, but they made Bonnie nervous. She mentioned them to her mother, who came to school one afternoon to see for herself. She saw the boys cruising, and got their license plate number. Through a friend in Juvenile Hall, she found out that the driver of the car had been called in more than once on suspicion of exposing himself to young girls. Nothing had ever been proven and she was unable to take any legal action, but she did go talk to two of the boys' parents. The cruising stopped. Bonnie's mom still thinks she might have prevented something traumatic from happening because she listened to her daughter.

Many young people face undue harassment by students and either cannot resolve it or are afraid to. If this is happening to your child, it may be because he lacks certain self-management skills, such as assertiveness. Assertiveness training, problem solving, and conflict management skills are all worth learning (assertiveness and problem solving are discussed in later chapters). They can add to your child's feelings of protecting himself. You may want to check your local community education programs for workshops and courses in these areas. There are also a number of books on these topics for parents and children. The Suggested Reading section at the back of this book lists some titles, and you may want to ask the librarian at your local public library (or at your child's school) to suggest others. Don't hesitate to talk with the school's counselors, nurse, and principal, or with other parents, about your concerns.

Learn about classroom rules, policies, and procedures.   The rules designed to govern physical safety in the classroom send a loud and clear message that all children are protected there. No doubt your child's teacher has certain rules posted for all students to observe. Rules like "No running, shoving, or hitting," as well as other safety rules (what to do in case of a fire or other emergency) make it clear to each student that the teacher values the safety of all the children in the room. Be sure that your child knows what the rules are (and why and how they are designed to protect) and that he follows them.

Learn about the policies that govern schoolwide safety. What rules exist for student safety in the school environment?

Again, be sure that your child knows what the rules are and that he follows them. If rules are lacking or not enforced, arrange a time to meet with the principal and your PTA to discuss what can be done.

Learn about school security. Security procedures are necessary in every school. The best ones are unobtrusive, of course. Measures to ensure physical security must focus on guaranteeing internal control of the school and external control of its perimeter. Take the time to talk to the school principal, groundskeeper, or security officer about what safety measures are being used on your child's school campus. Are there guards, or do teachers regularly walk through corridors and grounds? Does a patrol car come by to check out the parking lot during evening activities? Is the campus well lit at night?

School personnel will usually be very willing to tell you about security measures. If they are not, you might take their reluctance as a tacit admission that the school's security measures are not as good as they should be. If you can't get any information from the school, call your local police department to find out whether there have been any crime reports filed from the school—and if so, how many and of what type.

Once you have learned about school security measures, support them. If you are displeased with your child's school's security measures, say so. Tell the principal, superintendent, or members of the school board. If you can't get any satisfaction, consider requesting an editorial in the newspaper, or ask a local television station to investigate. Ask your community to back efforts to make your schools a safer place. The effort may have to begin with you.

Ask your child about his teachers. Listen to the stories your child shares about his teachers. Concentrate on his tone of voice. Does your child sound truly frightened, upset, or insecure? Does he seem embarrassed when talking about something the teacher said or did to him? Does he sound as if he is covering up anything? Ask about how other children in the class view the teacher. Sexual abuse or mental cruelty have a devastating effect even on children who are not directly involved.

○ IT'S UP TO YOU!

The first, most critical, and fundamental aspect of self-esteem is a strong sense of physical safety. A child's life revolves around two places: home and school. Take the time to talk about these places, to find out how your child feels there. Discuss his fears. There is usually a reason behind every insecurity. Talking about it with your child shows him how much you care and that you are taking steps to protect him. You make your child feel more secure, more worthwhile, more loved, and more appreciated.

Feeling safe at school allows your child to move on to being a learner and a friend. Hopefully, you have enrolled your child in a school where student safety is the school's number-one concern. Until your child feels physically secure, he will not be comfortable with himself nor face the challenges of childhood with normal curiosity and excitement. Once he is physically secure, he opens up and becomes more aware of all his inner potential—more willing to take chances and to become a fully developed person.

5 SAFETY: SAFEGUARDING YOUR CHILDREN FROM ALCOHOL AND DRUGS

O WHY DRUG AND CHEMICAL USE?

Perhaps one of the most frightening dilemmas parents face today is how to get their children through childhood without their using drugs. Drug use represents one of the greatest fears of parents: Alcohol and mind-altering chemicals can alter a child's life forever and totally destroy their self-esteem. Keeping our children drug- and alcohol-free is no easy task. Growing up in contemporary society calls for an ever increasing ability to endure anxiety, tolerate tension, overcome doubt, resolve conflicts, reduce frustrations, and manage stress. A child who uses drugs and alcohol is less likely to succeed at handling these challenges. While low self-esteem contributes to drug use, using drugs torpedos a child's positive sense of self.

Using drugs no longer scares children as it once did. Nowadays children—yours and mine—are more likely to imagine that drugs hold promise for short-cutting the problems associated with growing up. It doesn't just happen to *other* people's children.

Jay's Story

Jay, a high school student, tells it this way. "In junior high school all my friends would say, 'Jay, you're the luckiest guy, you have everything!' In a way, they were right. My parents were always very giving and loving people. They provided a good home for my sister and me. We had a nice house and things other people didn't have. Yet I never felt happy. Though my family was caring and warm, I felt like a stranger inside. Somehow I never felt as good-looking, smart, funny, and happy as everyone else was. I had a lot of good friends and was very involved in school. I was captain of the soccer team. I was really good at sports, and I knew it. But that good feeling was not a lasting thing. I was very insecure inside, and tried to hide it by being loud and disruptive in class. I tried to become the kind of guy I thought my friends expected me to be.

"In eighth grade I started to drink once in a while, hoping that it would give me a good feeling about myself. In a way, it did. It made me feel 'big' to be able to tell my friends how I got drunk over the weekend. I was surprised how easy it was to cover up my bad feelings and fool people, to make them believe I was a tough guy who wasn't fazed by anything. Even though I knew drinking was not a good idea, I kept doing it. My parents drink occasionally, and I used their liquor supply. They never did notice. Drinking didn't seem to hurt me, and besides, I kept telling myself it was better than doing pot, like some other kids I know. My perception of an alcoholic was the bum lying by the park bench or on the street who never did anything with his life. That person had nothing to do with me. I was a good athlete, a good student, and had friends.

"I'm not sure why I started up with pot. Maybe it was because all the kids had it in eighth grade, and besides, by now I was buying cigarettes from the ninth-grade boys and smoking; one kind of cigarette seemed no worse than another. One day a good friend asked whether he could copy a homework assignment and when I said in fun, 'It'll cost you,' he offered to pay up with a joint. I couldn't just say I hadn't done marijuana, with me being the big guy who was getting drunk and smoking and all, so I said okay to his offer. The first time I smoked marijuana I didn't get high or experience what I heard it was supposed to be like, so I just faked it. But the next time I used pot, things were different.

My friend and I were smoking after an evening high school football game, and I lost all awareness of time and distance. A part of me was really scared, but I also felt very aloof and free. I thought it was great just laughing and feeling strange.

"Dependence is a strange thing. You're sure you have everything under control, that you use drugs only occasionally—you know, when you 'need' them to help you handle the bad times in school and when your friends abandon you. But gradually you get pulled in. At the beginning of the ninth grade, I started to get high every morning when I arrived at school, and some days I'd just never make it to classes. Some friends and I would walk down to a nearby park, have a few joints, and then plan our day. I thought my life was terrific. I had a part-time job at a gas station; marijuana cost so little in my circle of friends. Twice the school called home looking for me. I told my mom that my job had called and needed extra help, and since the money was good, I went there (they agreed to my job so I could save up to buy a car). Basically I was a good student and mom didn't seem concerned. She covered for me and asked me not to do it again. Her whole attitude was that it was no big deal, that 'boys will be boys.'

"Soon I decided my old friends were boring, so I turned to older kids who were more exciting. Besides, the older guys had cars. Since I always had money and shared it for beer and grass, they were all too happy to have me along. They introduced me to some wild parties and some good times. I thought my life was really taking off.

"I still had my parents convinced that I was a great guy and that they could trust me. I bragged to my friends about how often I pulled the wool over their eyes. Sometimes I lied to my parents just to convince myself that I was capable of saying something and having it accepted. It made me feel I was trusted, and my parents found it easy to trust me. But as time went by, they couldn't help but see the changes in me, although at first they didn't understand them. I wasn't considerate at home anymore. I smart-mouthed my mom and dad, and actually made it a point to not do as they said. At times I would feel guilty for treating them the way I did. I was pulled back and forth between my friends and my family; I was always in conflict. Finally, I decided in favor of my friends. 'After all,' I told myself, 'it's my life. I can do whatever I want.'

"It was a bad move. The friends I hung around with weren't real friends—they were just convenient. I used them and they used me. I wouldn't hesitate to steal drugs or money from them, and they'd do the same with me. So there was no one I could trust. I started losing self-respect. I no longer cared how I dressed or whether my hair was too long, or how I talked in front of people. I made the soccer team each year, but often went to practice stoned and just sat on the sidelines. When I did play, I thought that I was really great and that the other guys were the reason we lost so many games. I knew I should be giving the team my best shot, but instead I convinced myself I never really had a chance with all the other good players and all.

"Not doing well at soccer felt the worst. My parents had stopped coming to games because I was on the bench so much. I think they assumed I would feel bad if they saw me not getting a chance to play. It was all very depressing.

"It was a vicious cycle. I would do drugs to feel better about myself, but I'd end up feeling worse, so I'd do more drugs. Getting high was no longer a thing I did to feel happy and have fun. It was a part of my life. I had to get high just to feel normal and not drained and burned out.

"My life began going downhill fast. I began to feel really scared, but I never expressed this to anyone. I just pushed my feelings down deeper, hoping they'd go away. To do this I had to harden myself, and I became insensitive to almost everyone. By now I was getting C's, D's, and F's in school. I was negative about everything. I was talking about what a pain my parents were, and how useless school was. I'd psych myself up about a concert for a month or two in advance, but when the time came, I'd be so high that I couldn't enjoy the music. I'd just sit there like a space cadet, waiting for it to be over. It seemed as if everyone else was having a great time, so I pretended I was, too, but none of my life was fun anymore, and concerts were no exception. The drugs had flattened everything.

"My last cry for help was getting in trouble with the law—and my parents were called to pick me up from the police station for disturbing the peace. I know it sounds crazy, but I was so relieved. I had been rescued. I would no longer need my big-guy/tough-guy act."

Could Jay's Fate Have Been Prevented?

It was a long way back to health for Jay. Alcoholism and drug addiction are tough challenges for anyone, and particularly for young people. Jay missed a crucial part of growing up. Drugs and alcohol can easily sabotage the emotional, physical, and social development critical in your child's formative years.

How can you prevent your child from sharing Jay's fate? Substance and chemical abuse is so widespread in contemporary society that it crosses all age and social and economic boundaries, infecting rock stars and homemakers, students and executives. Alcohol and drug use among today's children is so prevalent that no parent can afford to be complacent. As with Jay, some of the most unsuspecting youngsters become dependent on alcohol and/or chemicals.

When a youngster has obviously become dependent on alcohol or drugs, most parents react with shock and disbelief. How could a problem of such serious nature have infected their child? Other parents feel that drug or alcohol use is just a phase—all adolescents will experiment, and soon grow out of this kind of behavior. But this kind of passivity can be dangerous. The consequences of alcohol and drug abuse can be lethal.

O COPING BY CHEMISTRY

Young people must come to terms not only with how they feel about themselves in relation to family, peers, and teachers, but with themselves as well. Jay realized these images may not always be congruent. The struggle to balance the many competing priorities of school demands, social life, physical growth demands, and other daily life experiences must be done in a healthy way. Not all children succeed at doing so. To meet as many of these demands as possible, adolescents often depend on a wide variety of methods to squeeze more 'productivity' and up-and-on time from each day. They listen to tapes while sleeping, review lecture notes while eating, and often operate on less than adequate sleep and nutrition—and many take drugs.

Among the most popular drugs are those that provide a quick fix for an added edge of stamina, stimulation, energy, or creativity. Young people believe drugs provide a boost for confidence, mood elevation, relaxation, and overall coping with the demands of their multifaceted lives. Unfortunately, many of our young people have been led to believe that drugs and alcohol provide relief and solutions. It's estimated that over one-third of all U.S. adolescents use alcohol and illegal drugs. Many are unaware of the damage these substances do to their well-being. *Drugs and alcohol not only delay our children's ability to recognize that they are in distress, but also work against their ability to detect the underlying problems (cause) and gain mastery over them.*

Today's young people are more likely to use drugs and alcohol than any age group before them, and to do so at a far younger age. Even if they have never smoked marijuana, taken pills that were not prescribed for them, or used cocaine themselves, most young people know someone who has. Drug use is all around them, from the adult who takes tranquilizers to cope with daily stress, to older youngsters who sell pot at school, to movie idols who glamorize drug use on screen and off. The result has been an increased acceptability of drug use over the last decade, making it a rite of passage.

O GETTING STARTED: THE MAKING OF AN ADDICT

How does substance abuse start? Young people often introduce their friends to a drug or alcohol—show them how to use it, and convince them it will make them feel good. This sets the stage for a repeat experience. Before realizing their predicament, they are dependent on a chemical crutch.

The period following the initial introduction to alcohol and drugs is very deceptive because during this time a child often has the illusion that he can control his drug or alcohol intake, that the substances he uses are not addictive.

The progression to hard drug use often begins with what are generally referred to as "gateway drugs"—first the legal ones, alcohol and tobacco, then on to marijuana and other more harmful and addictive drugs. Polydrug addiction is also a major trend; its common denominator is alcohol. If a child begins to drink, the more likely it is that he will also use one or more drugs. Once drug or alcohol involvement begins, it can accelerate quickly, moving from occasional indulgence to dependence. Children—even more than adults—are highly susceptible to this snowball effect leading to polydrug use.

Predisposing Factors

While no one personality type is linked with drug or alcohol addiction, predisposing factors may point to youngsters at risk. Anything that accentuates the self-doubt that kids harbor about themselves or their abilities may subtly or inadvertently lead to alcohol or drug use. Other potent indicators that make a child vulnerable to the influence include:

- Major stress-producing events requiring special coping skills, such as the divorce, separation, or remarriage of parent(s); death of a parent, sibling, or friend; home or school relocation; loss of a long-standing friendship or love relationship; major entrance exams
- Poor self-image
- Family discord
- Sexual or physical abuse
- Lack of emotional and physical affection on the part of parents
- Disharmony in the child–parent relationship
- Parents who smoke, drink, use illegal drugs, or abuse prescription drugs.

Warning Signs That Your Child
May be Using Alcohol or Drugs

Long before they admit it to themselves, parents may see clues that they ignore, hoping the problem will go away. Childhood is a time of intense feelings and wide mood swings, and distinguishing their effects from those of drugs is not always easy. This is another important reason for remaining close and accessible to your child. No one knows the intricate habits and patterns of your child quite as you do; no one can detect changes as you can. With this in mind, watch for abrupt changes:

Peer group.   The child suddenly starts hanging out with a new group. He may begin to spend a lot of time with new friends whom he does not want you to meet. He no longer brings friends home and is secretive about who his friends are.

Personality.   Your child may suddenly exhibit extreme hostility, moodiness, or wild elation; he may be depressed or evince a "get off my back—leave me alone" attitude toward you or other family members.

School performance.   There may be a sudden decline in grades; tardiness or frequent absenteeism should not be overlooked or dismissed.

Performance at home.   There's a noticeable and persistent neglect of chores or routine responsibilities, or the work is done carelessly. He begins burning incense to mask odors from tobacco, alcohol, or marijuana.

Physical changes.   You see a sudden change in physical characteristics, such as reddened or bloodshot eyes, dark glasses worn indoors, persistent use of eye drops, a persistent cough, vomiting, frequent listlessness, drowsy behavior, staggering, morning headaches, loss of appetite, peculiar odor on breath and clothes.

Disappearing items or the appearance of drug paraphernalia.

- Disappearance of prescription pills from the medicine chest
- Tablets and capsules among his possessions
- Repeated requests to borrow money
- Unexplained disappearance of cash, cameras, radios, and jewelry or other valuable possessions—signs suggesting your child is desperate for drugs
- Large supplies of cement and glue or glue-stained plastic bags
- Bottles of cough medicine containing narcotics
- Bent spoons, syringes, eye droppers, and cotton balls
- A persistent sweet or lingering odor on clothing.

Before you can focus on helping your child deal with the problem of drug and alcohol abuse, you need to understand the nature of alcohol and drug use. Your knowledge will give you more credibility in discussing the issue with your children. A number of resources are listed in the reference section at the back of this book, and you may wish to check with your public library for additional resources. Speak with your pharmacist, who is an expert on drugs and their effects on humans. (Pharmacists are, typically, quite aware of the drugs frequently used by adolescents in the community, including those not sold over the counter (such as amphetamines).

Questions Parents Should Ask Themselves

Listed here are clues that may be danger signs of alcohol or drug use. Ask yourself the following questions:

- Is my liquor supply dwindling? If your child is abusing alcohol, your stock might evaporate mysteriously or turn into colored water. Unless you keep an inventory of your liquor, such practices may go undetected for months.
- Has my child's personality changed noticeably? Does he have

sudden mood swings, such as out-of-the-ordinary irritability, giddiness, depression, or unprovoked hostility?

- Is my child becoming less responsible about such things as doing chores, getting home on time, or following instructions and household rules?
- Has my child's interest fallen off in schoolwork, school, or extra-curricular activities, including athletics? Are his grades dropping? Often school performance will go down. In severe cases, a child may become a truant or even drop out of school entirely.
- Do I hear consistently from neighbors, friends or others about my child's drinking or questionable behaviors? An alcoholic youngster's or drug abuser's reputation suffers. Listen to these reports.
- Is my child in trouble with the police? Even one arrest for an alcohol-related offense is a red flag that may well signal alcoholism. A drug-related arrest is also cause for great alarm.
- Does my child spend a lot of time alone—in a bedroom or recreation room? Does he resent my questions about destinations and activities? A certain amount of aloofness and resentment is typical of adolescents, but when it is extreme, it can mean problems with alcohol or other drugs.
- Has my relationship with my child deteriorated? When a youngster has a drinking or drug problem, the first relationships to suffer are those within the family.
- Does my youngster "turn off" to talks about alcohol and other drugs or strongly defend his right to use them?

To persuade your child to abstain from alcohol and drugs will be easier if you both trust and respect one another. The most effective way to help your child become responsible about drinking or drug use is to divest both alcohol and drugs of their allure. The following suggestions have proved successful:

Help your child learn how to assert his opinion fearlessly and unashamedly.   It takes courage for a teenager to say, "No thanks" when he is with peers. Role playing can be a helpful tool here. Create a number of typical scenarios and rehearse possible dialogues with your child.

Help your child learn to communicate assertively. He'll need to learn to say "No" without an apology, argument, or excuse.

Teach the skills of moderation in connection with alcohol use.

- To fix a nonalcoholic drink that resembles a drink being served at the gathering.
- To sip it, not gulp it
- To eat prior to drinking
- To deal calmly and assertively with comments when he is challenged about his not drinking

Teach safety above all else. Tell your child that if his friend or date has been drinking too much, have someone else drive him home. If no one else is available, he should call home to get a ride or take a cab. If your adolescent drove but calls home for a ride because he was drinking, focus on the goal of having him arrive home safely. (Discuss the incident of drinking at a later and more appropriate time.) Reassure him that he can come back for the car in the morning.

○ CIGARETTE SMOKING

Most young people are well aware of the danger of smoking cigarettes. They also know that parents do not want them to smoke. Apparently these deterrents fail, since it is reported that 67 percent of all junior and high school–age youngsters smoke two to three cigarettes every day. Research concludes that virtually all sixth- and seventh-grade youngsters try smoking at least once. Fortunately, half lose interest without going beyond the experimental stage. It's estimated that of the 50 percent left, more than half will become serious smokers (smoking one or more packs a day) by the time they are in ninth grade. Experts warn that the most vulnerable period for addiction seems to be mid-adolescence.

Intervention Tactics: What Works?

Prevention begins at home. Bringing out the facts of smoking and health is up to you. Very young children who are taught the dangers of cigarette smoking almost always take the warning very seriously, even going so far as trying to coax smoking parents to stop. But too often the same youngsters upon reaching adolescence see nothing dire happening to friends and relatives who smoke. By then they have become unimpressed with scare tactics. Teenagers often take up smoking for reasons that are different from those that make adults light up. Teenagers respond differently to efforts to get them to stop, too. As with adults, if either physical or psychological addiction is entrenched, stopping is more difficult. Because adolescents usually smoke for different reasons than do adults, efforts to "unhook" them or to discourage them from taking up the habit require different strategies:

- If *you* have the habit, tell them how hard it is to give up smoking yourself. If you have tried unsuccessfully to quit, explain to your child how much more difficult doing so becomes the longer a person smokes. Avoid preaching, and remember that your child is sensing strong peer pressure and that the approval of friends is quite important to him.
- Know the facts about smoking before you try to discuss it with your teenager. If your child informs you that "everybody does it," talk about about health and well-being and the responsibility each person has to care for himself. If you catch your adolescent smoking on the sly, your first impulse may be to forbid it. Chances are this won't be very effective. There are too many opportunities out of your sight, so banning smoking is not likely to be much of a deterrent.
- The desire to smoke will fade with improved self-esteem.

Discuss with your child why he smokes or why he is thinking about it.

- Assure your child that he won't be an outcast if he says no to cigarettes. Talk about the role of peer pressure and ways to respond. You may wish to role play here, so that your child is able to rehearse the various ways young people offer cigarettes to each other and pressure peers into smoking to feel better about their own cigarette use. "It was really helpful when my parents showed me how to argue back," says Ken. "Last year friends would offer a cigarette and I accepted sometimes, though I often wondered why. I knew that I was afraid to say no because I thought they would think I didn't want their friendship. Through the conversation with my parents, I just started saying "no," and because I was so certain about it and was able to just tell friends that this was something I didn't want to do, they accepted it. It was a lot easier than I thought. I also got a good friend to quit by sharing the negative feelings I had about myself when I would slip up and smoke."
- If you feel you need professional assistance, take immediate steps to seek it.

○ GETTING YOUR CHILD TO SAY "NO!"

The discovery that your child is using drugs is a soul-shaking experience. After your initial response of shock and outrage, you may be tempted to react with pity and indulgence, or with rejection and even brutality. Don't. These responses will not be helpful to either you or your child. Experts say parents are still the first and best line of defense. "Parents have to take primary responsibility for their family's education about drugs and what drugs do to their kids," says Joyce Nalepka, president of the National Federation of Parents for Drug-Free Youth. It's not enough merely to tell kids to say "no." Parents have to explain the dangers and give kids mental ammunition to combat what is often overwhelming peer pressure. Here are the steps *you* can take to help your child avoid drugs, alcohol, and cigarettes:

1. Provide a healthy role model. Treat a nondrinking guest with respect. Don't pressure anyone to "have another." Commend business establishments who enforce "no smoking" on their premises.

2. Don't glamorize drinking or taking drugs.

3. Don't create the impression that the only way to socialize is with a drink, or that relaxation can be based on prescription (Valium, Librium).

4. Don't praise someone else's tolerance when telling stories about the guest who "drank everyone under the table" or used drugs as a way to relax.

5. Don't intimate that alcohol or pills are to be used to relax, alleviate anxiety, or counteract depression, melancholy, or tiredness.

6. Explain how alcohol is enjoyed socially to accentuate a good meal or celebrate a special event, though it is not a prerequisite in either case.

7. Communicate. Provide the honest facts about drugs. Scare tactics or hysterical exaggerations should not be used. Share your values and also point out what is and what isn't legal.

8. Get to know your child's friends and their parents. Provide responsible supervision at your house and check with other parents if there is a party someplace else.

9. Be aware of the early signs of drug and alcohol abuse so you can get immediate help, for the family as well as the child.

10. Encourage your children to get involved in activities that can give them a natural high. Sports, recreation, spiritual support, and volunteer activities can be real substitutes for drugs.

11. Participate. Form groups with other concerned parents. Join your PTA. Invite drug counselors to meetings. Talk with school superintendents, principals, coaches, physicians, church personnel, and local politicians to make sure that everyone is not only aware of drug problems, but also responsive to the threat they pose, and concerned about prevention as well as intervention.

What Should You Do When You Know Your Child Is Abusing Drugs?

This is one time when the ostrich defense can be lethal. If you look the other way, you can only expect the problem to get worse. Obviously, confront your child, but the best time is not when he is high or drunk. A forthright dialogue the next day is absolutely essential. Help your child see the necessity of licking the habit early on, because it's so pernicious.

1. When he gets back to normal and you can talk calmly, show your concern and ask questions. What is happening? Why?

2. Listen—without interrupting.

3. Examine your own attitudes about drugs and alcohol. Is it possible you are sending conflicting messages?

4. Talk with other parents about your teens.

5. Check out your schools. Are their rules and the consequences for disobeying them clear and consistent? What kind of prevention programs do they have? How pervasive are drug and alcohol use?

6. Find out what treatment opportunities are available in your area—in schools, mental health facilities, drug treatment agencies. Exactly what do they offer? How effective are they?

7. Confront the problem. When you see that your child shows signs of a problem, don't look the other way or, worse yet, pity him. At this stage, he needs your help, not your tolerance and acceptance of his weakness. Real parental love may best be demonstrated by helping your child help himself. Teach him to develop his own strength, to find other, constructive ways of dealing with his problems and feelings. If you find your child's problem is too much for you to handle, seek help. There are many programs that you and your adolescent can attend together, such as Alcoholics Anonymous. Information about AA as well as other excellent programs is given in the resource section at the back of this book.

How Can I Best Help My Child?

Honest confrontation is a must. Avoid recriminations about past lying, stealing, and breaking of trust. Focus on the present and the future. Get a grip on the problem, and, with professional help, identify its best remedy. Make it clear that you cannot shield him from the consequences of his habits/actions. Send a clear message: "You cannot drink or take drugs without consequences."

Most parents find it difficult to take this stance of "tough love." Your child may even need medical or institutional care during the initial phase of treatment. You may have to restrict contact with your child for a few days, or not permit him back to the house or neighborhood to associate with the same peer group. Rehabilitation is a complex and difficult process, often as hard on you as on your child.

○ IT'S UP TO YOU!

Helping a youngster kick drugs and alcohol takes time, persistent attention and continuing effort on your part. The best ammunition parents have to guard against the ravages of alcohol and drugs is the attitudes and skills we help our children acquire. Only then will our children respectfully adhere to the limits we set and understand and exhibit the strength and self-esteem we want them to have.

6
EMOTIONAL SECURITY: BUILDING YOUR CHILD'S EMOTIONAL SENSE OF SELF

The second building block of self-esteem is emotional security. Your child is emotionally secure if he isn't fearful of being made to feel unworthy and if he feels safe from intimidation or emotionally painful put-downs. Think how demeaned you feel when someone does something that makes you feel unimportant, says something unkind or sarcastic, or doesn't show respect or pay attention when you're talking to him. We often say thoughtless things to children that we wouldn't say to friends or coworkers. These put-downs tear down—and their effects are lasting. What children hear, they believe. The messages are later played back and become a reference for what a child believes about himself. This tape makes up a child's inner language. For better or for worse, that child has been programmed.

○ THE POWER OF INNER LANGUAGE

Our inner language has a powerful effect on us. It creates our reality. What is the nature of your language to your child? Do you encourage him and build his self-esteem? Does he hear that he's lovable, capable, and important to you? Positive or negative, these messages have long-term implications. I've worked with children who no longer rely on others to put them down—because they do it to themselves! Many will carry the scars of hurtful words from their childhood into their adult years. *Put-downs tear down.*

Maria

Maria moved from New York City to California. She had never had a driver's license in New York but couldn't manage without one in California. She asked her friend, Carla, to teach her to drive. Carla tells it this way:

"I couldn't believe it: At thirty-two years of age, Maria is an intelligent, well-educated, professional woman running an office. Yet every time I gave her an instruction she would do the opposite. I'd tell her to turn right, she'd signal left. I wanted her to make a turn, and for some reason known only to her, she put the car in reverse and backed up! If I weren't so scared, I would have burst out laughing. The strangest part, however, is that Maria didn't get frustrated. She kept shrugging and saying, 'Well, I never did have a sense of direction, and I'm just not very good at these things.' Now I've met Maria's parents and brother, and I have an idea where she got it from. Maria's parents were immigrants with no formal education. Maria got straight A's, unlike her brother, who was lucky to get C's. So the parents and brother salved their egos by saying that sure, Maria was smart in school, but she could do little else. Maria heard that so many times as a child that she believed it as an adult. It took me a month to get her to trust herself behind a wheel."

Miles

Miles, a sophomore in high school, had been told he was clumsy so many times that he believed it. Although he was a tight end on the football team and his running was a thing of beauty, he managed to knock over everything on the kitchen table at nearly every meal. His parents had thought he would grow out of his clumsiness as he got older and complained constantly about it. The more they complained, the more they reinforced the idea that Miles was, in fact, clumsy—and the more awkward he became.

Both Maria and Miles had an inner tape telling them all the things they weren't and all the things they couldn't do. They had heard the tape so often that it became part of their lives, something they accepted. Both of them had loving parents who tried their best to make their children happy and healthy . . . yet they were parties to making their children's lives dysfunctional. What tapes are you building for your child?

A Case of Self-Imprisonment

Several months ago I was attending a four-day event for my sixteen-year-old daughter in a distant city. The third evening was planned for just the hundred-plus young people in this competition, so we parents were on our own. I asked where I might have an informal dinner at an outdoor cafe and was told to go to Restaurant Row.

When I arrived, the parking lot was full, so I parked elsewhere. But I had to walk through that same parking lot. There in the very lot that was so full, was an old and very long Cadillac parked lengthwise, the driver oblivious to the painted lines, carelessly taking up four parking spaces.

Nearing the baby-blue, badly dented, and dirty Cadillac, I saw a very large dog hanging out of the window. He bared his teeth and snarled as I walked in the direction of the car. And there, right beside that furious animal was a tiny kitten—not much more than two months old—and not at all fearful of this big snarling dog! Getting closer, I saw a large woman sitting behind the steering wheel. Then, passing right next to the car, I noticed a curious sight: The car was packed full of clothes, much as if someone had scooped up armfuls of clothing and thrown them into the car. From door to door, dashboard to the back window, the clothes were packed solid. Obviously the animals had been lying on top of them for some time.

The sight was most unusual, and I couldn't help but want to talk to this woman. She and I glanced at each other.

"Hi!" she chirped in a friendly and lovely voice. Her eyes lit up, her mouth smiled, and her words danced as she spoke. She looked about thirty-five or forty, although it was difficult to determine with the weight she bore and her appearance in such disarray.

Sensing an invitation to entertain a conversation, I stopped, returning her invitation to share a moment. (I wanted so much to ask, "How on earth did you create this mess?" "What do you do?" "With those clothes packed in beside you like that, how long have you been sitting there?") How could she tolerate this?

"Hi," I said, returning the pleasantry. "It's a beautiful evening, don't you think? Are you waiting to join friends to have dinner here?"

"Oh, no!" she said. "I don't have any friends. I'll just be here in the car."

"How long have you been in your car?" I asked, trying not to stare at the mess.

"Oh, about two years now," she replied, smiling brightly.

"No, I mean, it looks as if these clothes were put in after you got in. They're packed in around your body and all. It looks like you've been sitting there for some time!"

"Well, honey, I have been here a pretty long time!" she assured me. "I live in here."

"You live in the car, really?" I asked, glancing at her oily and uncombed hair. "Well, what do you do when you want to shower?"

"Oh," she replied sweetly, "I simply go over there." She pointed with her crochet needle in the direction of the nearby hotel. "I take the elevator to the second floor and watch for someone to leave. Then I ask if I might use their shower facilities."

Wanting to see if she experienced success with this creative approach, I asked, "Does that always work for you?"

"Well, of course not!" she replied, sounding a bit shocked that I would be so naive as to believe that it would always yield a "yes" response. "You can imagine why some people might reject the whole notion. Some might fear that I would use their phone and charge up a bill. Others might be afraid that I'd stay the afternoon and they would be charged for another day. No, I don't always get a 'yes,' but sometimes I do!" She sounded rather pleased with her success rate.

She didn't look destitute, and by now I knew that besides her eloquent vocabulary, she possessed a very important social skill: She was friendly and outgoing. I pressed on. "Why do you live in your car?"

"Well, it's like this," she said, her head lowering and her voice changing to a lamenting tone. "My eleventh-grade homeroom teacher said I'd never amount to much, and I guess she was right. My dad said so too. 'Margaret,' he said, 'you'll end up a bum or marry one.' And I did. I married a bum, an alcoholic bum, and he left just one year after we were married. Then my boss fired me; I guess he thought I was nothing too. Guess I became what they said I would."

"Well, do you have family?" I asked, wanting to break the saga of how everyone had done her in.

"Oh, yes. My sister lives across town. She's a cop, but she won't give me any money. She won't even talk to me; she's so embarrassed by me."

Sensing we were back to square one, I asked, "Where else can you go to start over, to get a break? Can you seek out the assistance of a local social agency or a halfway house?"

"Are you kidding?" she said. "This town has those kinds of places for men, but not for women."

Now being a woman had added to her victimization. I was sensing that this was a very long and negative tape, so I moved on to an area that I was sure would get a positive response. Small doilies were stacked in three separate piles on the dashboard. She had a caftan of the same colors wrapped around her shoulders. "That caftan you're wearing is beautiful, and I see you're knitting something new. Do you take these knitted things to a store to have them commissioned for sale?" She had to make money somehow.

"No," she scowled. "Who would want these worthless things?"

I tried one more approach. "What are your goals?" I asked. "What do you want more than anything else?"

She lit up. "Oh, that's easy! I want to be able to take a bath any time, without having to ask. You know, I'd like to have my *own* place!"

Now we were getting somewhere. "Well, then," I said, "when I come here next year, where will I find you? Where will you be?"

"Right here, honey!" she said, smiling sweetly. "I'm not going anywhere." She looked sincere.

I excused myself for dinner.

Who imprisoned this woman?   Why couldn't Margaret transform her life? Why couldn't she reach her goal of having a place of her own? How could such a friendly, communicative, intelligent woman not be able to start over? Because Margaret was stopped by her inner language. Her tape was a destructive collection of negative statements reminding her that she "couldn't," "wouldn't," "shouldn't," and other life-denying messages that didn't serve her very well. Although Margaret had a high school diploma, a year-and-a-half of college at a four-year institution, and a job, and had once had a marriage partner—all the things that so many would want—life's everyday amenities eluded her. It's quite possible that Margaret sabotaged herself— that she was a party to making her life dysfunctional. Acting on the messages that contributed to her low self-esteem, she saw few options for transforming her life and, hence, she gave up wanting to forge ahead.

◖ HELPING YOUR CHILD BE POSITIVE AND OPTIMISTIC

I'm often asked by parents how to help children maintain a positive inner language, especially when they begin to give themselves negative messages, which serve only to defeat them. Negative self-statements such as "I can't," "I'm fat," "I'm ugly," or "I'm dumb" obviously do little to promote a positive sense of self. But you can turn this habit around to help your child develop a healthy tape and to reprogram an existing negative one. Below are the steps.

Empowering Your Child's Inner Language

Use positive language. What kind of language do you use? There are hundreds of opportunities to give praise to your child every day. Even when correcting your child, use positive and constructive feedback. For example, try the following.

"I love that you tell me what you and Gerry did today. I look forward to hearing the details of your science project. But the right way to say it is 'Gerry and I,' not 'me and Gerry.' When you use correct grammar, you make the story even more interesting."

"That's a great drawing you made. I love the colors you used. If you keep the colors in the lines next time, the drawing will be even better and Daddy and I will be even more proud of your work."

"Great job you did changing the oil in the car, son. How about finishing the job by cleaning up after yourself, and leaving the driveway without those spots? That way, I can focus on how smoothly the car is running rather than on how messy the concrete is."

Classify your language.   Teach your children to recognize and identify put-downs and compliments. My daughter and I call them zingers (put-downs) and fuzzies (compliments). There are times when we don't hear ourselves speak, when we don't know we are being hypercritical or sarcastic. That's when we say, "Now, that was three zingers in a row. It's time for three fuzzies, if you please."

TYPICAL (PERHAPS SUBCONSCIOUS) ZINGERS

"One of these days you might be a pretty good cook."

"When you try, you can keep your room clean enough."

"No one wants to hear all your problems with your friends; you're old enough to handle some of that stuff yourself now."

FUZZIES (COMPLIMENTS)

"My friends are all jealous of me when I tell them what nice things you do around the house."

"I look at you sometimes and wonder how I ever got so lucky."

"I think the hospital made a mistake and gave me some Nobel Prize genius's son, but they're not getting you back!"

Insist on positive language.   Insist on positive language from everyone in your home. The most obvious place to start is with the words you say to your child. Don't talk negatively about yourself or others, and request the same from others who are around your child. Post a reminder in a highly visible location, such as on a door, refrigerator, or mirror, until the message gets across to all family members. At a friend's house, a stick figure on the refrigerator door reads, "Harsh words can hurt too. Don't hurt anyone in this house." When anyone delivers zingers—the put-downs that tear down—it shows up on his door as a reminder of just how powerfully words can hurt.

Reinforce positive statements. Teach your child what a positive statement is. Many children have used put-down statements so often, they've actually conditioned themselves to say the negative. If you fear that your child is developing negative self-talk, reinforce what you want your child to tell himself. Focus on your child's positive statements and forget the negative ones for a while. It's easier to change behavior by focusing on the positive aspects instead of the negative.

Examples

NEGATIVE: Geez, when was the last time you brushed your teeth—Christmas?

POSITIVE: My mom gave me a package of hard mint candies. I'm eating one. Would you like one?

NEGATIVE: You never shut up and have to comment on everything all the time.

POSITIVE: I like how open and willing to communicate you are. People learn a lot from listening to you, but maybe you could listen to other people sometimes and learn from them too.

Teach your child how to receive and give compliments. Teach your child how and when to say, "I appreciate it when you . . . ," "I feel good about myself when I . . . ," "I really like it when you . . . ," "Thank-you," "Thanks for noticing," or "When you say that I feel good." Statements to compliment others are always welcome.

Eliminate the negative.   If your child is negative toward himself or others, say, "Remember, we say only positive things about ourselves," and be quick to point out the positive statements of others, or use a private code or signal between you and your child. Each time your child makes a negative comment, use a signal (such as raising a hand) to remind your child. Often children are not aware of how many negative self-statements they are making.

One put-down equals one put-up.   Whenever a put-down is stated, ask the sender to change the put-down into a "put-up." For example, if your son says to you, "My baseball coach is so stupid," tell him that's a zinger. Ask him for a "put-up." He may say, "I like my coach, but I can't always hit the ball!" or if he says something such as, "John is a big mouth who can't keep a secret even when I tell him to," tell your son that's a zinger and he has to say something nice about his brother such as, "John trusts me and tells me his secrets; other brothers aren't so close." Consistently enforce this rule to divert negative statements and encourage positive ones.

What Are Your Words and Actions Telling Your Child?

A respected child psychologist, the late Stanley Coopersmith, devoted his life's work to researching family conditions that promoted emotional security in children. He found that the most important factor was **unconditional love.** High-self-esteem children came from backgrounds that provided the kind of love that expresses respect, concern, and acceptance. Children were accepted for their strengths and weaknesses. It was clearly love with no strings attached.

○ IT'S UP TO YOU!

What are your words and actions telling your child about unconditional love and acceptance? How would you describe the health of your child's tape—his inner language? Is his tape one that will serve him well in his life? Is it working for him now? Is it destructive or in need of repair?

If he needs to replace his tape with a new one, will you help him do that? Words can hurt your child. They can also build him up, instill self-confidence and self-acceptance, and influence how he views himself and reacts to his surroundings for the rest of his life. Take the time, effort, and thought required to empower your child's inner language; it can be one of the most important factors in his life.

7

EMOTIONAL SECURITY: WHAT YOU SHOULD KNOW ABOUT YOUR CHILD'S FEARS

The second step in developing your child's sense of emotional security is assisting him in understanding and dealing with fears and insecurities, and in feeling capable of transcending them. This is especially important in the early years.

○ THE PSYCHOLOGY OF CHILDHOOD

Children are more vulnerable to specific anxieties at certain ages than at others. For example, at age fourteen a child's primary need is for unconditional acceptance of himself as an individual. He is more adamant: He wants to be accepted, no matter what. Long hair, green hair, or shaved hair, his actions will center on gaining approval and total acceptance for his individual sense of self. His goal is to differentiate from his parents by getting them to accept him on his own terms, and although he wants to be special and unique among his friends and peers, he won't alienate them too much because he needs their approval. In meeting his needs, he'll use whatever strategy works. We call this necessary and natural developmental stage **seeking autonomy.** This differs from a five-year-old, whose primary need is to be with his parents, preferably all the time. He'd like to spend the daytime hours with them and would like to sleep in their room at night.

84

His greatest fear is to be without his parents. He'll need a heavy dose of parental security because the next stage is to trust himself as separate and capable of accomplishment in his own right. We call this necessary and natural developmental stage **separation anxiety.** Whereas the fourteen-year-old seeks separation from his parents, the five-year-old is debilitated by it.

The particular stage of development your child is experiencing is one of the driving factors behind his behavior. By being aware of these developmental stages, you can better understand the work that your child must undertake at each stage (and consequently, his behavior) and then help your child learn acceptable ways to respond to the people and events in his life.

○ THE WORK OF GROWING UP: A CRASH COURSE IN CHILDHOOD DEVELOPMENT

What is the work of childhood? Each stage of a child's development presents its own set of tasks and demands, all focused on gaining self-knowledge—**selfhood.** The work of each stage is pretty well-defined. Although it's not possible to go through each age in detail here, there is a general overview below to help you decipher how each influences a child's perception of self. The Suggesting Reading section at the back of this book provides additional resources, and you may wish to consult your child's pediatrician or other child development specialists (child psychologists or your child's school nurse or counselor) for additional suggestions.

Age Two: Autonomy

Until the age of two, a child primarily views himself as part of his mother (or father if he is the primary caretaker). Upon reaching two, he develops the ability to be aware that he is in reality separate from her. This presents him with the task of establishing **autonomy**—separateness. The two words that best describe his new-found selfhood, that he is in fact a separate person, are "no" and "mine." Possession is the tool he uses to enforce that sense of separate self.

Implications for developing self-esteem.   Parents who have experienced their child's zealous work on this task of *selfness* without understanding it have no doubt at one time or another said, "He's reached the 'terrible two's.'" The two-year-old is neither a selfish or an obstinate child. He's looking for power and ways to assert it. Developing his sense of self is a matter of allowing him power and ways to be (safely) assertive. Give your child choices. For example, let him pick out which shoes he wants to wear, or how he wants to comb his hair. Let him decide which book you are going to read to him. In each instance, provide him with two or three choices, all of which you can live with.

The autonomy the young child develops at this stage lays the foundation for being able to value himself. Through his "work" he learns that he can count on his own abilities and to trust that he can assert himself—these traits are the forerunner of independence. If these tasks have been met with a fair degree of success, at age three he will be quite independent.

Age Three: Mastery

Having realized his separateness, the three-year-old goes on to master his environment. Mastery plays an important role in his perception of self: It influences his feeling of being capable (or not capable). His need for success in his endeavors at this stage is crucial. He labors over each of his accomplishments. He is slow and methodical and it takes forever to do each task. Needing feedback to know if he has been successful, he strives for recognition of these achievements ("Watch me, Mommy! Watch me, Mommy!"). That he has something to offer nurtures his sense of competence and proves his value—he is worthwhile.

The search for mastery stimulates curiosity. "Why, why, why?" he wants to know. His drive for discovering (learning) is insatiable—his capacity for learning is unlimited. He has an incredible ease learning languages and language-related skills. With vigor he explores his surroundings, observes people, and examines how he fits into each relationship. Needing to know about everything is a huge assignment for such a little person. It's also a time of sexual unfolding. Here the opposite-sex parent plays a major role in the child's sense of self: Boys will seek to attach themselves to the mother, girls to their fathers. They are looking to gain a sense of their maleness or femaleness.

Implications for developing self-esteem. Be patient as you answer a three-year-old child's repeated questions. He is exploring his environment and examining everything closely. Recognize his achievements with much praise and tangible signs, such as putting drawings on the refrigerator or elsewhere around the house. When you are chatting, repeat things he has said. If your child asks, "Why is the sky so blue?" respond with "Why do you think the sky is blue?" Show that you have, in fact, listened. Ask your child to tell you again about something he enjoys discussing, such as how or why he has drawn a certain picture or why he has chosen to use certain colors in the picture.

Age Four: Initiative

The four-year-old's task is developing **self-initiative.** This may involve something as simple as taking responsibility for putting his toys away after play or as detailed as making his own bed—complete with lumps and crooked sheets, lumpy covers and corners—or as complex as learning to tie his shoelaces. What's most important to him is his having taken it upon himself to do it—to attempt it, to strive. Initiative is the forerunner of motivation.

Implications for developing self-esteem. This child's attempts should be commended and allowed, whenever possible, to remain exactly as completed by him. Focus your praise not on the way the task was done, but on the fact that it was attempted or completed. If you want him to improve the way he does a particular task, show him, as opposed to telling him. Experience, not words, is the best teacher now. This will encourage further displays of his initiative while also encouraging self-confidence.

Age Five: Separation Anxiety

Parents are the name of the game for the five-year-old. At this age, the mother is the center of the child's world. He not only wants to please her, but he also wants to be near her, wants to talk with her, play with her, go to work with her, help her around the house or go along on errands, follow her around the house, and many times would prefer to be with her than with friends. This does not mean that the father is left out of the picture. While the mother is the preference, the father is definitely important too.

The five-year-old's adoration of his parents is unquestionably heartwarming. The result is almost totally parent-pleasing behavior. The basic framework is: "I want to be good all the time. I want to not do any bad things; I'll do whatever you say." Not only does he want to be good and mean to be good, but he also, more often than not, succeeds in being good. In his determination to do everything just right, he'll ask permission for even the simplest thing, even when he needn't, and he will then beam with pleasure when you smile and give permission. (Later in this chapter, I'll be using this age to illustrate a point, and you'll see the down side of this child's developmental needs.)

Implications for developing self-esteem.   Most important in this period is staying connected and helping your child recognize and realize that he is a person in his own right; that "separate" feelings are all right. Especially important is allowing your child the feeling of being good, doing right, and winning your approval. Because separation anxiety is very real to him, let him know where you are, that you are safe, and how he might reach you. When you are away for extended periods of time (two or more days) be sure to call and walk with your child, and reassure him that you will return, even if that sounds obvious to him. You might want to leave notes to be read to the child for each day you are gone. These can be little silly things such as:

Now it's Monday.
I hope you have a fun day.
I've been away one day.
When I come back, we'll have some fun play.

"Now it's Tuesday
An 'I-miss-you!' day . . .

and so forth. You might want to work your child's name into the poem. The idea is to give him a sense of time passing and that there is something to look forward to—namely, your return.

Age Six: Me-ness

"Self-centeredness" comes before "other-centeredness." While in the preschool stage, children discovered they were separate from their parents, although they still kept their parents as the center of their existence. At six, they must shift the focus from their parents to themselves. They now place themselves at the center of their world instead of parents or others. Although they appear to be self-centered, this is an important milestone in their development. They are now ready to undertake the task of being receptive to their own interests and attempting to understand them.

Implications for developing self-esteem. At this age, "I hate you!" means "I have to break away from you for now; I need to be momentarily independent, to do it myself." Allow your child reasonable room to make some of his own decisions. This doesn't mean that you let your child rule you or let him have everything he wants; it means that you show acceptance and empathy, while simultaneously setting boundaries and healthy limits. Present him with several options for doing things, again all of the options being those you can live with. Be tolerant of his boasting. If you have two or more children all close to this age range, make provisions to spend time doing different things with each child. Keep comparisons with others—brothers, sisters, friends, or the neighborhood children—to a minimum. Strive to build your child's individual sense of self by designing projects that invite him to discover a wide variety of learning encounters. When you see a particular area of interest, allow him to delve into it. Help him look for library books on the subject, or take him on an outing (such as to a museum) to explore this area.

Ages Seven and Eight: Sameness

Having established a *me,* the child moves on. Now the need to be separate takes a back seat to his need to feel *oneness* with his same-age, same-sex peers. As he makes the move from self to others, playmates are the new reflectors, and friends become more important. Mastery of social and physical skills becomes the common language to gauge how well he's doing with them.

Implications for developing self-esteem.   Children of this age should be encouraged to join same-age groups, provided with opportunities to develop skills in a variety of activities, and helped to learn healthy and positive ways to relate to others— namely, acquiring and maintaining friendships. Teach and reinforce the skills of fairness and cooperation. This is a great age to begin activities such as Girl Scouts, Boy Scouts, or similar activities that encourage same-age, same-sex friendships.

Ages Nine and Ten: Sexual Identity

A duality of needs exists for this child: He needs approval, direction, and affirmation from both adults and peers. At this stage the continued need to be with members of the same sex is a matter of sexual identity. Although outwardly this child may claim and exhibit contempt for the opposite sex, very often he has a secret girl-friend, she a secret boy-friend. Games of boys chasing girls or vice-versa are common. This is normal and is part of the task of forming sexual identity—a necessity in becoming heterosexual. His task here is to learn the ways of being masculine; hers, the way of femininity. This child also tries to get the feel of how males and females behave by imitating the same-sex parent. This too plays a part in his development of self: The task of discovering his maleness (or her femaleness) is his (or her) first healthy, safe attempt at romance, laying the foundation for future relationships.

Implications for developing self-esteem. There are two distinct phases here. First, the child needs to imitate the same-sex parent. This means the parent has a chance to perform those behaviors he wants the child to imitate, such as performing little courtesies (for example, holding out a coat for someone to shrug into or opening a door). The female parent can remember to say "Thank you" for such courtesies. It's at this stage that boys in particular need to learn the difference between being strong and masculine and being rough. Emphasize the importance of not hurting girls (or anyone) with their strength (this child is often rough and hurtful to pets or other small animals as a show of dominance—strength—and this behavior must be discouraged). Girls need to learn the difference between being feminine and being weak.

The second phase involves the child's developing a relationship to the other-sex parent. A little boy might be made to feel quite the gentleman by being allowed to pull out the chair for his mother at the dinner table. A father can praise a little girl on how beautiful she looks with her new dress or give her a corsage on Valentine's Day. This is a good age to introduce relationship books that give your child a sense of (sexual) security, a sense that it's all right to notice the other sex. At this age, little boys in particular might be teased if they show any attention to or affection for little girls. Having them read books that show how boys treat girls with respect and affection can reassure them that their feelings are normal and that they're not "sissy." Books that show healthy boy-girl relationships can provide healthy images of what it means to have and be a mutual friend.

Ages Eleven and Twelve: Refining Competence

This is a comparatively mellow time between the two major periods of pronounced growth. It's also a time for refining physical and academic competence. This period includes the important task of deciding what's important (meaningful) and what isn't. It's a period of trying on a lot of roles to see which ones feel right. Children will at times appear very rambunctious and, at other times, seem to be nothing more than bystanders, observing everything.

Implications for developing self-esteem.   Here parental modeling is all-important, as is having appropriate models in the classroom and in your child's activities. Teachers and coaches, for example, should be terrific people, worthy of being emulating. (Have you met them?)

This is also an ideal stage to involve your child in gaining skills, whether it's music lessons for one child or soccer for another. Children this age tend to have a natural curiosity and an almost uncanny ability to achieve in several areas simultaneously. Be sure to provide this child with a variety of opportunities for learning and excelling.

Ages Thirteen to Fifteen: Go for It!

All systems are Go at this stage. A child's need to be physical and his curiosity and ability to expand his understanding of the intellectual, social, and spiritual realms are remarkable. Everything is possible, and everything is explored and examined. It's a time of enormous growth in every way; as one stage is being left behind, dramatically a new stage (adolescence) is being born.

When viewing the scope of tasks that must be undertaken at this stage, it's no wonder that it's also a time of chaos. Building a solid sense of self and personal worth at this time is probably the toughest and most important task the child ever faced. These are uncharted waters: Learning seems to be a process of trial and error. One of the most difficult tasks is coping with the (physical) growing pains. Physical maturation—internal and external—occurs at an amazing rate. Key hormones are at work now, doing their job of moving this child from preadolescence to full-scale puberty. The awkwardness of physical growth is coupled with the psychic pain of feeling lonely and alone. That boys are about two years behind girls in physical development doesn't help. The two-year time span in development will even leave some girls out of sync with other girls, causing each to question just why she is (or isn't) growing in this way or that way.

Implications for developing self-esteem. We can best help the child of this age to maintain high self-esteem through stong support systems during his trials and tribulations and by avoiding making him feel guilty when his efforts don't work out. We can also help him understand the changes he is going through by discussing with him these changes, as well as the pressures he faces, and help him learn how to deal with them. The more we give the adolescent a sense of physical and emotional security, the better he will withstand the outside pressures to become what he thinks peers want him to be. Instead, he can develop along the lines of his own interests and talents and aptitudes.

The importance of your attention to your child at this phase of development can not be underestimated. This is your last easy attempt to build a strong and mutual relationship: What you do now will set the tone for your relationship over the next few years.

Age Sixteen: Excuse Me, But You're in My Way!

This age stands alone because there really is no other age quite like it! It's not uncommon for this young person to experience feelings of being confused, embarrassed, guilty, awkward, inferior, ugly, and scared, all in the same day. In fact, the teenager can swing from childish and petulant behaviors to being sedate, or acting rational or irrational all in the same hour; from intellectual to giddy—back and forth as he tries to figure out just who he is and what's going on with him. It's a time of confusion and uncertainty. Often these swings come complete with easy tears and genuine sobs, high-level in-depth sensitivity, great insights and sudden bursts of learning, and flare-ups of anger or boisterous and unfounded giggles. Raging hormones are responsible for ups and downs as well as for changing general sexual feelings from ambivalent to specific. The goal is to experience intimacy; the self-esteem need is to belong. The task is to learn about oneself as a sexual being, (hers, femininity; his, masculinity) and how one is perceived by the opposite sex.

This is a time of duality: He wants to be with others yet he wants to be alone; he needs his friends but will sabotage them if they appear to outdo him; he'll root for a friend out loud, but secretly wish for his demise. It's a time when he wants total independence but is by no means capable of it; he doesn't really want to live without his parents, although he believes they are roadblocks hindering his life.

This time of physical and emotional jumble is hindered by his inability to look ahead and visualize the long-term effects of present behaviors. To tell the child who is skipping classes that he might not be admitted to college; to say to the child who is not studying that he is cheating himself out of an education; to insist to the child who is stealing that it's all taxpayers' money is virtually meaningless. Today, this very moment, is what matters. Feelings of invulnerability and immortality lead youth to behave in reckless ways: The it-can't-happen-to-me attitude prevails as they drive too fast, have sexual experiences, and experiment with alcohol and drugs. This is truly a time of identity crisis—an age of frustration.

Implications for developing self-esteem.　Seek to understand your child's needs as those of a budding adult rather than those of a child. Expect a defiance of adult authority. Consider resistance to adults (especially parents and teachers) as part of the independence move.

He sees adults as hopelessly old-fashioned and naive. This helps him complete the act of pulling away and establishing courage for asserting independence and toying with the idea that he could manage life on his own. Most pronounced is his tearing away from the same-sex parent—especially if the bond has been a loving and close one. To emotionally "leave" this loving parent, he'll have to make him wrong (how could he possibly want to leave someone so wonderful?); he'll have to see him as the problem—at least for now.

A great many sixteen-year-old children actually do leave home (or threaten to) for three or more days during their sixteenth year. This is usually done for one of two reasons: (1) to coerce us as parents into providing them with more rope to be independent—to gain a bigger share of self-power to make decisions on their own, and (2) to shake us up, to see if we are really paying attention, especially in areas where they have taken a lot of rope and are frightened of their own activities. In other words, they need us there as safety nets.

Depending upon how parental power has been handled in early childhood, defiance need not come to all-out rebellion. This is a good time to learn effective ways to listen so that your child will talk, and to talk so that your child will listen. Learn how to negotiate with your child; fortify your relationship with your spouse, because you will both be tested (more especially the same-sex parent); be fair and resilient; and take your vitamins!

Ages Seventeen and Eighteen: Establishing Independence

The final stage of development in childhood is establishing total independence (as an individual person able to assert independence). In looking beyond being dependent on others to being self-dependent, this child confronts some pretty big (and frightening) issues. Their three tasks are:

1. *To determine vocation.* "What am I going to do (for work) with my life?" "Can I afford myself?" Answering this gives meaning to life and the future. Underlying this task is the self-esteem need to be somebody—to experience positive feelings of strength, power, and competence.
2. *To establish values.* The goal is to sort out his own values and decide which ones to keep and which ones to discard. This is the only way he can develop integrity. Perhaps most striking is his need to establish a workable and meaningful philosophy of life. Reevaluating his moral concepts will mean searching for his own personal beliefs, complete with facing religious, ethical, and value-laden ideologies. Developing personal convictions will be influenced by his level of self-esteem—especially if there is conflict in what he believes, what he was raised with, and what his friends find acceptable. Will he claim and stay committed to what is true for him? As he ponders the thought, he'll grasp and cling to sweeping idealisms, searching for their meanings as he tries them on for size.
3. *To establish self-reliance.* Accomplishing this task develops self-trust and confidence. Underlying this task is the self-esteem need to be oneself—being defined by his own self-perceptions and not through the role of student, athlete, son, and so on.

Implications for developing self-esteem. Show respect for this child as an individual. Don't expect him to be a clone of you, parroting each and every value of yours. Give him the respect you would give to an adult friend, especially if you disagree. Ask for his opinions on adult topics, such as current affairs. It is immensely flattering to be asked for an opinion or for help with a problem that is troubling you, like a job decision. You might ask for suggestions about dealing with a personal problem, such as a tiff with a friend. By getting your child to tell you his opinions, you encourage him to think through his own philosophy, to give it more form and substance, to develop it, and to put it into words. He sees that he has some problems similar to yours but others that are different. He sees that you respect him and learns to respect himself as well. Mostly, he learns to trust the process of making a decision, following through and evaluating the consequence. This gives him confidence in putting one foot in front of the other and going forward with his life.

The Challenge of Change (or, How Do You Keep Up with Your Child?)

Perhaps in reading these developmental tasks you nodded your head in agreement when you recognized your child's needs at a particular stage, amazed that children are predictable. That's because childhood is about learning and growing, and children do so in sequential fashion. Even so, children are always in transition, always transforming from one developmental stage to the next. A child is a person who

1. Is leaving behind the prior stage of development and moving on to the next developmental stage.
2. When scared or frightened, slips back into the security of the previous stage; when feeling secure, ventures on to try on the trappings of the next stage.
3. Is undergoing a rapid and intense period of physiological and psychological changes.
4. Wants to be independent but doesn't have a backlog of personal experiences to use in functioning independently.
5. Needs to express his needs and to have those needs taken seriously.
6. Has not yet formed a cohesive value system that would support him in what to live for, so this tremendously important anchor of security is not yet within his grasp.
7. Is locked into his financial and emotional dependence on his family.
8. Notices when there are discrepancies between the rules or values claimed by adults and adult behavior.
9. Has the same intense emotional needs and feelings as adults, with limited understanding as to what these emo-

tions mean or how to cope successfully with them (until we help him learn to do so).

10. Has a strong need for adult guidance as he constructs his own identity and tries to acquire a sense of selfhood that will sustain him.

11. Feels lonely and alone when his parents are physically and emotionally absent; he needs them to

- Show love and attention
- Listen and show empathy and patience
- Offer guidance and direction
- Allow experiences for positive growth through exploration
- Encourage separation and independence
- Help him cope with the crises at hand
- Model what it's like to be an adult

12. Lacking adult nurturing, becomes unable to construct a secure self-identity and becomes less competent to meet the challenges inevitable in daily life.

13. Becomes debilitated, in the absence of adaptive coping skills, by the ravages of stress.

14. Feels helpless when the family situation does not feel nurturing or supportive and turns to peers for the fulfillment of these needs.

Every child has the task of growing and changing—physically, mentally, and emotionally. Children need help every step of the way. Whether your child is five or fourteen, seven or sixteen, take the time to know him. Your child's needs give you insight into his aspirations and motivations and provide you with information that can help you help him overcome the stress, strains, and fears he encounters along the way.

○ THE (NEW) FEARS IN CHILDREN

Knowing about children's developmental stages is more than interesting. Used wisely, this information not only helps us to understand our child's behavior, but to help him develop a healthy self-concept along the way. This information is especially important to parenting in today's times. For example, the five-year-old suffers from separation anxiety when he's away from the parent. Separation anxiety isn't new; you and I had separation anxiety when we were five, and our children's children are going to have to get over being away from their parents too. But contemporary times have transformed many of children's normal fears.

Today five-year-olds worry daily about their parents' safety and not just their parents' whereabouts. In other words, the normal fears take on new meaning. The five-year-old believes that if his parent goes home to work (or stays at home during the day) that someone will come in the window (the door is still a safety point), and harm the parent. He believes that if the parent uses an elevator at work, someone will get into it and knife the parent; and, if the parent goes into a building that is more than two stories high, as on *Dallas* (and that's his frame of reference for this fear), there's a good chance of that building getting blown up.

The major insecurity of being away from a parent, then, is transformed into a fear of his parent's death. The five-year-old wonders whether or not a parent will survive the day in order to pick him up after school or come home at the end of a workday. "My mom is picking me up today," or "My dad is taking me to the zoo this weekend," he assures you. This daydream, or flashback, occurs three to five times an hour. Here your five-year-old is reassuring himself that Mommy and Daddy are still okay. It's his way of reasoning his parents' safety.

Not All Fears Are Productive

Your child is not at his best right now. He's preoccupied, the way you would be if you were going through a painful separation or divorce, had recently lost your job, or were experiencing the death of a loved one. Your mind would be preoccupied with sorting it out. Children can become emotionally distracted too. Here's what's at risk.

The transference of bonding and trust.   When a child comes to school, he has to transfer parental bonding and trust to the teacher. When the teacher says, "Sit down, let's . . ." your child needs to comply. He has to form a trusting relationship with the teacher, and that's important because it becomes a significant link to his learning. We know that students (of all ages) transfer onto the teacher the same relationship they have with a same-sex parent.

Acceptance of others.   Next, a child needs to show acceptance of others. When he looks around at other classmates, for example, he must conclude, "Gosh, there sure are a lot of kids in here. Rather than hit them, I think I'll talk (and socialize) with them!" We call this view of adjusting to others **socialization** in early childhood, **friendship** when children are older, **popularity** when children get to be teens, and **camaraderie** in adulthood. In the workforce we say they are team-players, have synergy, and so on. Acceptance represents respect for others.

Children suffering from stress and anxiety do not adjust well to other children: Sometimes they're selfish, rude or even hostile toward other children. They're not liked much by the other students either. They don't do well in groups, and because they've alienated other students, those children are unkind to them in return. For the teacher, dealing with self-esteem problems takes up valuable time that could be used for learning.

Learning.   We know that the major issue for the five-year-old is parental anxiety, so when he hears about other children in the stories we tell (or write for) him, he identifies; if we add pets, he's a little more interested; but, when we tell tales about a parent and child interacting together, we have entered into his emotional security needs and he becomes a captive and curious learner. We can increase his attention span from five to nearly ten to twelve minutes. Such programming helps us meet his emotional needs, while simultaneously developing his academic skills.

A reading list designed for your child by his teacher reflects the needs of each age of learner. The Suggested Reading section at the back of this book provides resources to help you learn more about these needs too. Additionally, you may wish to consult your local public library for information.

Why Are Children So Different (Fearful) Today?

Why does the five-year-old conjure up images of a parent being hurt or killed while they are apart? Increased hostile exposure to violence can be one cause. Having erased the dividing line between childhood and adult programming, television exposes children to images that disrupt their physical and emotional safety—images beyond what they are capable of handling. Having seen violence on television (or in real life), the young child transposes that image onto what he imagines could happen to his parents. If we believe that children do not pay a price for being exposed to violent and hostile messages and images, we misunderstand the nature of childhood and fail to understand the connection between a child's early sense of self and his adult years—to living functionally.

That's why you must monitor your child's television viewing. It matters. I remember, and perhaps you do too, a time when we slowly disclosed to children the adult contradictions and other personal and social realities of adulthood. We didn't swear in the presence of children and understood why we believed it to be harmful. But today we mostly ignore those common-sense practices, probably believing that one way or another, children will see and hear it all. We erroneously believe it doesn't matter . . . but it does.

A lack of self-restraint on the part of parents and the other adults around him greatly impairs his childhood years too. Returning to the example of the five-year-old, we know that at this stage of development, the child can't separate reality from fantasy. If a young child imagines a ghost is in his room, you don't put the ghost under the bed or behind the headboard, right? You put the ghost up in the corner (so to speak), where the child can "see" it. Then you give it a friendly name and tell your child that it's there to protect him. We create a fantasy to help the child deal with it because he doesn't have the capacity to make the fear go away. That's why the world of fantasy and imagination is used so often in childhood. It helps children make fears manageable.

Making Your Child's Fears Go Away

What can we do then? How can we help our children be psychologically healthy so that they are able to go on to other things—such as being a friend and a learner?

Parents are the key to their children's emotional security. Below are tasks that you must perform.

Dispel fears.   If your child is five, the first thing you can do in dispelling his fears is to take your child to your workplace. It doesn't have to be Monday morning at 8:00; it can be in the afternoon at 4:30 or on a weekend. The goal is to let your child see your workplace as a safe and orderly environment, and to give him reason to believe that you are safe there. Many children have never been to their parents' workplace; most children have no idea what their parents do during the day. The problem with this is that young children might think that their parents work with very dangerous people who carry guns and knives and so on. You don't want (young) children to believe that your life is in serious danger. Even older children are frightened when they believe that their parents' well-being is in jeopardy.

The unknown produces fears in children. This is true for all children, even the sixteen-year-old who is painfully aware (and often angry about) how much he needs adults. These anxieties keep children from the other productive work to be done in childhood, such as making and sustaining friends and, of course, learning.

Learn about your child's stage of development, and talk generally about it with him. This is especially important in the adolescent years, when development is so mysterious to teens and yet when they sincerely want to know what is going on. Today there are a number of good books for parents and their children, and these can be useful in helping you learn more about your child and ways to help him learn more about himself. Again, the Suggested Reading section at the back of this book provides resources, and you may wish to consult your local public library for additional information.

Monitor television viewing. You must monitor television viewing when your children are young. I advise parents to do so until their children are at least twelve years old. By that age, children are fairly agreeable about watching prerecorded (or rented or purchased) videos, so you have a good deal of control in monitoring what they are watching. For older children, point out that violent news may be disturbing; that a scary movie may be frightening; that positive images can create good feelings and can bring about feelings of happiness, and so on. Explain the importance of protecting their minds from unnecessary hostile and violent images (and music lyrics). Harmful insecurities are created as a result of the impact of these images on young minds.

Talk about your safety. Talk to your children about your safety while you are away from them and, most especially, if you travel and are away from home often. For example, describe your trip, making a humorous story of how you got to your destination, the people you met along the way, even the food you ate. This can be fun for you as well. Children, unlike adults, are not jaded. The minutiae that an adult would find boring is fascinating to your children. A special aunt of mine always traveled to far-away places. I remember including my aunt in my daily prayers as a young child, usually placing her before other family members, because I was certain she would fall out of a cab when it wheeled around corners, or that someone would try to steal her! I was absolutely enthralled when my aunt told me about power locks on taxi cabs, and soon felt that there was no way she could fall out of a car like that or be abducted. It made me feel very secure, and it wasn't too long after that I dropped her to the bottom of my prayer list!

If you make the same trip frequently, write down what you do or, better yet, take pictures. Have a few snapshots of your hotel room, of the airport, and of you in front of the office building. Your child can follow your trip as it unfolds and feel comfortable knowing where you are. If it's affordable, consider taking your child along on a trip to let him get a first-hand sense of what you do, and to see your safety.

Learn about the normal stress, strains, and fears of childhood.   Many fears are predictable at the various stages of childhood. Take the time to know what they are for your child. Such information gives you insight into the tools your child needs to manage his daily life. In one of my earlier books, *Stress in Children: How to Recognize, Avoid and Overcome It,* I examined the fears of children in each of the years of childhood and presented ways for parents to lessen the toll. (A summary of the information given in my previously presented book is in the table that begins on page 105.)

Take the time to be well-informed. When you reduce your child's insecurities, he is less emotionally encumbered. There are many excellent books on the behavior and concerns that arise at the various ages of childhood. Several are listed in the Suggested Reading section at the back of this book.

Be alert for symptoms that your child is feeling insecure. When a youngster exhibits physical, emotional, or behavioral symptoms that are inappropriate or unhealthy (such as fighting, swearing, hostility, or psychosomatic illness such as persistent stomach aches or headaches), it's time to find the cause. Watch closely for stress signs that show your child is not coping well, and then get help if you feel you need assistance to help your child. Your school counselors, family doctor, and your child's pediatrician are all potential sources of help.

Teach your child to manage stress. Managing stress is critical to your child's ability to move beyond fear in successfully managing the day-to-day events in his life and to cope with times of crisis as well. Being able to manage stress helps children to develop confidence in themselves and in their abilities to handle the stress and strains of childhood. He learns that he is capable and emotionally hearty; that he can cope; that he can withstand certain fears. His sense of self-esteem is enhanced as he finds that he can meet the challenges head on. See the table that follows for stressors that you'll want to teach your child about at each grade level.

THE STRESS, STRAINS, AND FEARS OF CHILDREN
(BY GRADE LEVEL)

GRADE	STRESSORS
KINDERGARTEN	Uncertainty of parental safety Fear of abandonment by parents Fear of punishment/reprimand by teachers, parents, or other adults
FIRST	Fear of loud noises, especially those of large trucks and buses Being struck by another student Fear of wetting themselves in class or in front of others

SECOND   Fear of not understanding a given lesson (won't be
              able to spell words for a quiz, pass a test)
              Not being asked to be a "teacher's helper"
              Fear of teacher's discipline

THIRD   Fear of being chosen last on any team
              Fear of not being liked by parents or teachers
              Fear of not having enough time to complete work
              Fear of being asked to stay after school

FOURTH   Fear that a friend will betray them, select a dif-
              ferent friend, or share their secrets
              Fear of ridicule by teachers or other students
              Fear of not being personally liked by teachers

FIFTH   Fear of being chosen first on any team (and being
              made an example)
              Fear of losing a best friend, or that a friend will
              share secrets
              Fear of being unable to complete schoolwork

SIXTH   Fear of the unknown concerning own sexuality
              Fear of not passing into middle school/junior high
              school
              Fear of peer disapproval of appearance
              Fear of not being liked by other students

SEVENTH   Fear of being selected first (and having to lead) and
              fear of being picked last (interpreted as being
              disliked or unpopular)
              Fear of the unknown concerning own sexuality
              (peers have shared wild stories or myths, com-
              pounded by television exposure and popular
              lyrics)
              Extreme concern and worry about emotional hap-
              piness and unhappiness
              Fear of not being able to complete homework/
              schoolwork/assignments task

EIGHTH   Fear of being selected last (interpreted as being
              disliked or unpopular)
              Fear of coming to terms with own sexuality (based

on bits and pieces of information concerning his sexuality, coupled with inner and outer stage of development)

Extreme concern and worry about emotional happiness and unhappiness

Fear of activities that require exposure of the body (gym class)

NINTH

Fear of sexuality (too much misinformation from peers)

Fear of activities that require exposure of the body (gym class)

Extreme concern and worry about emotional happiness and unhappiness

Fear of being challenged to a confrontation by someone of the same sex (getting into a fight)

TENTH

Fear of being disliked or unpopular

Fear that another peer will vie for one's sweetheart

Fear of not having derived satisfaction from schooling ("I'm not a good student" or "I don't do well in school, but I don't know why.")

Questioning of family harmony in relationships

ELEVENTH

Fear of "not being okay" and being ridiculed by class members

Fear of not having enough money

Fear that adults will interpret roles for them (as the child seeks to try on and define own values)

Concern over not knowing what to do in life

TWELFTH

Fear that adults will interpret roles for them (wants to clarify for self own values, goals, and relationships)

Fear of uncertainty (not knowing what to do next year—life outside of school)

Fear that preoccupation with self-needs (physical, job, career, personal, peer, or ego) results in deficiency in school role as a learner ("I just didn't take school seriously," "I don't think I learned anything," or "I don't think I'll make it in college.")

Knowing that stressors create problems for children in their school life allows you to talk about them and help your child learn effective ways to deal with them. When parents better understand their children's insecurities and help them find workable solutions, children can come to the learning experience less emotionally encumbered.

Stress affects you in three ways: physically, emotionally, and behaviorally. For example:

Stress affects me *physically*.

- My muscles get tense.
- My stomach feels as if it is churning.
- I have difficulty sleeping.
- I have sudden bursts of energy or I am extremely tired.
- I lose my appetite (or eat too much).

How does it affect you? _____

Stress affects me *emotionally*.

- I get nervous
- I feel sad or giggle a lot.
- I worry excessively.
- I feel bad about myself.
- I get angry easily.

How does it affect you? _____

Stress affects my *behavior*.

- I have difficulty concentrating.
- I become grouchy, irritable, blaming, or sarcastic with family or friends.

How does it affect you? _____

I feel *stressed* when

- I have an argument with my best friend.
- I don't have enough money for the things I would like.
- I feel that my appearance is not what I want it to be.
- I have too much to do and not enough time to do it.
- I don't know what to do in a given situation.

What causes stress for you? _____

Coping with Stress

Coping effectively means dealing with stressful events and managing your feelings (nervousness, tension, helplessness) in situations in positive ways. When you are able to cope, you feel in charge. Being in charge gives you the confidence to handle the situation. No one likes feeling out of control or powerless. The goal is to handle the situation in an acceptable manner.

Some kids cope by tuning out, running from, or otherwise avoiding situations. Others cope by hanging in there when they hit the rough spots, by facing stressful situations head-on, confident they can get back in charge. How about you? How do you cope with stress?

The stress cycle. When one event leads to another, a cycle of stress can begin. When you become overloaded with stress, you are likely to feel overwhelmed and out of control. That can lead to anger. Being angry makes it easy to yell at others or to blame them for your problems. But it's unfair to unload or dump your feelings on someone else. That doesn't mean you can't share your feelings, just that you must take responsibility in managing your response to stress. You can decide to cope with situations in a healthy and productive manner, or you can decide to let whatever happens just happen. It's up to you.

Below is how Robbie coped with his day yesterday. See if you can find reasonable clues to these questions: What do you think went wrong? How did one event lead to another? Could Robbie have stopped some of the problems from occurring? What could he have done differently to better manage his day? Have any of these things happened to you? How did you handle them?

Robbie

- Robbie sets his alarm for 7:00 A.M. but it fails to go off. He awakens at 7:35. Because Robbie is running late for school, he skips breakfast, forgets to feed the dog, and doesn't make up his room. His mother is upset.
- Robbie dashes for the bus stop. When he boards, he finds that his best friend is sitting with someone else. He won't pay attention to Robbie or tell him why he hasn't saved him a seat, as promised. It doesn't feel good.
- To top it off, when Robbie gets to school, he can't remember his locker combination; this makes him late for class, and he can't hand in his assignment on time. He is disappointed because he had worked so hard to complete it.
- His teacher says she won't allow him to go to the office to get help in opening his locker and won't accept the assignment because it's now late.
- Now that he has received a failing grade on the assignment he worked so hard on, he refuses to pick up the new assignment due tomorrow.
- As he is returning to his seat, he kicks the desk that he bumped into. The student behind the desk responds by saying, "Watch out, stupid!"
- Robbie shouts back, "Stupid yourself!" but the teacher catches only Robbie and says that he has to stay after school for thirty minutes.
- Because he stayed after school, he couldn't go to the 4:00 major league football game with his father. He had really been looking forward to that game. Now that he can't go, he is really angry.
- At home, his sister teases him about staying after school, and he responds by hitting her. That makes him feel even worse.
- Next . . .

Everyone has bad days, but what you want to get across to your child is that one event leads to another (positive or negative). Understanding how one event leads to another is the first step in coping. You can teach your child to minimize the harmful effects of stress by learning ways to effectively cope with it. Using the real events in your child's life, have him write his own script. He'll find it fun and will learn to connect the events so that he can begin to control the events rather than be a victim.

○ IT'S UP TO YOU!

The more we know about the psychology of each age of childhood, the more we understand our children, and the better able we are to lead them, to instill confidence, and to inspire them.

Being informed allows you to be alert for the symptoms that show your child is feeling insecure and to take remedial measures. That you want and are actively seeking to allay those fears will be evident to your child and, therefore, contribute positively to his self-esteem as he finds worth in this demonstration of your caring and love. He will feel connected to you, person to person (not just parent to child, or adult to youngster). He will feel that you matter as much to him as he matters to you and that the two of you are a unit. He'll feel part of the team.

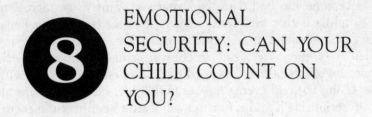

EMOTIONAL SECURITY: CAN YOUR CHILD COUNT ON YOU?

○ ARE YOU AND YOUR CHILD ON THE SAME TEAM?

Another fact that helps your child feel emotionally secure is the knowledge that you are there for him and that you will be on his side, no matter what. It doesn't mean that you always agree with him or that you take his side all the time, but that he knows you're on the same team. He can count on you—you value him and will want to see *his* side of things too. He needs to know that you are supportive of him, and that he can count on you to be in his camp. If you're in a relationship in which you feel that you can count on your partner, you know what a solid comforting feeling it is. And, of course, if you don't get the support you need, you know all too well that an important element is missing in the relationship.

Children Search for the Boundaries of Parental Love

Children cross-examine parents to see how much they are valued. They want to know the boundaries of your love. You have probably heard statements such as, "What would you do if I flunked a class in school?" or "Would you still love me if I did something wrong and got into trouble with the police?" Last year my sixteen-year-old asked me if I would "kick her out of the house" if she became pregnant. I explained to her that I would hold her close and together we would have to face and make many long-term decisions—all with serious consequences—and we talked about what those decisions were. She looked at me and said, "Well, my friend Jana is pregnant and her mother told her to get out. But Jana has nowhere to go and her mother said, 'You should have thought about that before!' I knew what you were going to say, Mom, I was just double-checking."

Queries like this from our children are pleas for reassurance. Children want to know if we will love them unconditionally or if there are strings attached. What makes this issue of letting your child know that you are there for him even more important is that at certain ages many children do feel lonely—moody and down—due to many of the hormonal changes that progress the body from one stage of development to the next. Because some of the natural stages of development contribute to your child's overall behavioral mood swings, he realizes that his behavior is erratic and wants to know you'll love him no matter what mood swing he's in. Sometimes he depends on you to love him when he himself cannot. These times are golden opportunities for you to say, "I will always love you. If you have a problem, you can always come to me. I may not support your actions, nor will I enable negative behavior, and I may be upset by what you have done, but I will still love you."

Does Your Child Feel Unconditionally Loved?

A child may be told that he's loved, but unless he *feels* that he is loved, he doesn't believe it. This leaves him insecure. It's pretty easy to recognize a youngster who feels loved. A small child might automatically climb into your lap when you sit down, certain that he'll be welcomed. He's confident that he will get kissed and hugged, that attention will be paid to him. Past experience tells him he can initiate this gesture, that it just might be perceived as doing you a favor.

An older child who feels loved is eager to share his thoughts with you because of the closeness you share, and because he knows that he can count on you to keep loving him, no matter what. He will be listened to. He can tell his side, no matter how dark the secret. He will be more likely to bring his difficulties to you and to seek your help in working them out. The child who doesn't feel loved buries his problems inside, exacerbating the problem.

Emotionally Secure Children Have Higher Self-Esteem

A child who feels your love also has greater self-confidence. He's not alone. He can count on your emotional support. As a result, he is more willing to take on challenges. His inner confidence is projected outward. He's willing to become friends with others because he knows he's worthy of friendship. In school, he participates in class because his participation is welcomed. A child who feels loved is less willing to tolerate cruel or negative behavior from others. He is likely to say, "Hey, I don't deserve to be treated this way. Stop it!" He'll stand up for himself. After all, he has an army of support (you) behind him. Now he can risk being assertive.

A child who doesn't feel secure in your love slinks away from the hurtful behavior, believing that he deserved it somehow. Or, hurt and angry, he slugs his way through, sometimes acting out what he was accused of being. This pattern, if repeated often, follows him into adulthood. Perhaps you remember hearing of an adult who went from one destructive relationship to the next but always ended up with someone else who treated him in the same inconsiderate way. Why does that person find it so hard to break the cycle? Does he feel that he deserves such contempt and disrespect? Is he initially drawn to the pattern of familiarity of low self-esteem in others—because he was somehow less lovable as a child—and still feels he isn't deserving of respect and appreciation now?

As Children Get Older, They Sometimes Feel Parents Love Them Less

Children frequently tell me that they are loved less each year as they get older. A fifteen-year-old girl recently told me how jealous and betrayed she feels when her parents shower her sister's four-year-old with love and affection. She said, "I feel my parents' love is contradictory. Because my sister's child is so small and cute and cuddly, they overwhelm her with attention. I know that I'm supposed to be acting like a grown-up, but I don't get that kind of attention any more. Why should I get less attention just because I'm older? It's not fair. I do things to get my parents to see how great I am, and all she has to do is smile and be cute!"

Every child (and most especially the child who feels unattractive and the adolescent as he struggles to become independent and his own person) needs the secure base of his parents. A teenager, for example, changes rapidly and has to feel that the new person he is becoming is just as lovable as the small child he left behind. This may be even more true if the adolescent is the oldest child, with younger siblings who are still in the "adorable" stage. Though your teen may not seek out your hugs and kisses as the younger child does, he still needs to feel loved and lovable. And for the younger child who feels he can never be as good as an older sibling who is held in high regard, he too needs to feel the power of your love. And you must express it in a way that shows sincere and genuine concern.

Georgia has a sixteen-year-old son, Jim, who is at the surly, leave-me-alone stage. He appears to prefer the company of his friends to that of his family and complains unceasingly whenever he has to "waste a weekend doing things with you guys." Many times Georgia's husband, Miles, becomes disgusted with Jim and stomps away, saying, "Just leave him alone; if he doesn't want to be with us, we don't want to be with him." Georgia agrees that she and her husband shouldn't force themselves on Jim by demanding that he spend time with them, yet she wants to make it clear to Jim how much they love him and want to include him in some of the activities. The steps she took are excellent for the rest of us to consider.

1. *Listen carefully.* Listen without prejudice. Listen tolerantly. Don't jump in with lectures or disapproving glances; allow your child time to speak, even if you don't appreciate all that you hear. Georgia would hear tales of her son and his friends doing things she considered a waste of time and energy and sometimes even bordering on dangerous. She kept listening rather than jump in to stomp on his values. She knew that as long as Jim would talk in her presence, she had an avenue of information about her son's life. Listening was the first step in showing her son how much Georgia cared about him and wanted to be involved in his life.

2. *Keep tabs.* You know how you feel when you have to keep reminding your spouse of something you had told him before: "Remember, I told you last week that Ann and I were going to this meeting and how much I was looking forward to it!" It's deflating not to have someone remember an activity that is important to you. This is even true for your children. They want to know that you think about them and recall their stories and tales. You can show your love for them by remembering and keeping up. Georgia impressed her son when she asked, three weeks after the fact, "So, did your friend Jose manage to raise his math score enough to keep from being cut from the basketball team?"

3. *Boast.* We all love to hear compliments. To a teenager, a compliment to his face might be embarrassing; to a small child, a compliment might be disregarded, not taken seriously ("Mommies always say that!"). However, when your children overhear you talking about them on the telephone to your friends and hear how wonderful you think they are and how proud you are of them, they just glow. When Jim overheard Georgia on the telephone telling her golfing friend, "Did I tell you the latest on my brilliant son? He even has his friends calling him at home for help with their math homework now! When I was his age, I was the one having to

ask for help; I don't know how I got such a bright son!" he felt great about himself.

○ YOU AND YOUR CHILD: REMOVING THE ADVERSARIAL RELATIONSHIP

One evening last year, after a workshop I conducted for a PTA, a number of parents gathered for a social. One woman in the group I was standing with, Dorothy, appeared to be on the verge of tears.

"Everyone else's children seem to do well, except my kid," she complained, not catching the irony in calling the other parents' offspring *children*, while labeling her own a *kid*. "My fourteen-year-old is a smart boy, but he's doing poorly in school. I told him he would have to stop being lazy and buckle down so he could get into a good college. But no matter how much I demand it, he won't improve his grades. In fact, he says he isn't going to school. I keep telling him he has no choice in the matter! I think he's doing even worse—intentionally. When I talk to him about it, he just shrugs. Ron is a really difficult kid! And I know he argues with me just for the sake of arguing. No matter what I say, he says the opposite. I'm beginning not to like my own son."

Dorothy had lost all joy in parenting her son. Worse, she felt her goal was just to survive until her son was out of high school. What should have been some of the most exciting years in the family's life were spent alternating between bickering and not talking to one another. She was constantly at odds with her son. The supportive relationship she wanted was, in fact, an adversarial relationship.

I talked with Dorothy several months ago. Here's what had happened in the months following:

"I finally went to a counselor because nothing else seemed to be working. I looked for someone who came with high recommendations and made an appointment. I was optimistic that he was going to help me get this kid straightened out.

"He asked me my feelings about Ron within the first few minutes of our first session. I told him how lazy, argumentative, and irresponsible he was. The counselor asked me whether my son knew I felt that way about him. I said, yes, he did; I had made my feelings clear in our many arguments. The counselor then shocked me by telling me that he thought I was irresponsible, immature, and rather stupid. I just sat there looking at him in disbelief. Finally, he asked how I liked hearing those things, how it made me feel about myself. I told him that I felt awful. He then asked me how I felt about him and whether I wanted to continue working with him. Of course, I told him that I had a pretty low opinion of him too and that I wasn't very motivated to come back.

"At that point, the counselor let me in on what he had been doing and why. He wanted me to see what it felt like to have someone I looked up to, someone in a position of authority, treat me with contempt and dislike and describe me in such negative terms.

"I heard what he said, but I was still so upset that it didn't quite sink in. Seeing my confusion and numbness, the counselor asked me to go home and write down all my feelings about myself, especially how I felt about myself when I heard him calling me those names. Then I was to write down how I felt about him when I first called his office and how I felt about him when he called me names. He said that I was to be honest and hold nothing back, then bring the notes with me the next week at my next appointment.

"I started with how I felt about him when he was calling me names, how I thought he was unprofessional, irresponsible, mean, cruel, and awful. I really got into it. Then I contrasted that with how I felt about him when I first contacted his office. I had high hopes of getting help and respected his professional qualifications. All those feelings evaporated as soon as he was so rude to me.

"As I was writing all this down, the purpose of the exercise finally hit me. The counselor was showing me how my son and I were relating. I was in the son's role, and he was in the parent's role. I was listening to someone whom I respected and looked up to—someone I expected to be on my side and help me—putting me down. It was a shock and an awful feeling. My gut response was to fight it, to do exactly the opposite of what he said and did. I was in an adversarial position with the very person whom I was supposed to be working with to bring about a positive outcome. It made me think, I can tell you.

"Then I wrote down all my feelings about my son. But now they were a little different. I mostly thought about how Ron must feel, hearing me call him names. I now felt more guilty than angry, more saddened than upset. I took the lists back to the counselor the next week and had a long talk with him. He said that, yes, I had gotten the point of the exercise. Then we did the exercise over again but this time he presented his case differently. Instead of calling me names, he praised me and my accomplishments. He told me how strong I was to seek assistance, how caring a parent I was to want Ron to have a good future. He went on and on. Finally, he gave me a few constructive suggestions, which I was happy to accept. I still was hearing the same things, but now I was willing to listen to them because I knew the counselor and I were on the same team, working toward the same goals, and that he wanted to help me. My self-esteem was left intact through the criticism.

"I took the lesson home with me. I started praising and encouraging Ron, complimenting him on his strengths rather than always lurking in the shadows waiting for him to make a mistake so I could pounce on it and begin another round of criticism. I began asking him what he wanted to do with his life, what he thought of his studies, how he felt about his performance in school. I asked him how I could be supportive of him in helping him achieve his goals. I listened instead of lectured. I encouraged rather than coerced. Soon Ron was telling me about good things he had done. It wasn't long before Ron's grades went up."

Dorothy and her son are no longer on opposite sides. She's enjoying her new relationship with her son, and he's more willing to work at achieving better grades and to take on the new challenge of learning. That leaves her feeling good about him and good about herself as a parent. She changed the adversarial relationship and is back to the joy of parenting. She laughed as she told me that now she and her son were each other's biggest fans. "Even though we disagree on some things, we have a great relationship, and it's a lot more fun being a parent than a referee!"

Ron's self-esteem was, quite naturally, threatened when his own mother, whose love and admiration and support he thought was absolute, began to attack and criticize him. Once his mother began encouraging him and showed support for what was important to Ron, his self-esteem went up. Slowly but surely, the positive self-concept replaced the negative one in his subconscious. He began to think of himself as good and worthwhile. He began a cycle of positive events: Think well of myself, do well; think even better of myself, do even better.

Can You Hear Yourself Talking?

Are you aware of what you are saying to your child? Ask yourself the following questions:

Do I find at least one good accomplishment per day that my child has done and praise him for it? "Brad, you really worked on your homework assignment tonight. You're such a diligent student." "Sheila, I noticed that you always talk to your fish whenever you feed them. You are so caring about your responsibility to them."

When I have to give criticism, do I make certain to criticize the action, not the child? "Chad, you didn't make up your room this morning. I want you to pick up after yourself every morning, please." Not: "Why are you so lazy? Am I asking too much for you to make up the bed? I've told you a million times; how often do I have to repeat it?"

Am I respectful rather than sarcastic and hurtful? "Randy, I'm pleased that you took the trash to the curb without my having to remind you a third time," versus "Oh, I see you finally got the casts off those two broken legs of yours. I completely lost faith in you that you would ever get around to taking out the trash."

Once an issue has been resolved, do I leave it in the past, or do I constantly bring up old wrongs, not letting them die even when they have been apologized for or remedied? "That's the fourth time this month you talked back to me." "That's the third time in a row you didn't do your chores on a Saturday morning." "That's the umpteenth time I've had to tell you not to put the dishes in the dishwasher without rinsing them." Do you keep count? If so, do you keep count of the good things as well? Consider this, "That's the sixth time this week you have made your bed!" or "That's the umpteenth nice thing you have done for your sister this month." "That's the third compliment you've given me today!" The second approach is likely to get the best results (and continued good performance).

Do I set positive expectations for behavior, or do I anticipate wrongdoings and criticize before anything has happened? "And I don't want you to shirk mowing the lawn this

Saturday as you did last Saturday!" "And don't be late as you always are!" versus, "I'll bet I won't have to remind you about mowing the lawn this weekend," or "I'll bet I can count on you to be on time." If you expect the worst, you might just get it.

The next time you are talking with your child, listen to what you are saying. Is the tone of your voice, your words, and your body language expressing disgust with the action or with the child? What message are you sending? Of course, the real question is, how is it working?

When you are letting your son's dog out because he took off with his friends again, it's easy to allow frustration to build up and explode when your child comes into sight. But how can you get the message across about the wrongdoing while still letting your child know he is cherished and loved, while keeping his sense of self-esteem strong?

The best way is to make it clear to your child precisely why you are upset. This sounds simple, but too often children, especially small ones, immediately assume that the parent doesn't love them anymore because they are bad. They don't think about having done something bad, but that *they* are bad.

Begin your comments by specifying exactly what is wrong. "You didn't let the dog out of his house this morning. I'm upset because I had to do it and was late to work as a result." It's fine to express your anger, but make certain the child knows it is directed at the action, not at him.

And don't cross your signals. Some parents blow up one second and then hug and kiss the child a minute later. How confusing for the child! He doesn't know what's going on. As long as the child has a solid core of self-confidence, he can understand and appreciate your discipline. You can express your underlying love with a statement like, "I bought you Prince because I love you and want you to be happy. I trusted you and expected that you would take care of him. When I had to let him out this morning, and it made me late for work, I was upset with you."

○ IT'S UP TO YOU!

The ultimate goal in helping your child feel emotionally secure is to make certain he understands that you love him and want what is best for him. His self-esteem is enhanced because he knows you care. When parents allow their children to get away with everything, the message being sent to the child is that he is not important enough to merit the time and effort required in providing honesty. Sometimes parents are afraid that by correcting a child we will drive him away. We see the confused reactions of small children and the withdrawal of older ones and become concerned. Just as children worry that we don't love them when we won't take the time to help them correct their actions, we adults can't help but feel that maybe we are losing our children's love and respect.

It's important for parents and children to have a mutual base of emotional security. In Chapter 18, I'll be discussing ways to build a solid foundation of love and trust that both parents and children can rely on.

9

EMOTIONAL SECURITY: SKILLS FOR EMOTIONAL WELL-BEING

When our love is without strings—unconditional—our children feel secure, validated, and affirmed of their intrinsic worth and identity. We make it easy for them to respect and love us and to want to cooperate. There are a number of specific things we do that convince and empower children to be on our side; one of the most influential is to have a vested interest in our child's emotional bank account.

○ OPENING A JOINT (EMOTIONAL) BANK ACCOUNT

With each relationship, we open an emotional bank account. Just as you can deposit to or withdraw funds from your account at the bank, you have, in effect, an account with your child. What you do and say can be a deposit or a withdrawal in the emotional account. Deposits are made through the positive and helpful and considerate things we do and say—courtesy, kindness, honesty, keeping commitments, and so on. Withdrawals are made through discourtesy, disrespect, swearing, hitting, being emotionally or physically distant. Here's how it works:

When I ask that my sixteen-year-old daughter honor her curfew and be in by 11:00, I mean for her to be in by 11:00. It's negotiable only in a few special cases. Mandate or not, should she choose to violate it, she could. That's out of my control and completely up to her. How will I get her to honor the curfew or, in unforeseeable circumstances, to call immediately to explain her plight? The best way is for her to want to uphold the curfew because she too values our relationship and doesn't want to break the trust she has with me. In other words, I'd better have a good relationship with her and, more specifically, I should have a positive balance in our account, in order for her to value the time (curfew) commitment. If I have a negative balance in the emotional bank account with my daughter—if I am in the habit of making promises but not keeping them, for example, or treating her unfairly, then because she is angry, she may make a withdrawal on my emotional account. By not being in on time or by not calling she knows she can cause me worry and anguish. If I keep making deposits in our emotional bank account, on the other hand, my reserves build up. Her trust in me becomes greater, and I can call on that trust if I need to. I can even make mistakes and other forms of withdrawals and be forgiven. But if I continually make withdrawals from the account without making deposits, the reserve is diminished. At that point I have little if any trust with her. I have to watch every step.

Emotional bank accounts are very fragile but, at the same time, very resilient. If I have a large emotional bank account, say an imaginary sum of $1,000 of emotional reserve capacity with my daughters, I can make small withdrawals of $10 from time to time and she will understand and overlook it. For instance, I may need to make a very unpopular, authoritarian decision without even discussing my decision with her. Let's say that Jennifer wants to attend a three-day camping trip and I'm not feeling comfortable with how the activity will be chaperoned. I may say, "No. You can't go. I will not support this particular activity." She may pout or be very angered. And she'll tell me so. My unpopular decision may cost me $100 in her eyes. But if we have a $1,000 bank account and I make a $100 withdrawal, I would still have $900 left. In other words, it's unlikely that she will go to her room, pack for the trip, and go anyway (though that is always an option with a sixteen-year-old).

I could also try to lessen the amount of the withdrawal. For example, I could explain why I did it—my reasoning and so on—thus possibly redepositing some portion of the $100. And I could work for ways to raise the cash to remove the negative withdrawal—perhaps I could suggest that she call up a favorite friend and invite her over for a special weekend. I might offer to pay for movies (without asking her to use her own spending money), or give permission for them to attend a special concert, or allow them a curfew later than usual—just to show my willingness to be compassionate about the fact that she isn't where she wants to be. Therefore, I may even get back twenty or thirty emotional dollars or some portion of the original withdrawal.

Do You Have a Positive (or Negative) Balance?

Your control over your child depends on your emotional bank balance. When withdrawals exceed deposits, the account is overdrawn. If parents threaten, yell, indulge, ignore, abandon, or neglect their children, relationships will deteriorate; discipline will be nonexistent or difficult. When children are young and susceptible to threats and manipulation, parents often get what they want in spite of their methods. But by the time the child becomes a teenager, a parent's threats no longer have the same immediate force to bring about desired results. Unless there is a high trust level and a lot of mutual respect, they have virtually no control over their children. There are no reserve funds in the account.

Making Deposits in Your Child's Emotional Bank Account

Because the emotional bank account is so important in the overall management and nurturing of children, what can you do to build up your account? Making deposits daily yields the best dividend. Only you know the best ways to reach your child, but below are the basics.

Understand your child. What would your child consider a deposit? Many years ago Margaret Mead told me a story about a gift someone had given her. She said, "It was something that was simply very unlike what I would ever use; it was the one color I didn't enjoy; it was not me. It was then that I realized that the person didn't know or understand me at all. I thought the gift a thoughtless one for those reasons."

At first I thought Dr. Mead's criticism was harsh, but later I realized how gift-giving, like deposits, should be very special to the receiver.

I remember agonizing over what I would give as a gift to a dear friend of mine who was getting married. As I was shopping, several beautiful crystal vases caught my eye. I reasoned, "If I were to receive one of these beautiful vases, which one would I want to receive?" (I had already made the decision that I would want to receive a crystal vase.) Finally, I chose the one that I would most long to have, but before I purchased it, I invited her to lunch in the large department store where I had seen it. After lunch we browsed a bit, and I deliberately directed our rambling to the department where the vase was located. "Aren't these lovely!" I remarked, trying to sound surprised and watching intently for her every expression. I wanted, of course, to see if she thought it was as regal as I did. "Well, I suppose so," she said, sounding quite uninterested. "But I really don't like vases. And to tell the truth, I really don't like flowers all that much. I sure hope I don't end up with vases for gifts! I'd just as soon get a toaster." I bought her a great toaster!

Maybe you've done something similar when you purchased a special piece of clothing for your child, only to find it hanging in his closet, unused, unappreciated, and ignored. You have to understand your child in order to know what he will consider a deposit. Is it time with you? Is it practicing kicking a soccer ball with him? Is it being pleasant to his friend (the one you don't like) when the friend stays overnight, without belittling your child or his friend? Is it tickets to a new movie? Is it helping him set and achieve a goal designed to bring about a special event or activity (like attending a special sports camp, affording tickets to a special concert, or going horseback riding, and so on)?

Remember the little things.   In relationships, the little things are big. Perform kindnesses and courtesies. Even small forms of disrespect and discourtesies make large withdrawals. Swearing is a withdrawal; showing concern when your child doesn't feel well is a deposit, and so on.

Keep commitments.   Children build their hope around promises. If you make and keep promises over time, that integrity builds a large reserve of trust. If you say you're going to call, call! If you say you're going to pick up your child this weekend, honor your commitment. If not, make sure he knows you won't be there. Whenever possible, you should be the one to tell him. Your reason for not being with him is important. If you say you're going to come to a particular activity (such as a game or school conference with a teacher), be there. Keep your word and honor his.

Sincerely apologize when you are wrong.   You make a deposit when you sincerely say, "I was wrong," "I'm sorry," "That was my fault," or "What I said was unkind." Children are very forgiving when you acknowledge that you have been unfair. But there's a limit. You can't talk your way out of something you've behaved your way into. Apologies lose their meaning when you keep repeating your transgressions. If you embarrass your child in front of her friends, acknowledge it, saying, "Ramona, I'm sorry to have embarrassed you in front of your friend the way I did. That was unfair." Such recognition not only reduces the amount of the withdrawal, but becomes a deposit as well.

○ RESPECTING YOUR CHILD (AND WHAT THAT MEANS)

An important part of emotional security is feeling respected. I've worked with parents who are more considerate to a friend or an outsider than their own children. One eight-year-old boy told me, "My dad yells at me, but when the phone rings, he's nice as pie to the person on the phone. When he hangs up, he begins yelling at me again in the same rude and mean tone."

Respecting children is more than an interesting and self-serving idea. It helps children to be respectful of others. It's how they learn respect. In my travels around the country, I find that children resent others for not treating them with dignity and respect, just as you and I do. My daughter tells me she feels that way, and I remember I did as a child.

Some adults tend to think that children should respect them because they are older, as though chronological aging is the primary basis for respect. That is a valid starting point but, just as for adults, it works both ways—you have to respect in order to gain respect. When children don't feel valued in this way, they speak out. Quite often, they are disciplined for verbalizing the honesty of this observation.

Getting Your Child to Respect You

If you think about who gets your respect and why, chances are your father or mother will come to mind. Hopefully. Surely, a teacher will. Think about how you learned the concept of respect (or didn't) because of them. I'll never forget the three things my mother did that showed me the meaning of being respectful.

• The family mailbox stood at the end of our long lane. To us children, its contents represented mystery and a sense of thrilling independence. Why? Because my mother didn't open the mail that came in the children's names. Although she had read her own mail by the time she had walked back up the lane, ours remained unopened. Even as a small girl unable to read, I got to open mail that was addressed to me and to look it over without her peering over my shoulder. Mom was wise enough to know that I would eventually bring it to her for reading. This practice continued from the day I was old enough to know what mail was to the day I left home. The message that this conveyed was, "This belongs to you. I respect that because I respect you." For me, the sight of mailboxes, especially those at the end of long lanes, retains a special meaning and reminds me of how much I respect and love my mother. To this day, I don't open my daughter's mail, nor do I toss out the junk mail that comes in her name before she has had a chance to look at it.

• The second thing my mother did was never to interrupt my sentences, even when she disagreed with me. I was allowed to express my thoughts. Because what I was saying was being listened to, I learned to choose my words carefully—she held me accountable for what came out of my mouth, always. To this day, two of my best habits are that I choose my words carefully, and rarely interrupt others. If I'm speaking and someone else interrupts me, I immediately (and automatically) stop talking (although when they are finished, I usually remind them what they did).

• And third, quite often Mom would set the table for the family with the good china. But I wasn't aware of its implication until one day when my aunt dropped in unexpectedly. My aunt looked at the beautifully set table and said, "Oh, I see you're expecting guests."

"No," Mom said.

"Well then why would you have the good china out?" my aunt asked.

"Because," my mom answered, "I've prepared my children's favorite meal. If you set your best table for outsiders when you prepare a special meal, why not for your own family? They are as special as anyone I can think of."

These were wonderful words and made a very lasting impression on me. It was also a very powerful sign of how my mother valued and respected each of us. And once again, I've retained this practice for my family.

○ EMPATHIC LISTENING AS A MEANS OF SHOWING RESPECT

Listening is a powerful sign of respect and an important way for meeting our children's deep need for emotional security. For children, listening means being understood. This doesn't mean that you necessarily agree with your child's opinions and ideas, but that your child has the chance to be heard. It conveys the message, "My ideas and opinions count. I matter." "Mom (or Dad) cares about me."

It's been said that a child's favorite parent is the one who has a listening heart. When a child is asked to name his favorite teacher, the teacher he considers to be the best listener is always named. Being listened to makes a child feel worthwhile. Unfortunately, we often interrogate children rather than listen to them. In a very real sense we decide what the conversation is going to cover. When we restrict our conversation to question and answer time, we close out the possibility of a conversation. Try using open-ended questions that allow your child to open up to you, such as:

- How long did it take you to learn those nineteen spelling words?
- What did you find most difficult about the six you missed?
- Why do you suppose your friend started that rumor about you? How do you think she feels about herself?
- What will you do now?
- How do you feel?
- Do you feel you can resolve this without my help?
- Is there anything you want me to do to help you?

Give your child's conversation the same respect you would give that of a friend. When a friend is confiding in you, you probably put down what you are doing and listen fully. Why would your child deserve less than your friends or even casual acquaintances? The next time your child is talking about something important to him, observe your listening style. Are you fidgeting and looking restless, or are you showing interest in what he has to say? Look at your child; meet his eyes. Give him your complete attention. Imagine how you would feel if you came home from work one day, bursting with big news of how well you did on a project and how others complimented you. You launch into the whole story. But it's obvious your spouse is bored and his attention is wandering. How do you feel?

Probably, you feel as if what you did must not have been such a big deal after all, because you can't even keep the attention of someone who loves you. You feel deflated. And you're an adult, aware of your feelings, able to isolate the action (the lack of attentiveness) from the intent—obviously your spouse never meant to hurt your feelings or disparage your accomplishment. Your child doesn't have this perspective. To him, you merely stopped listening. That means that he's not important to you and that maybe his accomplishment wasn't such a big deal after all. He feels a little less lovable, a little less worthwhile.

○ COMMUNICATION: A WILLINGNESS TO UNDERSTAND

The first rule in communicating effectively is to seek first to understand and then to be understood. It takes time and effort to understand others, especially children, and sometimes we feel we don't have all day to sit and listen. But in fact, it takes far more time to deal with misunderstandings and hard feelings. When we take the time to stay with the listening process until our child feels that we have understood, we have communicated many things: We want to understand; we care; we respect his feelings; we value his friendship; and we value our relationship. Our children (and marriage partners and business associates) spend a great deal of time, effort and energy fighting for acceptance from us, for being respected, and for a sense of their own worth. When we grant them this by sincerely seeking to understand, we find that almost all of their struggle will cease.

There are three ground rules for doing this.

- *Show empathy.* We can influence or persuade others only to the degree that they feel we understand and appreciate them and are seeking their interests as well as our own. Show that you are seeking to understand. While your child is talking, keep quiet for now and listen—without waiting for your turn to talk. This is the time to rise above seeing always through our own references.

  Autobiographical responses seldom have meaning for your child when he is angry or frustrated. The when-I-was-your-age lecture doesn't work because he realizes you've stopped understanding his moment. Save your stories for casual times when you are sharing a lighter moment, when a story, a parable, a metaphor, or a diagram is helpful in making your point and bringing it alive, and when doing so is a way to share what life is about (relationship building). Too often we do this before we take the time to listen.

- *Listen emphatically.* Listening emphatically means that you are listening so your child will talk. You are listening with your eyes and heart to his feelings and not just with your ears to his words. You want to see the world as someone whom you care about sees it. It doesn't mean that you feel as they feel. That's sympathy. The attitude of "I want to understand you" is enormously attractive because it keeps you open, and your child feels that you can be influenced. What he says has a chance of being heard and considered. Remember: The key to your having influence with your child is his perceiving that he has influence with you.

- *Be authentic.* After seeking to understand your child's point of view, you then need to express how you see it and how you feel about it. Know what you're feeling and express it simply ("I feel . . .," "In my opinion . . .," "As I see it . . .,"). Giving "you" messages ("Why are you so stubborn" or "You're so insensitive") only stirs up defenses and stops the communication process. Personalize the message. Own your words. At this point, avoid jumping in with how you would have handled or resolved it.

The following three-step process will help you practice this powerful way of influencing your child.

1. *Reflect the content of the communication.* Simply repeat exactly what is said. If your child says, "Nobody around here ever cares what I want!" you would say, "No one around here cares what you want?" Be patient and calm while you say this, and look at him as you say it.

Older children can become astoundingly dramatic during blow-ups. When your fourteen-year-old shouts, "You treat me like a thumb-sucking baby in diapers!" you can, while trying to keep a straight face, let puzzlement come into your voice as you repeat in a calm tone, "I treat you like a thumb-sucking baby in diapers?" The key is to repeat the phrasing, no matter how dramatic or absurd, to let your child know you have heard what he said. Perhaps in your repetition he will finally hear himself as well.

2. *Reflect feeling.* When we reflect feeling, we listen with our eyes to capture the nature and the intensity of the emotion behind the communication. In fact, your child may be saying a great deal more with his face, or with the tone of his voice, than the words alone convey. For instance, your child might say, "I asked Dad if I could get more money for washing the family car. He got mad and jumped all over me and said that money doesn't grow on trees. I can't do anything right. I might as well forget about saving for a car of my own." Reflecting the feeling, you might say, "You're pretty upset and feel completely misunderstood." If your child says, "I hate Mrs. Nelson. She kept us all after class because that stupid

John Jones was talking to the kid next to him." You could say, "You feel badly about being unfairly punished for someone else's transgression."

3. *Combine rephrasing content and reflecting feelings.* A small child in the middle of throwing a temper tantrum might exclaim, "I hate you!" Get down to the child's level, look him in the eyes, hold him in your arms, and in the middle of a big hug, say to him with a loving voice, "You hate me? No, we love each other very much."

You are not agreeing or disagreeing, only attempting to reflect your understanding of what your child says and feels. Sometimes it's obvious to both that understanding has taken place. There is simply no need to reflect or rephrase anything. Words would be out of place, perhaps even condescending or insulting. When you overhear the heated conversation of your son or daughter who has been rejected by a boyfriend or girlfriend, for example, you might walk over and simply put your arms around your child. Caring is the message.

Talking So Your Child Will Listen, Listening So Your Child Will Talk to You

"My seventeen-year-old son is so moody," a father commented to me in a recent parenting seminar. "I know he's really bothered by something, but when I ask him what's wrong, he just shrugs his shoulders and says, 'You wouldn't understand.' He just won't open up to me. I've told him over and over what he has to do."

I encouraged the father to try first to understand his son, rather than try first to get his son to seek his advice. He answered, "Oh, I understand him all right! What he needs is to show appreciation for all the things we do for him!"

"If you want your son to open up and talk to you, you have to listen so he will talk, and talk so he will listen," I said. "That means that you must work on the assumption that you don't really know what's wrong, and perhaps never fully will, but that you want to and, therefore, are willing to try."

The situation got worse, and soon the father had no choice but to listen. He did. The father decided to put the three steps into action. He sat down with his son, and let him talk. When appropriate, the father would look at his son with an expression that showed he was honestly trying to understand and repeat what the boy said. One conversation went this way:

SON: There's nothing fun to do. I feel so bored all the time. My friends are the same guys I've known since first grade and, besides, they all have girlfriends. I don't have a girlfriend; none of the girls want to go out with me. I'm tired of hanging around and being the only guy without a date. I feel dumb being with my friends when they are in couples and I'm a single.

FATHER: None of the girls want to go out with you? (The father here reflected the content of the communication, focusing on what appeared to be the most important point, the factor that was truly bothering his son.)

SON: Yeah, I've asked Janine and Tabitha and Marcy, and they all said no. I don't want to keep asking. I must be a geek.

FATHER: You feel that because these three girls turned you down, you'd be making a fool of yourself to ask anyone else? (The father reflects the feeling he hears coming from his son. It's not only the lack of a girlfriend that's bothering him, but also his making a fool of himself—of looking silly by continuing to ask.)

SON: Yeah, that's it. I mean, it's like I should get the message already. No one wants to go out with me, and I'm not going to keep asking just to keep getting turned down.

FATHER: It hurts when girls say no. I understand that sort of hurt, having been a single guy once, too. (The father gives his son a hug, and encourages him to keep on talking.)

The son was able to bring his fears out into the open, to discuss them with his father, who was very careful to be understanding but not ridiculing or patronizing. That is, the father didn't trot out bromides like, "You just have to hang in there" or "Those girls don't know what they're missing by not going out with a great guy like you." After talking for quite a while, the son began to see that things weren't as bad as he had felt, that maybe not going out with those girls wasn't the end of the world.

As the conversation progressed, he opened up even more and got to the heart of his real fears: that he was not worth loving; that no one, especially an attractive girl, would find him appealing and lovable. The father was able to reassure his son that those feelings and fears were natural and he reminded him of all the real friends he had, including girls. The father sensed that his son didn't want a sentimental, mushy "But-I-love-you-my-son" scene, and he showed his love simply by caring, listening, and being there when he was needed. The son felt that love and went away feeling much better about himself.

Listening as a Matter of Acceptance

The crucial dimension in communicating with your child is understanding, and building trust and confidence. When you listen, you make it clear that you care about your child's interests, concerns, needs, hopes, fears, doubts, and joys. Listening is accepting another person's ideas and feelings and being okay about the fact that this other viewpoint might be different from yours. Know that from your child's point of view he is right. Instead of saying, "I don't care what you think," say, "This is the way I see it." Say in a cheerful tone, "Good, you see it differently. I would like to understand how you see it." This conveys, "I see it differently," rather than "I'm right and you're wrong." Such language admits, "Like mine, your views and feelings are legitimate and respectable. You matter to me. I want to understand you."

Think back to the last time you had a misunderstanding with

your spouse, perhaps on a special occasion like an anniversary or a birthday. "I wanted you to take me out alone, not with your family and friends."

"I thought you liked my family and friends!"

"I do, but this was to be our special time together. I wanted something romantic, even just a long walk and talk. I need more time alone with you."

"Well, just last week you were telling me that we never went out with others and that you wanted more excitement in your life. I thought having a big group, a party, would be fun for you."

Miscommunication. Reading between the lines, they might be thinking:

SHE: Why couldn't he know I wanted to be alone with him?
HE: So now I'm supposed to be a mindreader? What does she want from me?

The Blaming Defense: Attack, Attack, Attack!

Many people don't accept criticism while they are listening. Instead they defend themselves by projecting blame onto the other person. Maybe you've heard this between your children:

HE: You broke my toy turtle!
SHE: Well, it was your fault for leaving it out on the floor for me to step on. You're always leaving your toys out on the floor. You're such a slob . . .

You might be guilty of using this attack defense with your children. Perhaps you feel uncomfortable about the lack of time you are able to spend with your kids and become offensive whatever they say.

CHILD: I'm going to Randy's for dinner tonight; we might watch videos afterward for a while.
YOU: Since when do you tell me, and not ask me, what you are going to do? And why can't you watch videos here with the family? You owe me some time too, you know.

It's important to listen without interpreting every comment as an attack on you. Unfortunately, many of us feel that we are not as good at being parents as we'd like to be and thus take any comment as an implied criticism. When you are listening to your child, focus on what he is saying. Leave your own self-justification out of it. You can lose a lot of what your children are trying to tell you if you are instead concentrating on building a defense, on saying, "Oh well, yeah, but there's a reason for that . . ." You are trying to learn from your children, not rationalize for them. You have no need to blame yourself. When you feel guilt, you naturally want to chuck it as soon as possible. That may mean projecting it onto your children, as in the examples above. You can easily sabotage communication if you fall into this defense-attack mode. Try listening without formulating your next comments.

Good Communications Don't just Happen

Unfortunately, just because you're the parent, you will not automatically be respected and honored by your child. Although some children are coerced into obeying parents out of fear, most bide their time until they are able to leave home and seek freedom—freedom from the tyranny of the parent.

You want to build a relationship of love and respect so that you can continue in your role of confidant and mentor for as long as you both want it that way. The following attitudes and behaviors are necessary for keeping the lines of communication open with your child:

ATTITUDES

- I do not question how important this is to you, or your sincerity.
- I care about our relationship and want to resolve this difference in perception.
- Please help me see it from your point of view.
- I am open to influence and prepared to change if necessary.

BEHAVIORS

- I listen to understand.
- I speak to be understood.
- I enter into communication from a point of agreement and move slowly into areas of disagreement.

Communication Breakdown Is a Credibility Problem

Communication breakdowns have largely to do with *credibility problems*. Parents might think that they see the world as it is, but their children see it from an incomplete, immature, and selfish picture. This viewpoint is communicated to the child, and he questions whether or not it's even possible to influence the parent differently. Believing it's no use, he is frustrated, and angry. He becomes defensive and hostile in communicating with his parent. After all, he has nothing to gain from entering into a conversation. He already knows the outcome.

Jason

Jason is a six-year-old boy, happy, cheerful, and energetic. Most of the time, he happily complies with what his family wants him to do. However, his parents now want Jason to take swimming lessons. Jason knows for a fact that the pool has no bottom, that he will drown, and that monsters and other things are waiting to get him if he goes in. He is not afraid of water in the bathtub or shower, because he can see the bottom and knows because of the clear water that nothing is lurking there to get him. However, a Y pool, so enormous and dark, is another matter entirely. He has tried to convince his parents, only to be patted on the head and told, "Honey, there are no such things as monsters." Jason becomes confused and angry that his parents won't believe him; he has never lied to them. He thinks that they don't care about him and are willing to toss him to the monsters to get rid of him. He stops talking and withdraws. He has already learned the lesson that adults can stop listening when they think they are right and you are wrong.

Ashley

Seventeen-year-old Ashley is best friends with Tiffany. Tiffany is considered a little "fast" by Ashley's parents, who can't see past the hard rocker look and too much makeup to the very nice girl below. It doesn't help that Ted, Tiffany's boyfriend, wears a leather jacket and smokes cigarettes. Ashley's parents have not specifically forbidden her to hang around with Tiffany but have made it very clear that they disapprove. Ashley, rather than go through all the hassle of that disapproval, often lies to her parents about whom she's hanging out with or just neglects to mention any names. She feels bad about deceiving her parents, but as she says to Tiffany, "Who needs this grief? They're not going to change, no matter how much I talk." The communication barriers have been set in concrete.

Four Barriers to Communicating with Your Child

There are a number of deadly barriers that most certainly will stop communication between you and your child. Avoid them; they'll do nothing but turn your child off from wanting to communicate with you.

- *Don't criticize.* Don't punish honest, open expressions or questions. If you do, you may run the risk of causing your child to cover up, or lie to protect himself. The greatest single barrier to open, honest communication is the tendency to criticize. "If you weren't so lazy, you'd keep your room picked up daily."
- *Don't hurry it.* "C'mon, C'mon. I don't have all day." Don't demand that your child disclose his heart and mind at breakneck speed. Abraham Maslow, the famous psychologist from Brandeis University, said, "He that is good with a hammer

tends to think everything is a nail." This is the wrong approach for understanding your child's mind and heart.

- *Don't misinterpret.* Sometimes we put our own misinterpretation on our child's behavior and guess his intentions. We discourage our children (and withdraw from the emotional bank account) with this tactic.
- *Don't judge.* Listen without judging. You want your child to feel that she can come to you with anything, a triumph to be shared, a problem to be discussed. You want to foster an environment of trust and enjoyment of each other's company. No one wants to participate in a conversation where one person is sitting on high, handing down judgment. If your child tells you of something she did at school and you're quick to judge, she will not be so quick to come back to you. This is especially true in terms of sharing problems. A child wants to feel that Mom and Dad are unreservedly on her side.

"You look down son. What's the matter?"

"Oh, I don't know. Nothing I guess."

"C'mon, you can tell me. I'm your father, and if you can't tell me, who can you tell?"

"Well, it's just that school seems so meaningless, so useless. I just hate school, Dad."

"What do you mean, you hate school? You had better change your attitude right now. When I was your age, I would have given anything to have had the opportunities you have. All you have to do is get good grades, graduate from a decent law school, and come into my law practice. You damn well better not blow it. Get a positive attitude about it, and don't let me hear any more of this nonsense."

Pause.

"Now, tell me how you're doing, son."

○ IT'S UP TO YOU!

Although love for your child is unconditional, your relationship is still one of give and take. One of the greatest opportunities for securing this mutual understanding and respect is through healthy communication. Listening with empathy will inspire your child's respect and willingness to communicate to and with you.

A child should be able to count on his parent not to criticize, hurry, misinterpret, or judge him when he comes to that parent with a story or a problem. This type of positive communication develops healthy parent-child relationships, while building the child's self-esteem.

If you want to be effective and persuasive with your child, start by demonstrating your understanding of his point of view. Then share your message clearly, graphically, and above all, in good will.

10 "WHO AM I?": HELPING YOUR CHILD ANSWER THE QUESTION

You've been looking at the importance of your role in helping your child feel safe and secure so that he can focus time, energy, and concentration on learning, growing, and building and sustaining healthy relationships. Physical safety and emotional security are prerequisites to being able to do that. By meeting those needs adequately, your child can now move on to the "Who-am-I?" question—identity—and evaluate his own essence. Helping your child develop a healthy image of himself is the third building block in self-esteem.

Here is a beautiful poem called "The Paint Brush" by Lee Ezell:

I keep my paint brush with me
Wherever I may go,
In case I need to cover up
So the real me doesn't show.
I'm so afraid to show you me,
Afraid of what you'll do.
You might laugh or say mean things
I'm afraid I might lose you.
I'd like to remove all of my paint coats
To show you the real, true me,
But I want you to try and understand
I need you to like what you see.
So if you'll be patient and close your eyes

I'll strip off all my coats real slow,
Please understand how much it hurts
To let the real me show.
Now my coats are all stripped off
I feel naked, bare and cold,
If you still love me with all that you see
You are my friend pure as gold.
I need to save my paint brush though
And hold it in my hand,
I want to keep it handy
In case somebody doesn't understand.
So please protect me, my dear friend
And thanks for loving me true
But please let me keep my paint brush with me
Until I love me, too.

Reprinted with permission.

Have you ever felt the apprehensions this poem poignantly illustrates? Most of us do from time to time. For children, however, it's ever present. With so many of us to please, each of us perhaps wanting something different, is it any wonder that as a child seeks to fulfill expectations of parents, teachers, friends, and coaches, he wonders "Who am I? What do I want?"

How your child sees himself and the way he thinks others view him play quite a role in what he will reveal to us. A child's sense of his identity is primarily formulated by five intertwining factors: his view of his actual, ideal, and public selves; his outer physical appearance; his feelings about inner and outer body stages of growth and development; how special he feels (or is made to feel); and his perceptions of how others see him. I'll examine the first three in this chapter, and focus on others in Chapter 11.

○ SELF-IMAGE INFLUENCES YOUR CHILD'S ACTIONS

We all have an identity. The question is, what do we see, and is this image a healthy and positive one? Sometimes it is, and sometimes it isn't. Children believe what they hear and act on it. I'm reminded of a story I heard Gail Dusa of the National Counsel for Self-Esteem tell recently at a National Counsel meeting.

A young boy came home crying because a classmate had called him a sissy.

"Why are you crying?" his grandmother asked.

"Because Paul called me a sissy. Do you think I'm a sissy, Grandma?"

"Oh no," said his grandmother. "I think you're a Ferrari."

"What?" said the boy, trying to make sense of what his grandmother had said. "Why do you think I'm a car?"

"Well, if you believe that because Paul called you a sissy you *are,* then you might as well believe you're a car. Why be a sissy when you can be a Ferrari?"

"Oh!" exclaimed the boy gleefully, feeling quite relieved. "I get to decide what I am!"

And that is what we need to help our children believe: Why be a sissy when you can be a Ferrari!

Unfortunately, and all too often, a young person believes his personal price tag reads "Damaged Goods" instead of "Valuable Merchandise." For example, the child who has been physically or emotionally mistreated (hurt or abandoned by those he loves) underestimates himself, or he exaggerates his self-worth as a way of compensating for low self-opinion. Sometimes this inner picture needs only minor repair; at times it needs to be fine-tuned or refocused, and sometimes it needs to be replaced by an entirely new picture.

Accurate or inaccurate, healthy or dysfunctional, our actions flow from this inner picture of our sense of self-worth. This is why a child who sees himself in a positive light acts positively; a child who sees himself as a problem child is usually in trouble; a student's perceptions of his capabilities become the baseline standard for his performance in school. A child's self-description definitely affects his potential—the inner picture is *very* influential. Luckily, you can help your child construct a healthy identity and even repair a bruised one.

The Actual, Ideal, and Public Selves

Selfhood is constructed by peering at ourselves through three separate windows, and assessing what we find there. We call these the **actual, ideal,** and **public selves.** These self-perceptions form one basis for how your child judges who he is.

- *The actual self.* A composite picture of how successful your child feels in each of his many roles—being a son, daughter, brother, sister, student, paperboy, friend, and so on: It's his overall picture of how he interacts in each of his many roles and how he is greeted in each of them in return. For example, he may think he's a wonderful son but not be very comfortable with his ability to make and sustain friends; he may feel good about his associations with friends, but inadequate in his role as a son.

- *The ideal self.* Made up of aspirations: It's the ideal of how he would like to be and who he wants to become: "I wish I were pretty . . . an A-student . . . thinner . . . heavier . . . smarter." Or it can be more definite: "I want to be a member of the baseball team . . . a lifeguard . . . make lots of money." It's the "When-I'm-rich" or "When-I'm-grown-up" ideas and his belief in someday having or being those things.

- *The public self.* The slice of image your child is willing to show to others: It's putting up a good front or disclosing only a certain image to others. He can be the one who decides what this will be, or he can be influenced by what others want him to be (popular, mean, spirited, and so on), or it can be based on who he imagines they want him to be.

Each of us forms a picture of ourselves in each of these three areas. What is of most importance is that this picture be in perspective. When great discrepancies exist in the overall balance, the stress experienced can be enormous. Those people whose lives are mainly lived out projecting only the public self, for example, can easily lose sight of how the other areas help serve to keep him safe. We can see this magnified in the lives of people such as John Belushi. Belushi's public self was that of a clown and a slob, like the character he played in the film *Animal House*. He put up the front of being a happy, exuberant, rather crass, uncaring, insensitive guy. The public was willing to accept him as such. They were less willing to accept him as a sensitive, romantic man. When Belushi tried to play a suave hero in the film *Continental Divide*, he was a flop. The public had decided which image of him it would accept.

Belushi knew that he had more to offer than a slapstick act. It must have been very difficult for him to know that the public didn't want to see more of him than that—that no one wanted to look past the humor to the intelligence and caring. Belushi's self-identity became more and more tied up in one self-window, to the exclusion of others. A toll, whether in inappropriate behavior, drugs, depression, or anything else self-destructive, is exacted for having a life out of balance.

What Is Your Child's Behavior Saying?

How does your child see himself? A place to start is by examining his behavior—it tells much about how he is feeling about himself. Dropping out of school, for example, tells more about the child himself than the degree of difficulty he is having with the school's curriculum, teaching effectiveness, school leadership, or the influence of peer pressure.

When the three aspects of identity are out of balance, your child doesn't know who he is or what he stands for. He's in turmoil. If he's acting primarily from his public self, for example, he may think he has to be popular—because others think he is and because they expect it from him (even if he feels uncomfortable in that role). He goes along with it, thinking it will please them. His actions are focused on gaining attention and feedback from others, and soon he'll say, "No one cares what I want." Passive-aggressive behavior or destructive coping strategies can result later on (denial, alcohol, drugs).

○ HELPING YOUR CHILD BUILD A POSITIVE SENSE OF SELF

Start by learning how your child sees himself, so you can determine how his actual, ideal, and public selves differ. Ask him to describe himself, using questions such as the following:

* What four words best describe you?
* How do you see yourself?
* What four words best describe how you would like to be?
* How do you think others see you? If they were to describe you, what would they say?

You'll notice that your child will enjoy talking about these things. He considers this to be a sign of real interest on your part.

There are other steps you can take to help your child build a positive sense of selfhood.

Model positive values. Parents are powerful models for their children. You need only to hear your young child talk to his doll or pet to know that he parents the doll (or pet) exactly as he has experienced your parenting. Is it "No! No! Bad dog!" for example, or "Here, let me show you how . . ."? Modeling is the way most of us learn. No matter how many times you say, "That's different; I'm an adult," or "Do as I say, not as I do," your child is going to act based on what he sees and hears. If you tell your child not to lie, but then have him tell lies on your behalf ("If that's Mrs. Peterson, tell her I'm not home now!"), you send out a contradiction, and he'll learn to lie, too. You might quit smoking so your child never begins. That's positive modeling. Remember, our values always show up in our actions!

Verbalize the benefits. Besides modeling the values you want your child to embrace in order to build a healthy identity, verbalize them. If you think of yourself in a negative way, your child will, too. On the other hand, if your outlook is optimistic, your child is going to be more pleased at his own reflection. When you say, "I felt pretty good about myself when I left here this morning. Others noticed it and wanted to be around me. I had a fun day because a lot of people went out of their way to talk to me," it sends a positive message to your child. Show him the connection between how good you feel about yourself and the positive outcome. Tell him how your good attitude affected your day.

You may want to play out "what-if" scenarios so he can hear the difference. "Hmmm, I wonder what will happen if I stay in this good mood all week: Will I accomplish more and have a better time?" By verbalizing the benefits of a healthy identity, you teach your child that he can be in charge of his attitude.

Speak positively about yourself. When you speak positively about yourself, you impart the message that self-respect matters—that you count. Your child hears you say, "I did a good job at the office today," and he is more likely to come back from school and say he did a good job himself. He hears you say, "I feel good about myself because I managed to stay with it and get it completed, even though it was a really tough assignment" or "My baby is cutting teeth and is really irritable. I was feeling frustrated, so I called a babysitter and took a walk in the park to calm down and to get into a better mood." Your child is going to say, "I did a good job at school, not responding to Frank's teasing about my being short."

Teach him that he can manage his moods. Teach your child that he can be in charge of himself. Help him learn that he determines his outlook; he can turn a bad day around. Everyone has bad days now and then. If you are in the middle of one and feeling the world is against you, stop to think about how your comments are influencing your child. You are in effect painting yourself as a victim who has no control over your life. When you feel you've lost a day or two with bad moods, say out loud, "Wait a minute. I am stronger than this problem. I can find a solution." Here you show your child that we all lose it now and then, but you can turn it around. When the bad time ends, when the problem is resolved, your child sees that it was in part because you believed in yourself. As a result, the consequences were positive. Your child can do the same.

The Importance of Your Child's Appearance

Another important part of your child's self-concept has to do with his physical appearance. At quite an early age, your child begins to form a concept of himself and others based on outer beauty, and to differentiate between what he considers to be attractive and unattractive. You may say, "It's what's inside that counts," but to your child, his appearance and physical features are an important part of his identity.

This awareness begins as early as three years of age when children stereotype others on the basis of physical attractiveness. Attractive children are looked at, smiled at, touched, and are asked to play more often than other children. Attractive youngsters are also named as best friends more often than other children.

Studies on the psychology of teaching show that teachers call on attractive children more often than unattractive children. Teachers define *attractive* as a generally neat and clean appearance. An attractive child has parents who have bothered to dress the child, to bathe, fuss over, and perhaps match a ribbon or socks to the child's attire. These children receive the most eye contacts by teachers, and they garner the most positive strokes (reinforcements) in the classroom, as well. This means that such children receive a good share of positive attention, which is a plus in helping them cope with the normal frustration of learning and, of course, in feeling good about themselves. These attributes (positive attention, stroking, touching, and verbal and nonverbal affirmations) are factors that contribute to helping your child become an overachiever or underachiever!

Stages of Growth and Development Influence Your Child's Perception of Self

As I travel around the country and speak to youth groups, I frequently ask, "Who are you? How would you describe yourself?" Youth of all ages automatically respond with thoughts about their physical being. "I'm five feet four inches, have green eyes, brown hair . . ." When I ask, "If you could change anything about you, what would it be?" again, most children, regardless of age, cite some characteristic of their physical being. "I wouldn't want to be so tall (or short)," or something to that effect.

So another sense of identity for children is gained by relating to their physical selves. That's because childhood represents the most dramatic stages of growth and development over the life cycle, making children painfully aware of their physical dimensions in comparison to other students. As children grow and develop, the body makes a number of growth spurts. At times these changes are minor: An eight-year-old girl may gain four to seven pounds and grow three to four inches within a twelve-to-fourteen month period. An eight-year-old boy will gain five to six pounds and gain two to three inches of height. Sometimes these changes are dramatic: A thirteen-year-old will gain, on the average, fourteen to twenty-five pounds and grow about three to five inches in height during a twelve-month period. Whereas an eight-year-old boy will gain five to six pounds, a fifteen-year-old boy will gain between ten and fifteen pounds and gain ten to twelve inches in height. In other words, each year of life brings about its own set of growth demands. Such changes create for the child a new image of himself.

Hormones Have a Life of Their Own

In addition to outer features of physical growth, organs enlarge and mature in their functioning, and a number of hormones are set in motion to trigger body development and maturity. Added to this are the chemical changes produced in the brain, each announced by their own set of behavioral side-effects.

Children feel these changes inwardly, and compare themselves to others outwardly. With each stage of growth and development, a "new" (not always improved!) child emerges. As Becky, a ninth grader, said to me, "Will the *real* me please stand up and stay around for longer than a few months! I can't keep up with these constant (body) changes, and I'm not so sure I can handle my constantly changing moods, either!"

The "Who-am-I?" question, then, becomes a serious question of battling self changes. We need only look at similar populations who have had to come to terms with a body image that is somehow different. For example, for the individual who becomes physically disabled, the pregnant woman, the grossly overweight person, or the severely scarred or burned individual, coming to terms with the altered physical image is an important task in the acceptance of self.

Helping Your Child Develop a Healthy Perspective

Hormones aside, you can help your child gain a healthy perspective of identity in the important areas described below.

True fitness. One of the best ways to help your child develop a healthy sense of identity is by helping him learn the importance of health, fitness, and wellness, and how to maintain them. Pay attention to your child's overall state of inner fitness, as well as to his outward appearance. Nutrition, exercise, rest and relaxation come into play here. Your emphasis on nutrition at home and bedtime curfew, for example, matter. It sets the tone for just how important these habits are to maintaining body wellness.

Second, check to see what physical education and health courses are provided at your child's school. They may range from nonexistent to a well-developed state-of-the-art program. For example, Will Baker, a health educator, heads up a program where each child's overall health is evaluated at the beginning of the school term. This includes the child's inner health (such as cardiovascular fitness) and outer health (such as monitoring of caloric intake). Young people learn about respecting and taking responsibility for their health and wellness. In addition, parents are given a copy of the overall evaluation of their child's physical condition with suggestions for helping their child learn how to safely get and stay in shape. The school maintains complete health and fitness profiles on each child and is thereby able to track and monitor the child's health throughout his school years. What does your school offer? How can you be supportive of such efforts? If your school does offer ways to show the importance of fitness, support it. If it doesn't, you can help get a program started.

Appearance.   Clothes do count. Children who do not dress like the other children (including those who are overdressed in comparison with other children) feel different and have negative feelings about themselves. That's why many private schools request that students wear a uniform and why some public schools have dress codes. Dressing alike puts students on an equal footing.

Just as you have an acceptable standard of dress at your place of work, so does your child. Are you familiar with his? You should ask these questions:

• When was the last time I observed my child at school with his peers?
• How does his overall appearance compare with that of other classmates?

- How does my child look in relationship to his peers?
- Is my child clean and well-groomed every day?
- Have I imposed restrictions that are unfair?
- Is my child over-dressed?
- How does my child feel about his appearance?
- How would my child say others describe his appearance?

Making sure that your child looks like the other children doesn't have to mean having a big emphasis on clothes but, rather, seeing to it that your child is neat and clean and feels good about his appearance. After that, reassure your child that he doesn't need exciting packaging to be loved and accepted. You want to help him accept himself (to gain a greater sense of personhood in a realistic, self-assuring way) and not to have all of his self-perceptions come from his physical being.

Help your child gain insight into the growth stages. Self-knowledge provides understanding. Young people too need to understand more about their stages of growth and development, particularly at key times of dramatic growth. This self-knowledge can prevent many of the destructive behaviors we see them impose upon themselves. For example, seventh grade and eighth grade girls are serious offenders in using diet pills and often engage in bulimic and anorexic behaviors as a way to control the normal weight gain that is associated with this stage of development.

You can imagine why they are alarmed: While prior stages show only a slight change in growth and body weight gain from year to year, suddenly there is dramatic gain, and a girl's perception of her image is, "I'm fat and ugly." When she is not emotionally ready for these dramatic changes (when she has perception warp of the image she sees in the mirror), she can get into some serious negative and self-destructive behaviors aimed at controlling her weight. There are a number of books that you can read to get more information to help your child. Several are listed in the Suggested Reading section at the back of this book.

○ IT'S UP TO YOU!

When a child possesses self-knowledge, he makes friends with the face in the mirror. He is less likely to belittle himself and sell himself short. He's able to "knock and find somebody (himself) home." He's the child who decides for himself what his choices are—that he isn't going to abuse drugs and alcohol, for example.

You know the awesome responsibility you have as a parent. Along with the overflowing love you have for your child is a tinge of fear, of insecurity. All of us wonder what type of person we are helping our child to be. Are you helping your child to balance the three separate forms of self-perception: his public self (the mask he wears for others), his ideal self (what he aspires to be), and his actual self? You've taken a good first step by learning more about these selves and understanding the role they play in your child's development and sense of self-esteem. Chapter 11 discusses how assertiveness—not aggressiveness—can enable your child to move ever closer to his ideal self.

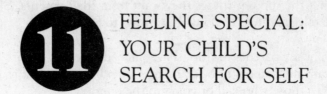

11

FEELING SPECIAL: YOUR CHILD'S SEARCH FOR SELF

The other two key factors in helping your child construct the "Who-am-I?" question are helping him feel a sense of self and getting a clear perception on how others see him. These two factors are important to your child because it's in these areas that he checks to see if his own emerging sense of self is met with acceptance from others.

Remember that your child's first perceptions of himself come from you. He sees his reflection in your eyes. If you believe your child is well-mannered, intelligent, and capable, and tell him so, he believes he's well-mannered, intelligent, and capable. On the other hand, if you tell him he's not, he believes he isn't. Either way, it's likely to end up a self-fulfilling prophecy. Children are very intuitive. You've probably noticed that your child has a long antenna and understands not only what you say, but is also pretty good at reading your body language too. He can sense your attitude toward him, and it influences how he feels about himself.

○ HOW SPECIAL DOES YOUR CHILD FEEL?

All children need to feel special, especially to their parents. Earlier I shared with you the results of a poll of what children

157

said are the top ten things they want from their parents. Six of these ten areas had to do with wanting to feel special:

- I want my parents to think I'm somebody special.
- I want my parents to be warm and friendly to me, just as they are to those who call or come to the door.
- I want my parents to be more concerned about me.
- I want my parents to know the me that nobody knows.
- I want to say what's important to me (and to have those views be valued).
- I want to be part of a happy family.

Helping Your Child Feel Special (but Not Spoiled)

How do you help your child feel special? Take a moment to ponder this question now. What are the things you say and do that builds this important sense of self? Would he rate them to be as important as you would?

Children say we parents do it best when we recognize and take notice of what is going on in their lives (especially subtle things)—when we are paying attention. It's the little things that are the big things. This is not to imply that you spoil him by bestowing favor after favor, or gift after gift. For example, teens do not deserve to be given a car just because they turn sixteen or because all the other parents are giving their children cars when they earn a driver's license. Children rarely appreciate such gifts—and generally take them for granted—showing little gratitude to or respect for the parent who gives them. Should you choose to give your child a car, that's your prerogative. And when the right expectations are set forth in advance, it can turn out to be a good experience. However, parents should know that feeling special is an inner feeling. For example, you might say, "Your school pictures are being taken on Friday. What will you be wearing? Do we need to wash and press a blouse or would you like us to shop for a new sweater to wear that day?" or "Your next baseball game is tomorrow at four. Would you like me to be there, or should I wait and take off early next week so I can be at next Tuesday's big game?" or "I'll help you work toward achieving your goal of having a car. Let's set some goals now to bring that about."

If you don't take steps to let your child know you are interested in him and what's going on in his life, he is going to turn to outside sources to get his need to be somebody met. You can help your child feel special.

Tell your child that he is special to you.   I say to my daughter, "You are so important to me, Jennifer," followed by "here's-why" statements. "I enjoy your friendship so much," or "I can always count on your support," or "You make me feel so happy and proud that you are my daughter." Such statements are more meaningful than the overused "I love you." (But if you rarely tell your children "I love you," by all means, say it!)

Talk about why you're happy to be his parent.   Don't give your child the feeling that he is a burden or that you're stuck with him. Remember, he'll live up to your expectations. You want him to feel special, worthy, and able to stand up and be counted. These postures he learns from your attitudes about him. "Jennifer, I love being your mother because you are such a loving daughter. Parenting you has been one of my greatest joys. It has been fun to watch you grow, and to watch you learn how to do things. I have really enjoyed getting to know you and to learn what is important to you."

Show acceptance.   We all have strengths, and areas where we don't do as well. Help your child to feel good about his strengths, and to know that the areas where he doesn't do well are accepted too. He shouldn't have to feel reluctant to go out for football if it's unlikely he'll be a star player. Working hard to get on the team and being a team member should be acceptable too. We don't always get to be number one in everything. Focus on the positive: "Pete, spelling may not be one of your strong points, but you work hard at it. That you do your best is what's important."

Encourage your child to take pride in his achievements, both great and small.   Experiences are personal. Your child must enjoy and be proud of his own accomplishments. He doesn't always need to depend on others for approval. Help him learn the value of self-satisfaction. "Rick, you must be proud of yourself for keeping your temper when your little sister was giving you a hard time this morning. You've really become good at not yelling back. I hope you know how grown-up you've become."

Teach your child to enjoy his own company.   Teach your child the importance of taking time out to be alone, to examine his own thoughts and feelings about himself and his life. Encourage him to get involved in activities he can enjoy by himself (for example, crafts, reading, or individual sports). Teach him to take time alone for his thoughts. "Susan, sometimes being alone is good because it enables you to take the time to think things out."

Teach your child to trust his feelings.   Encourage your child to pay attention to his thoughts, to trust his feelings, and to act on what he thinks is right. Teach him that being happy and fulfilled is a process—an outcome, not a goal. "Nell, I am so glad that you trusted your instincts about not going to that party. I realize it was hard for you, because some of your girlfriends went. But that type of party can get out of hand, and you might have been in over your head. I'm proud of you for being mature enough to give up what looked like fun because you recognized that in the long run, it wasn't right for you."

Teach your child to respect himself.   Help your child to value himself and not try to be someone else. Encourage him to explore and appreciate his own talents, interests, and ideas. "Alise, you don't have to play soccer just because Laurie does. You are much more gifted in other areas, such as music. There's nothing wrong with playing the piano rather than playing goalie, if that's what you're best at. Laurie probably would drive us all out of the room with her horrible music, so she takes mercy on us and doesn't try to be what she's not. If you want to play soccer, that's fine, but don't force yourself to do it just because you want to be like Laurie. Be yourself."

Teach your child to love himself.   This is achieved by accepting and learning from mistakes (and not overreacting to them) and by accepting his successes and failures just as those who love him do. Teach him that he must become his own best friend. "Juanita, it's not the end of the world because you failed the math test. You can always try harder the next time. Besides, look how well you did on your spelling all year long. Not everyone is cut out to be a rocket scientist; maybe you'll grow up to be a great writer and then look back and laugh at your struggles in algebra. There's so much that's wonderful about you, honey; let's focus on the positive. Think of what you would say if this had happened to your friend, Linda. You wouldn't let her go around moping, would you? You'd talk to her about all the great things that you love about her. Well, it's time to be a friend to yourself. Tell yourself all your strong points for right now."

○ IS YOUR CHILD INFLUENCED BY WHAT OTHERS SAY AND DO?

A child's self-concept is the single most important factor in determining his response to peer pressure. A child with a poorly constructed identity is frequently influenced by others. Not believing in himself, he often conforms or mimics others and uses negative statements when describing himself and others. Lacking confidence, he is dependent on others and all too anxious to please them, and he is willing to misbehave in order to attract attention. He is uncomfortable with praise and is likely to deny wrongdoings for fear of rejection. He frequently goes out of his way to be different, dressing to extremes to draw attention.

On the other hand, a child with a healthy self-identity expresses individuality without alienating others. He's comfortable accepting praise, and makes positive statements about himself and others. He'll stand up for himself. In the presence of peers using drugs, for example, he is more likely to say, "Hey, I don't do that stuff," or something else that conveys he's not going to participate and will stay committed to his decision—without putting others down, or judging them. He can't be easily swayed—he'll do some thinking for himself.

You can help your child develop a stronger sense of identity by helping him clarify and sharpen his self-picture. There are a number of skills to help him do this. Resources to help young people develop effective self-management skills can be found in the Suggested Reading section at the back of this book. You may also wish to consult with your child's teacher.

Confronting Others Confidently: Assertive Choice

Helping your child to develop assertiveness skills will enable him to confidently confront situations that would typically produce anxiety or frustration or cause him to deny his feelings. Assertiveness skills enable your child to assert his rights without using intimidation or being intimidated. There are times when he'll want to tell others how he's feeling, what he thinks is important, and what he is willing or is not willing to do. He'll need to be able to do this in a way that is accepted by others and gets his point across effectively.

Your child needs to learn how to do this appropriately. Perhaps he's learned that by shouting, pouting, ridiculing, and being intimidating he can get what he wants. Or, he may have learned that by being a sweet, likable "I'll-do-anything-you-want" type of person, he can get others to respond to him in the way he wants. But to be properly assertive means to value yourself—to act with confidence and with authority.

Assertion is communicating in a way that others will listen to and not be offended by. It's giving them the opportunity to respond in return. It's a manner that is direct, self-respecting, and straightforward.

How assertive is your child? Listed below are the nonverbal and verbal cues.

• *Eye contact.* The assertive child will have direct eye contact with you. This doesn't mean he'll stare you down without blinking; it means he'll look you in the eye and hold the contact fairly steadily throughout the conversation.
• *Hand gestures.* The assertive child will use hand gestures to help emphasize the content and importance of what he says. Of course, it doesn't mean making wild gestures with his hands.
• *Posture.* Posture can also indicate assertiveness: sitting or standing straight when communicating with you (not hunching over), shoulders back, head up.
• *Voice.* Speaking up and not mumbling is being assertive. Sometimes you hear a person make an assertive comment and then ruin the effect by either dropping or raising his voice at the end. For example, "I want you to be more truthful with me." This by itself sounds fine. However, if instead of waiting for a response he says, "Okay?" the assertiveness of the statement is lost. Other phrases that can detract from assertiveness (particularly when delivered in a whiney voice) are, "You know?" or "You know what I mean?" Being assertive involves knowing when to stop talking.
• *Owning your statements.* One hallmark of assertive behavior is the making of "I" statements, such as "I feel," "I like," "I wish," "I would appreciate," and "I need." The passive person puts responsibility on someone else, often finishing a statement by asking, "Don't you think so?" or "Is that okay?"

Getting your needs met means that you communicate successfully—that you are direct and straightforward without causing others undue pain. People respect honesty, even criticism, if it's presented in an open, caring, and kind way. Statements that affirm what you are feeling and what you need imply taking responsibility for yourself.

Assessing Your Child's Assertiveness

How good is your child at communicating his needs? Does he let others know how he's feeling? A good way to test your child's ability to stand his ground is to use the following questions (or similar ones) in probing his skills. Select a time when the two of you are feeling especially close. Most parents find that the best time to do this is when you are in the car together or window shopping, and are leisurely and not hurried, anxious, or rushed. Below is a list of questions to begin with; you may wish to modify this list for your child.

1. Another student asks to cut in front of you in a line. You don't want to let him cut in. What do you say or do?
2. Your brother or sister wants to watch a special TV program. He or she walks over to change the channel. What do you say or do?
3. A classmate asks to copy your answers to a test. You don't want him to. What do you say or do?
4. The teacher asks the entire class to stay after school because someone was talking. You don't want to take the blame for something you know isn't your fault. What do you say or do?
5. Your sister wants to borrow your favorite cassette tape to play at her friend's house. You're afraid it will get broken or lost because your sister is careless with her own tapes. What do you say or do?
6. You are watching a TV movie scheduled to end in minutes. Your dad/mom comes in and says you must go to bed immediately. What do you say or do?
7. Your mother tells you that you have to baby-sit for your sister this afternoon. You have already made plans to go to the movies and had gotten permission from your mom earlier in the week. What do you say or do?

8. What do you do if another person is calling you names?
9. You don't understand a problem the teacher has just explained. What do you say in asking for help?
10. Your mother is in the car honking the horn for you to hurry so she can get you to school. You have not fed and watered your pet rabbit yet. What do you say or do?

○ LOOK WHAT LOVE CAN DO!

We have all had those introspective moments when we ask ourselves, "Who am I? How have I changed through the years? What am I up to? What is my role in life?" We all do a check-and-balance periodically. But for a child, the "Who-am-I?" question looms large every day. He has to be able to make sense of his existence, to know where he fits in.

A child's feeling of worthiness shapes his identity. If he feels worthwhile, he knows that he has a place in your world and can be confident later of going out into the wider world.

○ IT'S UP TO YOU!

Helping your child to feel that he is special and that life is to be valued can be used as the first step in helping him with his search for self. When you show acceptance, encourage pride in his achievements, teach the importance of alone time, and help him to trust his feelings and respect himself, you pave the way for developing a stronger sense of selfhood in your child and for helping him clarify and sharpen his self-picture.

12 AFFILIATION: THE BELONGINGNESS NEEDS

In a popular song, the line "People who need people are the luckiest people in the world" reiterates the reciprocal human need to be with others. Most of us seek out the company of those whom we consider to be important to us. This is especially true for children, who are dependent on us—especially in the early years—for most of their needs. Children need to be needed. Approximately one million adolescent girls become pregnant each year and, of those, nearly 85 to 90 percent elect to keep their babies rather than give them up for adoption in the belief that a baby will provide the kind of unconditional love and acceptance that they perceive society does not. A feeling of belonging is important to achieving as well. The research on school dropouts clearly substantiates that a feeling of being unaffiliated—of not belonging—is the second leading cause of leaving school before graduation. We know that young people who do not feel they belong are more likely to

- Have difficulty making and keeping friendships
- Be easily influenced by others
- Be low achievers in school
- Be uncomfortable working in group settings
- Isolate themselves from others, and become even more lonely
- Depend on behaviors such as bullying, showing off, being uncooperative, withdrawing, ridiculing, and being insensitive to the needs of others

- Experience learning difficulties
- Be identified as juvenile delinquents
- Plan a pregnancy because they want someone to love
- Drop out of school
- Be more likely to experience mental health problems in adulthood

This is contrasted to a child with a sense of belonging who is able to

- Initiate new friendships
- Show sensitivity toward others
- Cooperate and share with others
- More easily achieve peer acceptance and be sought out by others
- Feel valued by others
- Express happiness
- Excel in school

While you don't want your child to be totally dependent on you or others, neither do you want him to be wholly independent—to feel that other people don't matter. A sense of interdependence (a healthy sense of reciprocity) is the ideal.

○ LOVE'S STRONGEST BOND: CHILD AND PARENT

I find that many parents are initially surprised to find out just how important they are to their children, especially as children get older and seek the friendships of others. Yet when children are asked to list the five most meaningful people in their lives, both girls and boys name parents as number one. While the first person they list is their favorite parent (the parent with a listening heart), the second person they name is generally the other parent (sometimes even in cases of separation or divorce).

The number-three spot goes to a favorite teacher—although this spot is sometimes shared by a step-parent or school custodian. The fourth person named is another teacher—but this time it's the teacher whose teaching style matches the child's learning style (providing the teacher also encourages the child and sets expectations for the child to develop his strengths). In fifth place, girls list their grandmothers, followed by a sibling (male or female), and anyone else who might serve as a support system. Boys list an uncle, a grandfather, and then a sibling (they'll list a brother first), in that order. Peers rarely show up in the top five until children are fifteen-and-a-half years of age or older.

Why do you think that's so? It's because peers, for the most part, are situational friends. You might be my friend because we're neighbors or because we share a locker or a class together, are on the same team, or get assigned to do a special project. But these friendships rarely last very long. Indeed, some won't even survive a few months.

You see, the influence of friends and peers (these are different) is closely tied to the process of socialization (learning how to interact with other young people). This experience is less than fulfilling in many cases. Nearly 37 percent of elementary school-children are not named as a friend by anyone in their class, and 29 percent receive no nomination from anyone in the school setting. They get even fewer votes as they get older. This is not to imply that when friendships end they will be painless. Children experience much hurt and turmoil when they break up, and friendships are always breaking up for children.

○ FRIENDS ARE NOT MORE IMPORTANT THAN PARENTS

Many parents erroneously believe that their children's friends are more important to them than parents are. However, it's only when parents are physically or emotionally distant that children will turn to their peers for acceptance and belonging—at any cost. This is when peer groups become the most influential and potentially the most dangerous.

If you have a teenager you might be thinking, "My days of influence are over. My child barely listens to me anymore and cares only about what his friends say. And then there's the TV and stereo. I might as well be chatting with a brick wall for all that he hears me." Those of you with very young children might be thinking, "My child is so active that he never stops running around long enough to slow down and listen to me. The only time I seem to have any influence at all is when I'm in a bargaining position—when I have something he wants or needs."

How You Influence Your Child's Choice of Friends

You affect your child in many ways. There are the obvious ways, such as determining what he eats, how much exercise he gets, and what activities he participates in. To some extent, you determine your child's appearance (by refusing to let a ten-year-old dye her hair or by insisting that a teenager bathe, brush his teeth, and wear clean jeans). Hard as this may be to believe, you also influence your child's choice of friends. It's not that you decide whom your child will like, but you do have an effect on which children your son or daughter meets. For example, when you go with your daughter to Girl Scouts, you meet a different group of youngsters than when you go with her to swim team or when your daughter is free to roam anywhere without restrictions or boundaries. By selecting one school over another, by buying a house in a particular neighborhood, or by knowing about and steering your child into attending certain functions, you directly or indirectly shape your child's experiences, which all contribute to his expectations out of life.

Why should you be concerned? Because the influence of others helps shape the opinion your child will form about his own sense of self-worth.

You Aren't the Only One Influencing Your Child

That's why you want to know with whom your child is spending large amounts of time, especially at the high school level. Be aware of the others in your child's life and what influence they exert over him. The most obvious are teachers. Yet as children get older, many parents stop meeting their child's teachers. Have you met your child's teachers? Do you know who they are? Can you put a face to the name when your son starts complaining about "Mr. Lopez, who expects us to memorize a book a night" or "Mrs. Harrison, who has a cow if the homework is even one day late." There are also athletic coaches or club sponsors who spend time with your child. When a child quotes the coach verbatim, you need to find out what sort of person the coach is. The same goes for teachers or adults who sponsor club activities. Attend school meetings where these individuals are introduced, or head up a parents' night, hosting a meeting in your home, where you can talk informally with the sponsors.

Don't overlook other adult influences, such as the parents of your child's friends. Think of how many hours you spend chauffeuring your child and his buddies around and how many times you have come home to find other children sprawled in front of your TV. If you feel you have an extra child or two around a lot, spend a moment with their parents when dropping off their child. Take a few minutes to talk on the telephone when they call to ask when their child is coming home. Remember, it's normal for every child to view his friends' parents as cool and more permissive than you are. Take that with a grain of salt . . . but check it out to be sure.

○ MAKING CERTAIN THAT YOUR CHILD FEELS BONDED TO YOU

There are very few households that have full-time mothers at home cooking and a working father and husband who knows best these days. Even so, you still need to let your child know that you are there for him. Parents need to figure out how to fulfill the meaningful time our children need with us. I see this unfulfilled need as a number-one reason why so many of them are unhappy.

Quality Time Versus Quantity Time

It's been estimated that, on the average, parents of children ages four to eighteen spend less than five minutes of meaningful conversation time each day with their children. Significant conversation is different from, "Did you take out the garbage?" "Did you do your homework?" "Did you make your bed?" or "Did you feed the dog?" The answer to the question of which is of greater value, quality time or quantity of time, is "neither." It's special bonding time—it's about developing personal and emotional well-being between parent and child. It's connecting, with both parent and child feeling it.

At a recent seminar I conducted for parents and teens, a mother and her son sat together in the front row. She said to me, "My sixteen-year-old has his own phone line, a TV in his room, and the latest in clothes. He's still not happy, and he misbehaves. What's this kid's problem?"

To break the heaviness of the moment, I turned to her sixteen-year-old son and asked in fun, "Well, what *is* your problem?"

"My mother!" he said in an instant reply. After the laughter died down, he added, "She doesn't care about me."

"Why do you say that?" I asked. "What does she do or not do that gives you that feeling?"

"Well," he said, speaking softly now, "I've had nine soccer games, and she hasn't been to one of them. And when my Spanish teacher scheduled a conference with her, she didn't show up. She doesn't really care. Her life is more important than mine. Her boyfriend is more important to her than I am."

"Yeah, let me tell you!" chimed in a boy a few seats over. "My father's always telling me how busy he is whenever I ask him to spend time with me. On Saturday I asked him if we could go practice kicking a soccer ball in the backyard. He said he didn't have the time, but when his friend called and asked him to play tennis, he was gone in a flash. He'll spend time with others before he'll spend time with me!

Does that sound familiar?

Creating a Better Bond with Your Child

Are you unknowingly turning your child away? It's often the little things that win the biggest points. There are things you can do to help your child feel powerfully bonded to you.

Show an interest in your child.   What are you doing to help your child feel connected to you? A busy parent sometimes needs to be creative. My daughter, a tremendous athlete, goes from one sports season to the next. I sometimes go up to school just to watch her in practice sessions. Why? Because even though I can't always make all of her regular games, I know that the most important connection is for her to feel that I'm interested in her and not just interested in whether the team wins. My being there at practice represents interest in her. She doesn't have to be a star to get my attention. I make it clear to her that she's worthwhile. I need to show her that while I'm a busy person, she counts in my life.

Talk about your bond.   How are the two of you doing? In what areas does your child want more attention? In what ways have the two of you created interdependence. Ask, "Of all the things going on in your life, what's most important to you right now? How's it going? How can I be of help?" Before you ask him to respond, see if you know what he'll say. Are your responses the same?

Participate.   If you don't feel you are participating enough in your child's life, your child probably has the same idea. But you can turn this around. A little honesty is a good place to start. "Jimmy, I have been so busy lately that I haven't taken the time to follow you in your activities. And I miss it. I enjoy being with you, and I have fun every time we're together. I'm going to come to your game tonight, put next week's game on my calendar, and not let anything get in the way of my being there."

Demonstrate love and acceptance. You can't simply assume that your child knows you love him; you must show your love. Your child doesn't want to hear, "Of course I love you. I'm your mother, aren't I?" He wants to know that you love him because he's worth loving, not because parents are supposed to love their children. He wants to feel it. There are many different ways in which you can express this love.

• *Verbal expressions.* Tell your child you love him. Say the words directly—don't hint at them. There's no need to be coy or cute or to worry that you'll embarrass your child (as long as you don't get mushy in front of his friends). Say "I love you; you mean everything to me" as often as you feel it. Make remarks such as: "You're such a wonderful son, Bill," "Have a good time, Jennifer, and take care of yourself for me." "You're so important to me, Roger," or "I like to be with you, Mary Louise." These are significant statements to our children, because from these remarks children draw conclusions about how connected they are to us and get an idea of how that feels to us.

From these incoming statements, your child formulates opinions about his strengths and weaknesses. "Am I really good at spelling?" "Do others like my ideas?" "Am I attractive?" "Am I a bad boy?" "Does my father really think I'm important?" "Am I really stupid?" These evaluations are also made when our children interact with others; that's why you want to know who your child considers important.

• *Nonverbal expressions.* Your nonverbal expressions are as important as what you say. Remember, children can tell whether there is sincerity or hypocrisy in the air. Your facial expression and body language communicate your love and bonding to your child almost as directly as your words do. Even newborns can sense our love and acceptance of them.

- *Empathic listening.* When we listen (and don't just wait for our turn to talk), we are telling our children that they are valuable and worthy of our time and attention. We show empathy when we respond to what they are feeling and not just to what they are saying. Sometimes just a few minutes of your undivided attention can tell your child all he wants to know about your acceptance. Your listening actions say, "I take you seriously. I care about you. You can always come to me."

- *Touching.* Touching is a very powerful way of showing your feelings of love and acceptance. Taking your child's hand, patting him on the back, stroking his hair, straightening a collar, or simply touching his arm expresses your love and pride in your child.

- *Show acceptance.* Accept your child for who he is. He is not a younger version of you, nor a clone of his brother. He is himself, and he wants to be accepted for his individual strengths and weaknesses. Acceptance can be felt in little things, such as putting your arm around your child and drawing him into the circle when you are talking to other adults. When you show that acceptance, your child knows that you recognize him for himself.

Ask for your child's opinion.   Consulting your child shows your connection to him. Mark, a thirteen-year-old boy, said the times he feels the most important is when his father consults him. "Yesterday Dad asked my opinion about whether to wear a certain tie or another to a very important business meeting. He was in a hurry, and he actually came into my room to ask. And it was a very big meeting too. My opinion really mattered to him. It was a great feeling!" Being consulted made Jeff feel that he counted, that his father considered his input a valuable one.

○ IT'S UP TO YOU!

Affiliation, the sense of belonging, of being bonded to those you love and accepted by others, is an essential element in building self-esteem. For children, the most important bond is that between parent and child. Your child must feel not only that he belongs to you but that you belong to him and that you care about him. You build a sense of affiliation by your actions as well as by your words. You further show him you value him when you talk about the bond between you, participate in his life, and demonstrate your love and acceptance of him. These displays may be made verbally or nonverbally, through touching or empathic listening, as long as you are genuinely interested in and accepting of him and love him.

13

BELONGINGNESS: HELPING YOUR CHILD MAKE AND SUSTAIN FRIENDSHIPS

Although you have more influence than anyone else with your child, you aren't the only one who influences his perception of self. Your child's self-opinion is also based on what others say to him and how he is treated by them. From these experiences, as children win acceptance and experience rejections, they arrive at a verdict about themselves. There's an ancient Chinese proverb that says, "A child's life is like a piece of paper on which every passerby leaves a mark."

Although in the early years your child's primary relationships consist mainly of you—his family—soon that circle is expanded. He learns to be part of a group. A youngster with a positive sense of self is more willing to make friends and join in making new friends. The insecure child will stand back and hope that someone eventually approaches him. He may stand there alone for a long time, then eventually figure, "Other kids don't like me," and become even more of a loner.

○ POPULARITY IS ABOUT PEOPLE SKILLS

One of the factors that erodes self-concept is a child's inability to make and keep friends. Popular children are popular precisely because they know how to make friends and interact with them. Through successful interactions with others, they come to feel appreciated and accepted. The goal is not so much to have popular children as it is to help your child gain confidence in social encounters—to get his needs for belonging met in a healthy interdependent (vs. dependent) way.

What It Takes to Be a Friend

An impressive number of social skills are needed to establish and maintain friendships, especially to gain entry into group activities with other children. Group membership is not automatic. Your child needs a good array of interpersonal skills in showing approval and support of others. Yet, while showing group membership, he needs to be an individual with his own style—without alienating others.

Learning to be a friend takes practice. That's because friendships are filled with customs, rituals, and rules—all a part of a dance for socialization. Many children will go along with almost anything, because to be alienated—to be left out—is painful. To be on the outside—not to belong—is a constant reminder that he's not liked and accepted. And the rules for belonging are always changing. Rules that worked in the early years of childhood don't work in the upper elementary years. Younger friendships were easier: A child who was good at baseball found acceptance in the sports group. If he had a bicycle, he was part of the street fun. Moving from childhood to adolescence is a real culture shock, because the rules among even friends change regularly.

Initiation rites, as well as acts of rejection and exclusion, can be devastating to children. To manage this maze and game playing, and most especially to avoid becoming a victim of negative peer influence, your child needs a strong sense of self, so he can figure out not only what to do, but also how to do it with his self-esteem intact. Socialization is not always an easy task for children to learn on their own (although many adults think it comes easy for children). You may have to help your child acquire some skills.

I'm amazed that we don't teach a course in school to help students learn interpersonal and social skills in dealing with each other, especially in the face of the cultural diversity and language barriers that exist in schools today. This is even more true for those children who are bused from their neighborhood into new school settings and then returned home. This child is an outsider at school and when he arrives back home in his own neighborhood. When students are in emotional chaos, they are not the best learners.

○ CHILDREN NEED SKILLS TO MAKE AND SUSTAIN FRIENDSHIPS

We must teach our children about the nature of friendships, how to have mutually satisfying relationships, and how to manage the influence that others exert over them. It helps for us to understand a bit about the nature of young friendships.

The Nature of Children's Friendships

Friendships fall into two camps: Kids call them the outsiders and the insiders. Psychologists call them the external and internal groups. Regardless of their names, you can help your child understand more about friendships, assess the value he places on friendships, and develop skills to successfully interact with others.

Outsiders are characterized by convenience and availability. Friendship is based primarily on physical proximity, cooperation, and ego fulfillment. What makes this category of external friendships so painful is that when the friendship ends, the unsuspecting child (the one who has been "used") feels betrayed.

• *Physical proximity.* The availability of someone who lives down the street or is in your child's French class provides your child with opportunities (mostly of convenience) to "use" the other in a time of need. This is situational friendship only, and rarely does this friendship possess the elements necessary for building a satisfying relationship. The Suzy who used to share her lunch with Patti won't even sit at the same table with Patti now that they no longer share the same reading group.

- *Cooperation toward personal goals.* Children like other children who cooperate with them in their attempts to attain personal goals and rewards. In this friendship, the child has little time for the child who hinders (or contradicts) his getting what he wants. It's not uncommon for an aggressive child to develop a friendship for the duration of a project and then drop the friend as soon as the project is over. There are some variations here. Let's say your child's teacher selected two cocaptains for a spelling contest. Whereas children ages four to seven will choose their best friend (defined as the one sitting next to them that day), for their team, children between the ages of eight and twelve will choose the best spellers to be on their team (the loyalty extends only until the end of the spelling contest, however). Children between the ages of thirteen and fifteen will choose the children they secretly admire and would love to be near (but probably this is as close as they'll get). Baffled by the change, the left-behind child doesn't understand what happened. How could he be so *on* only to be so *off?*
- *Ego fulfillment.* Children side with those who like them, see them in a positive light, and promote them. John, for example, may value Jimmy's company because Jimmy is constantly boasting about John's successes. It doesn't mean that the friendship is mutual, however, only that the friendship serves the purpose of meeting ego needs (John's). When it's over, Jimmy is devastated. Having relied on reference power (someone else's power to be "somebody"), he's really alone now.

Insiders are characterized by friendships in which mutual feelings in three or more of the following areas exist.

- *Respect.* Your child says, "I'll check with Melody. She'll know what to do."
- *Trust.* Trust promotes loyalty. ("I know I can count on Sally—she never lets me down.")
- *Understanding.* There is a sense of what is important to each other—they know why a friend does what he does. ("I know why he's upset.")
- *Enjoyment.* They genuinely enjoy each other's company. ("I always feel good when I'm with her.")
- *Acceptance.* They accept each other as they are. ("That's just Jim. That's the way he is.")
- *Confiding.* Friends share feelings with each other. ("She tells me things that no one else knows about her.")

Is Your Child Liked and Accepted by Others?

The first questions children ask as they enter a new classroom have little to do with teachers or the academic curriculum. They ask, "Who is in my class?" "Who will I sit next to?" "What are their names?" and "Will they like me?" Social acceptance dominates their thinking. The need to belong can put enormous stress on a child, particularly if he is not considered to be one of the group; yet many children go through school with few friends, and many are without friends entirely. Earlier, I shared with you the percentages of children named as friends or potential friends as seen by classmates. With the exception of tenth grade for girls and ninth grade for boys (loyalty is strongest during these years), fewer and fewer children get named each year as a friend by other children.

You can't always be there to assist your child in his relationships with other people, but you can help him develop the skills he needs to make and sustain friendships.

Help your child understand the nature of friendships.   You can help your child understand the nature of friendships and the value he places on them. If he understands more about the simple psychology of these interactions with his peers, he will feel more confident about his ability to relate successfully to others, without feeling that he is abandoned because he is unlovable, or unworthy of his friends' company when the friendship changes or falls apart.

Books such as *Friendship Is Forever, Isn't It?* help children examine the nature of friendships and the influence friends have on them. You may want to refer to the Suggested Reading section at the back of this book for resources or ask your child's teacher for the recommended reading list designed with the age of the child in mind. In addition, your local public librarian will usually have posted a recommended reading list for each age of child.

Help your child develop an awareness of the cultural diversity of others. An awareness of the differences in others can help your child develop a greater tolerance for other people, making him more capable of a broader range of friendships. Your child will need to learn that not everyone has the same interests, opinions, feelings, background, or capabilities as he does. Understanding this helps your child develop a balanced and healthy sense of self.

Help your child develop an awareness of the capabilities and backgrounds of others. Show an appreciation of the diversity, talents, and aptitudes of others. Make a special effort to point them out. Read your child stories about leaders and followers, rich and poor, uneducated and educated, and high-achieving people. Teach, by modeling, a nonjudgmental manner. Watch what you say. Prejudice is often passed down as an attitude from parents to children.

Encourage your child to invite friends over. Children from homes where parents allow other children to come and visit are candidates for being popular with their friends. A meeting place (to hang out) is one of the requirements of friendship. Encourage your child to invite other children over, but only when you are there to supervise.

Encourage friendships.   Does your child have a difficult time with a particular aspect of friendship-making? Ask:

- Does my child have friends?
- Who are my child's friends?
- What group does my child associate with?
- Do I suggest he invite friends over?
- How do I treat his friends when they come over?
- Do I offer to pick up and drop off friends?
- Is he invited to their homes?
- What skills can I help my child develop so he will be liked and accepted by others?
- Why is my child having a repeated problem with his friends? Maybe you notice that he's always standing on the fringe of the group and is rarely included. Why is that?
- Is he capable of initiating a conversation—does he feel that it's okay for him to start the conversation?
- Does he make eye contact? Does he smile? Does he show warmth and acceptance?
- Does he trust himself as a good friend?

Talk with your child about his feelings about being a friend, and then share with him that it's okay to start a conversation first, to look at people directly, and so on.

Ask: Is my home conducive to have friends over?   If your child doesn't want others to come over, it may be because he's embarrassed about something in the homeplace. "My sister throws her underwear in the laundry basket in the hallway where you enter the house. No way will I take the chance that my friends will see it," said sixteen-year-old Chad. When I was in high school, there was one particular boy I wanted to date. He was "a real cool dude." But I felt embarrassed by the way our screen door looked, tattered from six children opening and closing it over the years. You know what? I turned that boy down for every date he ever asked for. There was no way I was about to let such a guy see that door. And I was certain that if I had told my parents that the reason I was dateless for the prom was because of that screen door, they would have thought me silly. Ask your child about how he sees his home. There's a good possibility that he has a few complaints that, like the laundry basket in the wrong spot, can be rectified.

Ask: Is my child invited to the homes of other children? Kari, an eight-year-old, was popular at school and frequently had her friends over to play in the afternoon. Her mother, Judy, was very protective of Kari and carried it to the point where she rarely allowed her daughter to visit classmates' homes. Eventually the child's friendships became strained. While it's important to familiarize yourself with the parents of your child's friends, where they will be playing, and what supervision they will receive, it is equally important to let your child make test flights from the nest.

Building Skills for Ending Friendships

Your child needs to know how to make and sustain, and sometimes end, friendships. Talk about how he's feeling. **Role-playing** is an effective way to help your child learn how to handle a particular situation, as well as to evaluate the pros and cons of what to do. It also helps you steer your child toward the strategies you want your child to choose. Best of all, this practice helps your child commit to the choice (decision) he has made. You help him by confronting his decision head on. Below is an example of how role playing works.

The scenario: Sixteen-year-old Julie has been asked by Ron to go to the school dance on Friday. However, she has now decided she doesn't want to go out with him. Too embarrassed to call him up and tell him, she doesn't have the courage to confront him. So she decides to stand him up—to simply not be at home when he comes to pick her up. You want to convince her that's not appropriate and to teach her a better way to undo her date. You also want to increase her ability to confront Ron, without backing down once she gets Ron on the phone or meets with him face to face. Here's how role-playing might go:

Test run 1: (Your child represents herself; you represent Ron.)

JULIE (pretending to phone Ron): "Hello, Ron?"
PARENT: "Hi, Julie!"
JULIE: "I'm calling about the dance tomorrow night."
PARENT: "Oh, I know! I'm so excited about it! My dad said I could borrow his car instead of using my old beat-up one. Guess what, Julie! I'm taking us to dinner before the dance. And, oh, I bought this really great new shirt and sweater in your favorite color! It's going to be so much fun. I'm so excited. I'll pick you up at 6:30."
JULIE (unprepared for Ron's enthusiasm and afraid to disappoint him): "Oh, okay." (She hangs up the phone, really disappointed in herself.) "I don't care. I'm not going out with that nerd!" she yells. "Now I'm stuck with having to go out with him. I'll be so embarrassed. I'm not going to be seen with him. I'm going to the movies instead with Marsha!"

Test run 2:

JULIE: "Hello, Ron?"
PARENT: "Hi Julie!"
JULIE: "I'm calling about the dance tomorrow night."
PARENT: "Oh, Julie, I'm glad you called. I'm really sick. I won't be going to school tomorrow, and I won't be able to go to the dance. I'm really sorry. I hope I didn't ruin your weekend plans. Can we talk about it at school on Monday?"
JULIE: "I'm sorry to hear you aren't feeling well, Ron. Yes, we can talk next week." Julie hangs up the phone, surprised and

pleased that she didn't call when she was angry with herself and take it out on him.

Test run 3:

JULIE: "Hello, Ron?"

PARENT: "Hello, Julie!"

JULIE: "I'm calling about the dance tomorrow night. I know it's very late to back out, but I really have to. I hope you'll have time to make other plans."

PARENT: "Well, I'm sorry to hear that, Julie. I was really looking forward to going. Are you sure I can't change your mind?"

JULIE: "Yes, I'm sure, Ron. I really must say 'no.' I'm sorry."

PARENT (sounding disappointed): "Oh, c'mon, Julie. Don't say 'no.' Say you'll change your mind, please? You know I can't find another date this late in the game!"

JULIE: "I really must say 'no.' I'm sorry."

PARENT (sounding disappointed but accepting it): "Okay. Bye, Julie. Oh, Julie, if you change your mind, please call me back. Okay? Bye."

There are, of course, many more likely responses. But do you see how this kind of rehearsing can help your child build his confidence in handling situations that have potentially stressful outcomes? That was an actual role-playing scene between a parent and daughter in a workshop I ran. As Julie explained when the exercise was over, "Getting practice on how to handle the situation was really helpful to me because I didn't know how to tell Ron that I had changed my mind about going out with him. To tell you the truth, before I role-played this with my mom, I was just going to not be home when he came to pick me up for the date. This exercise helped me see how standing him up would have made him feel really awful and, as you said, rejected and humiliated. But you know, I didn't really think I had the nerve to call and cancel, even though there was no way I was going to go out with him. Role-playing gave me the confidence to carry on the conversation I should have had in the first place."

The next phase would be for Julie and her parent to reverse roles, with Julie playing the part of Ron and her parent playing Julie. This helps her build confidence in her ability to assert her decision even further. Such preplanning reduces the likelihood that she'll be overwhelmed at the time of confrontation. It also provides your child with an opportunity to assess her understanding of the situation and test her ability to implement it under stress, such as when Julie really has to confront Ron about breaking the date. And, as importantly, by exchanging roles, your child gets to put the shoe on the other foot—to put herself in the other person's place. Give your child the skills to interact with others in a positive way.

○ IT'S UP TO YOU!

This is part of helping your child understand the nature of friendships. Helping your child with his social skills and people skills offers assistance toward forming friendships. Consequently, this develops your child's sense of belonging, the fourth vital ingredient in building a child's self-esteem.

14 COMPETENCE: HELPING YOUR CHILD FEEL CAPABLE

The fifth building block in self-esteem is competence—a sense of being capable. Being capable is an empowering feeling. When your child feels he has mastery in several areas, he's more likely to feel confident overall. It's this attitude of capability, more than IQ or opportunity, that determines your child's willingness (motivation) to do other things. Children with an attitude of "I can do it!" are willing to go the extra mile, so they usually make it to the finish line. With an increased sense of confidence, your child expects to do well—and actually does better. Each success stimulates your child's efforts, and he soon has a storehouse of positive reminders of his being capable—he feels like a winner!

○ HELPING YOUR CHILD FEEL LIKE A WINNER

Seeing himself as a can-do person will serve your child well in many ways. When he makes a bad judgment call or a mistake, rather than being debilitated by it, he puts it behind him and moves on. Because he erases it from the error column (and instead talks about what he learned from it), the outcome is a positive growth experience for him. This attitude is central to doing well in life, as Gail Sheehy's findings reveal in her book *Pathfinders*. Sheehy wanted to know why, when they encountered crisis, some people were debilitated by the trauma, while

187

others found creative ways to remove the obstacle or jump the hurdles and continue on their way to achieve satisfying and nourishing lives. Sheehy's research reveals ten characteristics of people with a high degree of life satisfaction. Of those ten qualities, one very important point stood out: Highly satisfied adults said they rarely felt disappointed or cheated by life because they were able to learn from their experiences. Nearly everyone of these individuals had failed at something in a major way, but all had recast the experience in their minds. They had erased the outcome from the error column and came to see the experience as a plus. "What I learned from that experience . . ." was a common statement made by all. The so-called "bad experience" was found to be a useful one—so much so, that they rated it near the top of the ten attributes of satisfaction.

THE TEN CHARACTERISTICS OF HIGHLY SATISFIED PEOPLE

1. My life has meaning and direction.
2. I have experienced one or more important transitions in my life and have handled them in a positive way.
3. I rarely feel cheated or disappointed by life.
4. I have attained several long-term goals that are important to me.
5. Personal growth and development are important and ongoing for me.
6. I have mutually loving relationships in my life.
7. I have many friends.
8. I am a cheerful person.
9. I am not crushed by criticism.
10. I have no major fears.

Exactly the opposite was the case with low-self-esteem people, who described their crises as personal failures and destructive experiences and saw themselves as victims instead of people in charge. These individuals did not see themselves as capable of transforming a disappointing experience into one that would allow them to go forward with their lives. Many were angry that life had dealt them such a fatal blow. Few saw how they themselves had engineered their own fate, and even fewer took responsibility for what had happened. Unwilling to pick up the pieces and go forward, many had actually dropped out of the workforce, abandoned their spouse or children, allowed their health to deteriorate, and began coping through a cycle of chemical or substance abuse.

Your Attitude Affects Your Child's Performance

We know that a child's attitude about his abilities are integrated in the performance of everything he does. That doesn't mean that if your child has a good attitude he will do well in everything but, rather, that he will approach his experiences with zest and zeal. Teachers say, for example, "He is an eager learner," or "He is really motivated," or "He'll do well because he expects to." This willingness to succeed—even in unfamiliar terrain (such as when attempting something new and difficult)—means that he is likely to succeed. See the box below for positive characteristics of a child who feels capable.

CHARACTERISTICS OF A CHILD WHO FEELS CAPABLE

- He is eager to try new things.
- He wants to try it again—to self-correct—when he has met with failure.
- He accepts challenges.
- He uses mistakes as a learning tool.
- He knows his strengths and leads with them.
- He shares opinions and ideas freely.
- He displays good sportsmanship.
- He has effective coping strategies for handling defeat.
- He recognizes accomplishments and achievements.
- He gives himself positive self-statements and encouragement.

Compare this to a child with a low self-concept about his capabilities, and you'll see just the opposite. The low-self-esteem child magnifies his weaknesses and failures and ends up with little incentive to try again. His attitude of "Why try, I'm just going to lose again anyway?" begins a self-defeating pattern. The message he gives himself is: "I won't be able to do it. I can't do it." Not feeling capable, he acts helpless. He's dependent on others, even in areas where he is competent. He is unwilling to take risks, has an overriding fear of failure, and is a poor loser. He uses negative self-statements ("I'm so stupid") and discounts or discredits his achievement ("I was just lucky"). How can such traits possibly lead to feelings of inner peace and joy and to experiencing outer achievement and success?

Luckily, you can help your child develop a greater sense of capability.

○ WHAT ARE YOU SAYING TO YOUR CHILD?

The most obvious place to start is by examining your speech, the words you say to your child. What are you saying to your child? Is it positive and encouraging? Or not?

Imagine that your child has just finished cleaning his room. You had not told him specifically to do it, but he knows that keeping his room clean is his responsibility and that Saturday mornings are reserved for chores. He comes to you and says his room is clean. You go in to check it and find that the bed is poorly made, there are clothes jammed under the bed, the desk is cluttered, the closet is a disaster area, and the window sill has a layer of dust. What do you say? Let's suppose that you are not in the best of moods this morning, so you say:

"I thought you said you cleaned your room! Do you call this a clean room? It looks like a pig sty! Look at this mess! I want you to start over again, and don't come out until you have cleaned it up. You know better than this. You're just lazy. I had to tell you five times last weekend to clean your room and three times the week before! Your sister always keeps her room clean; why can't you be more like your sister? Start again, and don't come out until you get it done right."

What message have you sent? First you began with sarcasm. How would you feel if your boss came over to you at work and said, "This report is junk! Start over, and don't leave until you finish it." You would probably be discouraged and disheartened and probably would not want to redo it.

Next comes the name-calling. You labeled your child lazy. That doesn't even seem a fair comment, because he had, in fact, done the cleaning. No one wants to be the object of name-calling, and when you call him lazy, you not only criticize your child, but unfairly make it sound as if he didn't even try. Perhaps worst of all, from the viewpoint of a youngster, he was compared to his sibling and found wanting. Then you told your child to start again and not come out until he got it right. What a depressing thought—start over again! Starting over has the connotation that everything that has gone before is totally worthless and useless. What feelings is he left with? He has been attacked. He considers himself lazy, incompetent, and worthless. What a message to send. Do you think he will start over willingly?

Your comments, when negative, do little to build self-confidence and inspire renewed efforts. Remember, your goal is to increase your child's sense of responsibility—because he feels capable. And you want him to do the task willingly, because he sees himself as capable. Your language of encouragement is the first reason why he will do that.

Try this approach:

"Son, I'm pleased that you have done the cleaning without my having to remind you about it. That shows a lot of maturity and self-discipline, which are good qualities of yours. But there are several things you must yet do. There are clothes under the bed. They should be hung in the closet or folded neatly and put away in the drawers. The papers and school supplies on your desk will need to be put away too. I would like you to start working on those things now. If you would like, I will help you. I remember how great it looked last week. Would you like that, or do you want to come and get me when you are finished?"

Here you begin with positive language, saying that you appreciate your child's efforts. Everyone wants to be appreciated and feel worthwhile. Next, offer praise. Praise is the language of encouragement. Mention his good qualities as they relate to the task at hand. This reinforces his sense of being capable. At this point, your child is feeling good about himself, even though his room is not meeting standards. You then give the constructive criticism and guidance that you know your child needs, without making it an attack on him personally. Critique the job, not your child. Tell him that the job was poorly done, not that he is a poor worker. Give him something concrete to deal with: There are clothes under the bed; he can do something to change the situation. He is not left feeling that he is bad, only that he didn't do a good enough job this time, and can the next. His self-esteem is intact. In the previous example, you attacked your child personally and he was given no direction at all. Though he feels bad about himself, he hasn't learned much about shouldering the responsibility for the care of his room.

And finally make a point of giving encouragement, so he feels motivated to redo the work, rather than forced to redo it. The result may be the same in both cases (a clean room), but now your child is going to feel good about himself when he is finished, rather than feel resentful and put upon. That's what a sense of capability is all about.

Building Your Child's "I Am Capable" Language

Below are some ground rules for developing the "I Am Capable" language in your child.

Begin on a positive note.   We are always correcting children's behavior. Think of it as positive and constructive feedback. Ask yourself, How can I make my point (get my message across) and still leave my child feeling good about himself? How can I phrase my comments so that my child knows I am telling him this because I love him and want to help him and because I know he can do better? In other words, how can I keep my child's self-esteem high while still changing the unwanted action? Start with something positive. Your child needs reinforcement throughout his formative years, and it's you who can best provide it.

Criticize the action, not your child.   It's okay to criticize the activity, but don't demean your child in the process. Suppose your nine-year-old has been told to come straight home from school. Instead he goes to a friend's house and doesn't call to tell you where he is. By the time he gets home, an hour late, you're almost frantic. What could you do to criticize the action and not the child? What could you say?

> "Tommy, I love you, and because I care about you, I set rules to help me to know that you are safe. One of the rules we agreed on together is that you are to come home right after school or call if you want permission to go to a friend's house. Today, when you weren't home at the usual time, I became worried. I called around and found . . ."

Here the parent informed her son of why and how the rule allows the parent to be responsible about her son's safety. She made it clear that the rules help him, too, not just his mother. By following the rule and letting his mother know where he is, he enables her to come to him and give him help if need be.

If you want your child to keep the rules willingly, emphasize why they are important. You want to change the improper action but leave your child feeling that the reason for the whole conversation is that he is important to you. For example, it would be useless to have your child hear, "You are an incredibly irresponsible person; I can't count on you to do anything right." As soon as your child hears the name-calling, he'll tune you out. To him, you are just griping as usual. No one wants to hear himself be put down. In addition, you will have defeated your own purpose by not making the connection in your child's mind between your criticism and his actions. The purpose is not to vent your own irritation, but to help your child realize what he did wrong, so that he can take action to change the situation in the future.

Call your child's attention to what he does well.   What one thing is your child very good at doing? Being capable to a child means that he can do something on his own. While young children are wholly dependent, they too need to see they can accomplish something separate from Mom and Dad.

Remember how proud of himself your child was when he first learned to tie his shoelaces, or made you an ashtray in art class, or drew you a special picture, or took out the garbage without being told to? Part of his pride stemmed from the fact that he was able to please you, but an even larger part came from the fact that he did something on his own that was worthwhile. He was able to produce, to give.

When your child experiences success at one task, he is willing to move on to the next. Think of the little child who looks at a new bicycle and wonders if he'll ever be able to climb up that big thing and not fall off. After many unsuccessful attempts, he masters it. Before you know it, he is pedaling around the block. Soon you can take off the training wheels. Again, he surmounts the challenge. Many bandages later, he's an expert. Soon, he's putting roadblocks in the way for a little challenge! "I am capable of doing this if I put my mind to it; I can accomplish whatever I set out to do," is an empowering message children send (or don't send) to themselves. Grade levels in school are based on this concept. Courses are offered in sequence, increasing a child's skills in one area before progressing on to another using test proficiency as a way of making certain that a child has mastered a concept before introducing another. He also moves from one grade to the next, a sign of accomplishment.

The same is true in your family situation. When your child was small, you probably assigned him easy chores, like setting the table or putting the dishes back on the shelf, and praised him disproportionately for those small tasks. As he got older, you assigned more and more responsibility. Encouragement and positive reinforcement is an effective way of building capability and helping children have a desire to go forward.

○ TAKING RESPONSIBILITY ENHANCES YOUR CHILD'S SELF-ESTEEM

Give your child responsibilities in the family. No matter how young a child is, it's a great boost to self-esteem to feel that he can make a contribution to the family. Young children can set the table, pick up toys, turn on the garden hose, or put water out for the dog. Older children can assume responsibility for a whole project, from seeing what's needed to getting it done. Yes, you can do these things yourself. But you'll cheat your child out of the self-esteem-enhancing experience of being needed and of having his efforts recognized and appreciated.

By tailoring the task to the child and then gradually adding more responsibility, you build your child's sense of competence. If your child is very young, start out with tasks in which he has a strong chance of success. Let your child do something that shows your confidence in him. Feeling more accomplished, he begins to feel worthwhile. He then progresses beyond whatever bounds he had set in his own mind.

Example: "Maria, you must water the plant in your room every Saturday morning. It needs water on a regular basis in order to live. Let's use this glass as a measurement of how much water you should give it. If you water it each Saturday, it will look beautiful and do well here in your room, and I can depend on you, too." (If your child is very young, be sure she knows when it is Saturday.)

The consequences, that the plant might die without her attention, and then the emphasis of what a good job she is doing are going to encourage her to be diligent with the plant care. Be sure to praise responsibility. Do *not* praise what wasn't well done.

Example: "This plant looks wonderful. You had the responsibility of watering it, and you did a very good job. You are a responsible daughter."

Whether she is responsible or irresponsible, she will remember the word when thinking about or describing herself. You want her self-concept to include the idea that she is a responsible person, capable of being depended upon. This makes her feel better about herself.

As children get older, we challenge them with new responsibilities to help them achieve an even stronger feeling of competence.

Tommy

Tommy's responsibility was to feed and water his dog, Rex, each morning before his mother took him to school. Although Tommy agreed to do this chore, his mother had to remind him every morning and then follow up to make sure it was done. She tried everything to get him to do it—from shouting to bribes, from allowances to a contract complete with checklist posted on the refrigerator door. Nothing seemed to work for very long. We talked about her overall goal.

"What do you want him to do?" I asked.

"Well, I want Tommy to take care of this responsibility every morning and to do it willingly and cheerfully," she said. "I want the dog cared for by Tommy."

Because her approach wasn't working well, we talked about a new one. This time Karen was to wait until she and her son were in the car and on the way to school before she asked him if he had fulfilled his responsibilities.

"Did you feed and water Rex this morning, son?" she asked.

"Yup!" Tommy replied. Karen knew that he had not, but rather than criticize him, she started in on the plan to get her son to really commit to this responsibility.

"That's good. You know Rex really depends on you. And he loves you so much. Why, he barks and runs to you the second you get home. He waits patiently for you all day. And I know how much you enjoy playing with him. Gosh, he sure has been a good friend to you, hasn't he? Well, he's a pretty big dog, and it gets so hot during the day, that it's good that you fill up his water bowl each morning. That could prevent him from getting sick—even dying—in the hot sun. He needs his food too."

She went on and on, reminding her son about the good times between Rex and Tommy, some of the particularly special times, and talked about ways in which the dog was dependent on Tommy. Never once did she criticize Tommy. Her goal was not to induce guilt, which at first you might think her approach implied, but, rather, to assume responsibility so that he could get to the place of feeling that he could depend on himself to care for his pet.

Her son was very silent on the way to school that day. Karen dropped him off, then went home and fed and watered the dog before she left for work. At about 1:00 that afternoon, she got a call from the school saying that her son had spent much of the morning in the nurse's office complaining of not feeling well. He did not have a fever, but he seemed disturbed by something.

Tommy was feeling remorseful about neglecting his responsibility to Rex. But something more happened. It was that day that Tommy signed the agreement in his heart to commit to the responsibility of caring for his dog. It was the last time his mother had to remind him. It was this approach, more than nagging, bantering, or threats, that had made the difference. Isn't that what we really want? Don't we want to help our children sign agreements in their hearts?

Praise is the language of encouraging responsibility in children. Responsible children feel good about themselves. The following section discusses helping children learn from their mistakes in such a way that they'll want to try again.

Helping Your Child Learn from Mistakes

Henry Ford was right when he said, "Failure is the only opportunity to more intelligently begin again." I see so many young people who have experienced so little success that they're afraid of making even more mistakes. These youngsters won't initiate friendships that appear too difficult to strive for, they don't go out for activities in which they think they won't do well, and they won't take a course in school that they think will be too difficult. Many schools have a rich curriculum with excellent courses designed for students to gain access to some very exciting skills, but unless these courses are mandated, many young people won't sign up for them. And so many parents distance themselves from the schools (never realizing how rich the schools' curriculum really is) and so are unable to counsel their children into courses that might otherwise help them become as capable as they could possibly be.

I often share the Thomas Edison story of success versus failure with young people to help them feel it's okay to keep trying after they've made a mistake. Edison didn't create the electric light on the first try. He didn't wake up one day and say, "Today's goal is to create the electric light." Edison failed—and failed—and failed. Finally an associate of his said, "Edison, you should give up. You've failed thousands of times."

"No, I haven't failed thousands of times," Edison replied. "On the contrary, I have successfully eliminated thousands of ideas that do not work!"

This analogy applies to helping your child build his sense of competence. Be encouraging. Research has shown that when teachers write specific comments of encouragement on a test or other assignments where a child didn't do well, the student improved on the next test. When students do not receive positive and helpful comments, they fail to improve on future assignments. This is true for both good and poor students. By receiving feedback from us in the form of constructive encouragement, young people know specifically what to do in order to improve, but just as important, they *want* to do better. And although you offer praise for your child's achievements, your child must see the value of his own work too. Teach him to acknowledge himself in the process.

Are You Giving Your Child (Enough) Gold Stars?

You and I need to feel successful, and children are no exception. But in order for your child to succeed, he must first believe he can. The more negative the statements he hears from you, the lower his self-esteem becomes and the less willing he is to try again. The more positive they are, the more he tries, and the better he does. He needs positive feedback and praise in order to be encouraged. Teachers are implementing this concept when they give gold stars to praise good work at school. All children need and deserve a chance to have gold stars and happy faces decorate their papers—at home too.

Like teachers, you can give gold stars. Is your child getting all the gold stars he needs from you? See the box below for some ground rules for giving gold stars.

GROUND RULES FOR GIVING PRAISE

- *Effective praise is personal and individual.* It need not be heard by everyone. Be sincere and share it heart-to-heart with your child. "You did a wonderful job washing my car, son. Although that's what you get paid for doing, I want you to know how much I appreciate it. Thanks for being so thorough."
- *Praise must be immediate.* The best time to give praise is when it is deserved. Keep in mind that the longer you delay your praise, the less effective your words will be.

- *The praise must be deserved.* Be sure that the praise you give is deserved or you will lose credibility with your child. Your child knows whether he really earned it. "Even though you failed the exam, Brad, I'm impressed with how earnestly you studied. I know you did your best. Next time, I know you'll do better."

- *Praise must be behavior-centered.* Praise specific behaviors and not just positive attributes. Stick to what your child did. Telling a low-self-esteem child he is sweet or nice doesn't fit his inner self-image and, consequently, the praise will be met with disbelief. For this child, it's important to relate the praise to a behavior. "Lola, when you asked your friend to step outside because he wanted to smoke, you showed good judgment."

- *Be specific.* The most effective praise is very concrete; it lets your child know exactly what was done well. When you see good behavior, don't say "Great!" but, rather, "Jerome, you did a nice job picking up your clothes and hanging them up." Specific praise lets your child know what he did well and, as a result, he's more likely to repeat the behavior.

- *Use praise consistently.* All children need praise, especially low-self-esteem children. Giving praise one or two times is not enough for children with low self-esteem. Their internal image is so ingrained that you need to repeat the praise for similar behaviors two or three times before the message is internalized and accepted. Don't feel that you're becoming a broken record; praise frequently for the same observed behavior. Younger children (or low-self-esteem children) tend to forget their praiseworthy moments.

- *Use awards and rewards.* Praise can be more than words; it can include awards and rewards. These are different from bribes. Bribes do not necessarily enhance self-esteem. A reward, on the other hand, especially if it's unexpected and spontaneous, shows your child that he did something special and that he deserves something special. It puts him in the spotlight for a moment and lets him feel his accomplishment. You tell him that what he does makes a difference, that he can affect others. "Sherman, you are doing so well at keeping your studies up. I'm going to treat you and a friend to an evening at the movies. You tell me when you would like to go."

○ IT'S UP TO YOU!

It's been said that the primary reason for being fired or released from a position is not because the employee didn't possess the capability necessary for proficiency for the job but, rather, because the person lacked motivation—the desire to do a good job. We can say the same for some children.

Children who lack the motivation to work toward course proficiency, for example, often end up dropping out of school. Yet many of these children can do the work required of them, but won't. If you've ever looked at a child and thought, "If only he knew how capable he is," and "If only she knew how bright she is"—you get the idea. Developing this attitude of being capable is an integral part of the effective life skills you give your child.

It begins by what we say to our child—developing that "can do" attitude. We must begin on a positive note; criticize the action, not the child, and call attention to what she does well. Therefore, to foster feelings of competence in our child, which is vital to both her success and self-esteem, we must use compassion, patience and thought, when speaking to her. In the following chapter we'll look at developing competence in your child's world of work.

15
COMPETENCE: UNDERSTANDING YOUR CHILD'S WORLD OF WORK

Your child will spend approximately 15,000 hours in an educational system from kindergarten through twelfth grade. From the time your child is five years of age until he is eighteen, nearly eight hours each day during the week will be spent in the school environment or on school-related activities. At the end of your child's formal school career, he will be a twelve- or thirteen-year veteran of a mandated educational experience. Is it any wonder that a big part of your child's feeling of competence stems from his performance in a place in which he spends so much time?

○ YOUR CHILD'S ORGANIZATION

I have always been amazed at how relatively little parents know about the real nature of the school experience. Some parents are surprised to find out that in many ways a school resembles the fast-paced and pressured environment of a business organization. The demands on your child as a student in school and the demands on you in the work setting are quite similar. You might also think of school life in this way: Being a student is your child's occupation, learning is his role, education is his career, and school is his organization. These facets encompass your child's world of work.

Unfortunately, parents don't receive a school career manual similar to the job manuals that many companies issue to employees, informing them of company policies and ways to maneuver successfully through the maze of organizational life. Although a school district often provides a brochure on the district's discipline policy, this simply spells out the procedures for taking action against your child when he has violated the rules. Both parents and children need more information.

For many children, school is an intense and frustrating experience. Many parents can't understand why children find it so difficult, but all the same, many children feel they can't (or won't) make the grade. Some drop out psychologically and others drop out physically. (Chapter 4 describes some of the emotional stresses encountered there.)

But school needn't be such a difficult experience for so many children. We can help them learn adaptive ways of dealing with it. Again, parents are the key. Helping your child develop skills in managing his world of work is more likely to result in experiences that lead to strengthening his self-esteem, rather than to a debilitating sense of self.

Things You Can Do to Help Your Child Manage His or Her Workplace

You can't always change the way the school operates, and you may not always be able to change the way others treat your child. But there are some things you can do.

Help your child become organized. Your child will need the appropriate tools for working. Every child needs a quiet study area that is safe from interruption and equipped with a good light. He'll need a desk and a bookcase. Shop for pencils, paper, and the standard supplies he'll need in his role as a student. Set up a file and show him how to use it. This filing cabinet can be the standard kind, or it can be as simple as a large cardboard box divided with inserts for separating files in terms of contents

("Great Articles: Save for Future Book Reports") or by class or subject area ("English Exams," "English Notes to Use for Studying for the Semester Exam," "English Papers Handed Back," and so on). What's important is that you help your child learn the system of getting organized. He is, after all, a career student and, depending on his age, will be for years to come.

Next, get a large month-at-a-glance wall calendar to record work assignments and school-related activities. This makes it easy for a child to notice when he needs to be focused on particular projects and assignments and when he's free to schedule social activities. It also helps him to feel like a professional doing a job.

This should be *his* work space—not a shared space, if possible. It doesn't have to be a large area: just a space that he associates with doing homework (productivity). Not having a place to work or the tools to do it is a big reason why many children don't want to do their homework.

Set parameters on study time.   During study time, there should be no TV, stereo, or phone calls. Phone calls can be made after homework projects are done or between studying different subjects as a way to take a break. If your child needs to clarify an assignment by talking to a fellow student, a two- to three-minute call should be sufficient. If your child is in high school and has unrestricted phone privileges, discourage lengthy phone calls during study time. You want to teach your child the power of uninterrupted concentration. Explain to him why this is a good practice.

Agree on a regular time for studying.   Whether you decide that this time is immediately after school or after the evening meal, keep it consistent when possible. This routine helps your child to do his homework consistently day after day, and takes away his excuses for not having the time to do it.

Help your child to identify his work style.   Your child may be able to complete all her studying and homework in a single session, or he may do better if he studies for twenty minutes, takes a break, and then comes back to it. Every child is different. What is important is that he recognizes his own style and optimum pattern for producing his best work. You can help your child identify his work style by pointing out the rituals that you go through before you are ready for productive work (for example, organizing your desk and sharpening all your pencils).

If he's overly tired or unwilling to get into a particular assignment, what rituals help prepare him for productive work: putting on a good tape, a brisk walk, a ten-minute bike ride? Help your child learn how to renew his energy and channel it to the tasks that need to be done. It varies for each age of child, and you're the best judge of your own child. When my daughter was in fifth and sixth grades, for example, I would allow her to take her bike to the local minimarket and buy fifty-cents' worth of junk food. She couldn't do too much damage with fifty cents, but she did get a surge of energy (my intention) from riding her bike there. I would time her to see if she could get there and back in fifteen minutes. It worked! By the time she came running excitedly into the house to see if she had won against the timer, her little body's endorphins (internally produced chemical compounds that, through exercise, trigger a natural high) were in full flow and ready to provide her with renewed energy. She was then ready to do her chores and to do homework before dinner. When she became a seventh grader, she would no longer buy that, and I had to look for new ways to get her ready to confront two hours or more of homework.

Look for ways that work with your child. If you know that he is simply too tired, don't force it. He won't be productive if he's unable to summon the needed energies.

Show an active interest in your child's school work.
When you show interest, you convey the message that you care about your child's school career, that attending school

is purposeful, and that learning is important. You show interest by asking meaningful questions. If you ask, "What did you do in school today?" and your child answers, "Nothing," ask more specific questions based on what you know is being taught. Rather than ask, "How as your day?" (to which he would probably reply, "Fine") ask about what he is learning. Ask him:

• Do you feel that you are improving?
• What contributed to your good grades as well as to your poor ones?
• What is your favorite subject? Why?
• Is the A a mark of achievement, or was the work too easy?
• Did you get the D because you didn't understand the material or because the finals were taken the day after your three-day band trip out of town and you weren't prepared for them?

Ask these questions even though you may feel you know the answers. Become familiar with the courses your child is enrolled in, and know what's being taught and what's expected of your child.

• What books will be read?
• How much homework will be required?
• What major long-term projects can be anticipated?
• Is your child likely to need help with any special projects?

Remember, school can be tough for A students too.

Your attitude is all-important. Children do as their parents *do*, not as they *say*. If you get excited about new books and new ideas, your child will too. A half an hour a day reading and talking to your child will make a big difference. A brief conversation now and then showing that education is important to you will influence how your child does in school.

Determine which on-the-job skills your child needs.
Use clues from report cards, teacher conferences, and aptitude tests to become familiar with your child's strengths and weaknesses so you'll know where you can help. Is he lacking a particular skill that is holding him back? Can you obtain special tutoring for a problem area? Is there a physical problem, such as with eyesight or hearing? Is there a particular learning disability?

Ask about his "coworkers."   Who are his friends at school and why? How much time do they get to be together in favorite school activities? Do they eat lunch together? Who are the good students and why? Which are not such good students and why? Has he noticed that he's a better learner when he feels like a friend—and a better friend when he's feeling successful in school? What are his thoughts about this realization?

Talk to your child about his teachers.   Think about the teachers you had in school, the ones you liked and those you didn't. How did they make you want to learn? Were some teachers so exciting that you looked forward to their classes? Did a few teachers even talk with students rather than lecture them day after day? Did you notice that in some classes time flew by, but that in others you were often daydreaming, waiting for class to be finished? Does he like his teachers? Why or why not? What teacher(s) does your child find exciting and why? Children sometimes choose a career because of a special teacher. Who is this special teacher for your child?

Teach time-management skills.   For most children, whether in elementary, junior high, or high school, there never seems to be enough time away from school to cope with assignments, friends, extracurricular activities, and family and have time left over for themselves. Even during the school day, one of the greatest pressures on your youngster is time. A very important step in helping him learn to manage his time is to set up a daily or weekly to-do list. It should not be a long and detailed list, but it should contain those things that he wants to accomplish each day (or week).

Priority setting is also important. Show your child how you set priorities and that your management of time allows you to do the things you want to do. Help your child to generate his to-do list, and then delineate the one or two tasks that are the most urgent. Set a timetable and estimate the length of time necessary to perform each task. Break long-term projects down into manageable parts so he can begin on them instead of wait until the last minute to do something he won't be able to complete in a short period of time. Some variation on the following planning form works for most students from second grade up.

DAILY PLANNING SHEET

Today's date:

Subject area:

Assignment:

When due:

Don't forget to:

Help your child with homework judiciously. When children become students, parents often become "students," too. Helping your child can be a very frustrating and tension-filled experience for both parent and child. Not all parents are able to help their children with homework. If you find that you are unable to help your child—for whatever reason—find an outside source who can. Children enjoy working with others, and this can alleviate the tension and additional constraints on parental time. For example, teenagers and college students enjoy working with younger children.

When you are helping your child with homework, here are some things to keep in mind:

- Have patience. Allow your child to learn at his own pace.
- Encourage your child to do his best work, but recognize that this work may not necessarily be A-level.
- Let your child know that you are proud of him for doing his best.
- Allow your child time to relax between difficult or long assignments.
- Praise positive efforts as well as work achievements.
- Don't name-call when your child is having a rough time grasping a concept.
- Don't become discouraged.

Tutor your child. In addition to daily assignments, there may be areas where your child needs special help in acquiring a skill. Tutoring your own child is often a difficult undertaking. I've not met too many parents or children who have enjoyed one another during parental tutoring. Remember, the goal is to enhance your child's sense of capability while preserving the relationship between the two of you.

When you're ready to help, this approach works best: "Michael, I talked to your math teacher this morning. She told me that you were doing well with simple equations but that you were having some problems with graphing. I can help you with graphing. How does that sound to you?" This opens lines of communication. Remember that you want him to want the extra help too. You want his participation and his commitment to do better. Without them, you may be the only one working for improvement. Here are some special considerations when tutoring:

- *Sit next to your child rather than across from him.* When you sit side by side, it's easier for both of you to see the lessons, and the physical closeness helps encourage a friendlier relationship.
- *If you find that the tutoring session is unpleasant for you or your child, don't get discouraged, and don't react.* Listen to your child. His reaction may be based on fear of not being able to do the work, while not wanting you to know of his fear, lest you be disappointed in him. For example, if you find that he's giving you just any old answer in order to get you so frustrated that you'll leave him alone, you might say, "Let's go slowly. I'll be patient while you think this through. I have lots of time to help you."
- *Be sure that the directions you give are presented slowly and clearly.* For some children the major difficulty is not in mastering the subject matter but in following directions.
- *Work through one step at a time.* This keeps your child's attention on the work and gives you a closer look at where the difficulties lie. For example, if you are doing addition problems, present them one at a time rather than ask your child to do a page of fifteen or twenty equations at once.
- *When your child speaks to you, or when you are speaking to him, be sure to look at him.* It's sometimes easier to *see* confusion and frustration than it is to *hear* it.
- *Don't skip any problems.* Wait for an answer to each problem. This helps your child develop the habit of confronting challenges rather than avoiding them.
- *Minimize your use of negative phrases such as, "That's wrong."* Respond to a wrong answer by restating the question and supplying your child with more clues to help him get the correct answer. After he gets the correct answer, it's useful to go over the question in its original form without the clues but with praise.

Make homework fun!　There is no need to be too serious. It's much more enjoyable to work together when you can gently tease each other or make silly puns. Personalize the lessons with humor. Parents of small children know how much the child enjoys it when the parent is wrong: "You mean K-A-T is not how to spell 'cat'?" You can carry it over into any subject. Pneumonics (memory devices) can become works of art between parent and child. I still remember my uncle Ray teaching me the divisions in biology—Kingdom, phylum, class, order, family, genus, species—with "Kinky People Come Over For Great Sex!" Twenty-five years later, I can still rattle them off!

Follow your child's progress.　Your child's performance appraisal (report card) tells you how he's doing overall. However, remember that bad grades don't suddenly materialize out of nowhere. If you've been watching weekly reports (grades on papers and tests) you should have some idea of how your child is doing.

Even if your child's report card isn't as good as you would like, look for something positive—a grade raised in math or a teacher's comments about how hard your child is working, and show your child that you are as pleased with his success as you are concerned with his less successful efforts. If you ground your child because of a bad report card, or if you yell and scream and tell him he is lazy or stupid, you're not doing anything to improve his grades; in fact, you're probably making the situation worse. Be proactive. Start with something you can make a difference in, now.

Meet your child's "boss."　Meet your child's teacher at the beginning of the term. Many parents feel uncomfortable about contacting their child's teacher and even more anxious if the teacher calls to request a meeting. Such feelings may be related to associating the teacher with the parents' own childhood, when the teacher may have been a strong authority figure who defined what was right or wrong and who passed judgment on us or was overly critical.

Keep in mind that most teachers are parents, too. They often come to parent-teacher conferences with their own apprehensions and uncertainties about how they will be viewed by *you*, the child's parents. Understanding the perspective of the teacher, as well as your own feelings, will help to make your relationship with the teacher productive and enjoyable.

Schedule a "business meeting" (parent-teacher conference). Some parents believe that parent-teacher conferences occur for one of two reasons: Either their child is behaving badly or their child is having serious problems keeping up with schoolwork. Conferences are held for these reasons, but they're not the only circumstances that prompt conferences. Conferences may serve a variety of functions, including to report on the child's progress; to compare the teacher's understanding of the child with that of the parents (when the teacher has noticed something in the child's behavior that could be of concern); or to ask parents for specific help (for example, when a child is having difficulties with schoolwork that may be related to the home environment).

Remember that teachers aren't the only ones who can schedule conferences. You can take the initiative too. If you have specific questions, or if you want to know generally how your child is doing, or if you think there's a problem, make an appointment with the teacher immediately. Call the school to set it up. Don't expect a teacher to leave class to speak to you, but do expect that the teacher will get back to you within a reasonable period of time. If you don't hear from the teacher within two days, call again, because messages have a way of going astray. If after your second call there is no return call, ask to speak with the assistant principal. (If you speak a language different from that of the teacher, ask if the school will provide an interpreter.)

Is Your Child Involved in Too Many Things?

Watch for the over-involvement syndrome—children can experience job burnout just as adults can. It may be due to an after-school job that takes up too many hours, or it may be caused by too much time spent with friends, on dates, or in other activities. Is your child trying to do too much at once? Discuss with your child which activities can be cut back. Your child will be relieved that you have intervened.

What Teachers Wish Parents Would Do

In the book *Talks to Parents: How to Get the Best Education for Your Child*, the National PTA lists the ten things that teachers wish parents would do. If it were your report card below, how would you do?

TEN THINGS TEACHERS WISH PARENTS WOULD DO

1. Get involved. Parental involvement is the greatest correlation to student learning and school improvement.

○

2. Provide resources at home for learning. Parents should have books and magazines available and read with their children on a weekly basis.

○

3. Set a good example. Parents should show their children that they believe that reading is both enjoyable and useful. They shouldn't spend all their time in front of the TV.

○

4. Encourage their children to do their best in school. Parents need to show their children that they believe education is important and that they want their children to do their best.

○

5. Emphasize learning. Too many parents get caught up in only supporting their child's athletics and in preparing their children for college. Support learning too.

○

6. Support school rules and goals. Parents should take care not to undermine school rules, discipline, or goals.

○

7. Use pressure positively. Parents should encourage children to do their best but not pressure them by setting goals too high or by scheduling too many activities.

○

8. Call teachers early if there is a problem . . . so there is still time to solve it. Don't wait for teachers to call first.

○

9. Accept their responsibility as parents. Don't expect the school and teachers to take over all the obligations of parents. Parents should teach children basic discipline at home rather than leaving this to teachers.

○

10. View drinking and excessive partying as a serious matter. This takes a toll on students' classroom performance. While parents are concerned about drug abuse, many fail to recognize that alcohol is the drug most frequently abused by youngsters as well as adults. Children can't learn in an altered state.

○ IT'S UP TO YOU!

"Whether you are a middle-class suburbanite, a minority parent living in the slums of a major city, or a resident of a rural area—whether you are a doctor or a dish washer—your involvement will mean that your child will learn more and do better in school," says Ann Lynch, 1989–91 National PTA president. Children whose parents are actively involved in their education often score higher on achievement tests than do students who have more ability or greater social and cultural advantages but whose parents are not involved. The U.S. Department of Education confirmed: "What parents do to help their children learn is more important to academic success than how well-off the family is." These and other similar reports give testimony to how important you are in developing your child's school competence.

16 COMPETENCE: SKILLS FOR HELPING YOUR CHILD FEEL CAPABLE

Competence is more than just doing well scholastically. Children also get a sense of how capable they are by their ability to manage their emotional lives. This is especially important because children often think that parents, teachers, or friends cause them to react the way they do, that someone else is responsible.

○ CONTROLLING INNER THOUGHTS (AND BEHAVIOR)

Help your child to believe that he can be in control of his emotions. Teach him that thoughts determine behavior. You've no doubt experienced this principle in operation. You're driving along in your car and begin to think about an unpleasant confrontation you had with someone a day, a week, or a month earlier. Soon you're driving faster and you're clenching the wheel tightly. Recalling the incident produced the same emotions as if it had just happened.

As you've no doubt observed, some people feel, act, and then think—when they would be well served to think, feel, and then act. We have to remember that our self-esteem comes from what we do as well as from what we think. Perhaps you have heard someone say, "I can't help the way I feel. It just happens." This assumes that thoughts and feelings occur independently and are not under our control. However, the opposite is true. Rarely does a feeling just happen. There is a direct connection between thoughts (and feelings) and behaviors. Let's look at this in operation:

Mary Beth told her son he had to turn the television off. She said, "I know you wanted to see that television special, Jon, but you won't be able to. It's 7:50 and your homework isn't done, and you haven't taken care of your dog yet. You know those things have to be done first." Jon begins to process this message. Below are two possible scenarios of Jon's thinking.

JON'S THOUGHTS: "Mom is mad at me. She knows how much I wanted to see that television special. If she cared about me, she would let me watch it."

JON'S FEELINGS: Upset, angry, defensive.

JON'S BEHAVIOR: He stomps off to do the chores, shouting how unfair his mother is.

Here Jon assumes that it is his mother who made him upset and angry and that he, therefore, has a right to be defensive. After all, she did reprimand him. In this case, Jon is thinking irrationally and it affects his behavior in a negative way. A different and more positive scenario might be as follows.

JON'S THOUGHTS: "I wish I had completed my chores. My homework is due tomorrow and my dog depends on me for care. It's not too much work, and I knew I was supposed to finish it before the program."

JON'S FEELINGS: Rational, responsible.

JON'S BEHAVIOR: "I'm sorry, Mom. I should have completed my chores before my friend came over, and I should have told him I would have to visit another time because I wanted to watch that special tonight. I really do want you to trust me and feel that I can be counted on. Can I watch the program as soon as I care for my dog? Then I can complete my homework after that. Okay, Mom?"

Helping your child learn the connection between thinking and behavior can have high payoffs. Besides being easier to parent, children learn that they are capable of emotional self-management. Help your children see that it's not so much the event that determines their behavior as how they think about it.

Knowing that the way they think determines the way they feel may require some changes in their usual ways of communicating.

Dean receives a low grade on his first math test. He tells himself that he is dumb and not capable of doing the work. He believes that failing this one math test means that he will fail on all his others. So he skips math class on the day of his next test. Just as Dean's coping style was affected by what he has told himself about his abilities, what your child tells himself can work either for or against him too. Beliefs that work against him put limits on what he will attempt to do. Dean's beliefs about math are dysfunctional. Beliefs that enhance or improve your child's coping ability work for him. Your child must be able to distinguish between the situation itself and what he says to himself about it. It doesn't make sense that Dean should skip math class because he failed one exam. Unwanted or irrational thoughts can be changed to positive ones.

Thought-Stopping Skills

Once your child is aware of how his inner thoughts work for or against his ability to achieve and excel, he'll want to be able to change the negative thoughts. This procedure is called **thought-stopping.** What this means is that you visualize a stop sign whenever you start telling yourself limiting statements. This stop sign acts as a signal to stop thinking dysfunctional thoughts. In the previous example, Dean told himself that because he failed a math test, he would fail again; therefore, he skipped class to avoid repeating an unpleasant situation. The last phase of thought-stopping involves thought substitution. Dean would visualize a stop sign and then generate as many positive thoughts as possible, such as:

- Just because I failed one test doesn't mean I'll fail all other math tests.
- Failing a test doesn't mean I'm dumb.
- I should study harder next time.
- I could attend review sessions and ask for extra help if I feel I need it.

Help your child learn how to reshape negative messages by focusing on the things that he does well. The goal is to get him to think about the approach he brings to his school-work, his relationships, and his life.

Rescripting Negative Messages

Another way you can get your child to turn the negative thoughts into positive ones is by getting him to write a sentence about something he doesn't like about himself and then rewrite the sentence, this time using a positive rather than a negative statement.

EXAMPLE: School is hard for me.
REWRITE: I enjoy all my subjects except algebra. I did well in math class, but I don't yet understand all the concepts of algebra. I need more help in that class.

EXAMPLE: I am unpopular.
REWRITE: I'd like to be friends with Karen and Debra, but I'm not certain they want my friendship.

When children feel they can be in charge of determining their behavior, it helps them feel capable. If your child thinks that he's not a good student, he will probably find school difficult, and this will contribute to his not liking school. Likewise, if he seeks someone's friendship but doesn't get it, he may feel unpopular. Changing, rewriting, or rescripting the way he thinks about himself is a vital skill in developing competence, because when he sends mostly positive messages to himself, he is more likely to have the courage to go forward when things get tough. When your child does well, he starts that wonderfully contagious success cycle that contributes to his excelling in his day-to-day work and in his relationships with you and others.

○ SOLVING PROBLEMS, GENERATING ALTERNATIVES, AND EVALUATING CONSEQUENCES

You can help your children learn and acquire skills that will change their helpless feelings to can-do ones. Taking responsibility and gradually exerting more influence over their own actions helps children feel capable. Children who previously floundered when faced with a dilemma now find they have resources to take charge. They are able to make decisions and choose what the outcome will be.

A good place to start with your child is helping him learn how to solve problems, generate alternatives, and then evaluate the consequences. Finding a solution and getting out of a dilemma is made even more difficult when your child isn't sure what the problem is, only that one exists. In groping for a solution, your child may act impulsively or make rash decisions.

Effective problem-solving is a four-step process that involves identifying the real problem, searching for sound solutions, and recognizing the consequences, trying them out, and then evaluating the outcome. This approach works with teens and with young children. Examples for both age groups follow.

The process begins by asking four simple questions:

1. What is the problem?
2. How can I solve it, given the possible consequences?
3. What is my plan?
4. How did I do?

Fifteen-year-old Sonja has invited Jennifer to her house for an overnight stay. Jennifer, also fifteen, has told her parents of the plans and has asked for permission to stay out overnight. Upon learning that the plans include dinner and an at-home evening (and being assured that Sonja's mother will be there), Jennifer's parents grant permission. However, when Jennifer arrives at Sonja's house after school on Friday, Sonja informs Jennifer that her mother will not be home and that her eighteen-year-old brother and his friend have offered to drive them to the movies.

Let's analyze Jennifer's problem:

---

1. WHAT IS THE PROBLEM?

Jennifer has accepted an invitation to an overnight stay based on certain criteria, and she has permission based on those criteria. Sonja changed the plans without notifying Jennifer or Jennifer's parents. Jennifer does not want to break the trust with her parents, but she wants Sonja to accept her—and she also wants to go to the movies. Jennifer's parents are out, and she cannot contact them at this time to get approval of the changes.

---

2. HOW CAN SHE SOLVE HER PROBLEM, GIVEN THE POSSIBLE CONSEQUENCES?

ACTION: She could go along with Sonja's new plans without telling her parents.

CONSEQUENCE: She will break the trust she and her parents have established.

ACTION: She could wait until her parents are home to get permission to accept the new plans.

CONSEQUENCE: It will be too late to go, and everyone will be tired of waiting for the decision.

ACTION: She could tell Sonja that the new plans sound interesting but that she cannot go along, because she has accepted the overnight invitation based on a prearranged set of criteria and that she is certain her parents would not approve of the new plans.

CONSEQUENCE: She will take the responsibility for her decision and run the risk that her friend will mock her.

ACTION: She could call Sonja a liar and a poor friend to put her in this predicament.

CONSEQUENCE: Sonja will feel offended, and the friendship will be strained.

ACTION: She could leave a message on her parents' answering machine, telling them of the change in plans, and go to the movies.

CONSEQUENCE: Jennifer's parents will most certainly feel taken advantage of and may not allow her overnights in the future.

3. WHAT IS THE PLAN?

As parents, we'll select the ideal response. Let's decide that Jennifer will tell Sonja that the new plans sound interesting but that she won't be able to go without first checking with her parents.

4. HOW DID SHE DO?

If that were the case, great! Sonja was relieved to not have to follow through with her own revised plans. She had felt that her mother too would be upset when she learned of the incident.

Now you need to help your child examine the likely outcome of proposed actions by asking a question such as, "If you do that, what would happen?" This question is often followed by "And then what would happen?" Generate as many alternatives to the problem as you can, and then help your child assess the potential impact of each option. Your goal is to help your child learn how a different choice of action leads to a different outcome. Below is an example for a younger child.

---

1. WHAT IS THE PROBLEM?

Danny called me stupid and it made me mad!

---

2. HOW CAN I SOLVE IT?

ACTION: I could call him stupid.
CONSEQUENCE: He will stay angry.

ACTION: I could punch him.
CONSEQUENCE: He might hit me back.

ACTION: I could tell him how angry it makes me.
CONSEQUENCE: He would understand my feelings.

ACTION: I could ignore it.
CONSEQUENCE: He might continue to call me names.

---

3. WHAT IS MY PLAN?
(Ask your child, "When will you do this?")

ACTION: I'm going to tell him to stop name-calling. I'll tell him on the bus tomorrow morning.

---

4. HOW DID I DO?

I was very nervous, but he seemed friendly, as if he wasn't mad at me at all, so I said I didn't like to be called names and that I wouldn't do it if he wouldn't. He said okay! It was great, and I didn't get into a fight. Danny said he was sorry. I think we're going to be good friends now.

○ IT'S UP TO YOU!

Too often, children feel powerless and become victimized by others. You can help your child develop the skill to treat others and himself in an emotionally healthy way.

An important part of self-esteem is feeling able to cope with the stresses of the everyday challenges of growing up. As a parent, you directly influence how competent your child views himself to be. This means helping him be prepared for situations in which he might find himself, both socially and academically. It means helping anticipate and develop strategies for coping. It means becoming involved, yet standing back far enough to let your child learn by doing. As you observe how your child is doing, you learn to understand what he needs and how to help him develop his own strategies for fulfilling those needs.

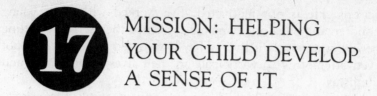

17 MISSION: HELPING YOUR CHILD DEVELOP A SENSE OF IT

And so the spiral toward the development of a healthy self-esteem continues. The sixth building block for helping your child gain a positive sense of self is a sense of mission—of being purposeful. Feeling purposeful is an inner knowledge that your life has meaning.

Children with a sense of mission develop inner well-being because they have in mind specific aims or intentions of what they want to do and be. Because they have a vision, they have direction. This is not to say that they know at age eight that they want to be a gardener or an engineer, but they do know if they are drawn to music, people, animals, healing, and so on. Each time your child focuses on what provides meaning for him, he's energized in the process. Inner peace, appreciation, and greater self-knowledge are the outcome.

Young people who have discovered interests that are of importance to them are vibrant, optimistic, and have a zest for living and doing what's necessary to realize their needs and goals. Because what's going on seems exciting, they are self-motivated and self-directed.

A child who feels that his life has no meaning is quite different from a child who feels purposeful. Not fulfilled, he is listless, aimless, and often turns to others for self-fulfillment. If his needs are met in a less-than-satisfying manner, he begins to blame others for his plight. He stops being accountable for his actions. He is not motivated. I've worked with both young children and older ones who have resigned themselves to feeling powerless about their lives. They have opted to be victims, not even attempting to participate in their lives in an active and vital way.

Helping your child find purpose and meaning is a critical element in developing his self-esteem. It is also essential in attaining vibrant health and well-being, and it is important to motivation, ambition, and achievement.

○ A SENSE OF MISSION ENHANCES YOUR CHILD'S SUCCESS IN SCHOOL

A sense of mission can actually raise the level of your child's performance in school. The Coleman Report, a comprehensive investigation of American education that regularly reports on the nature of U.S. schools, concluded that the degree to which a student feels his life has meaning is the second most significant determinant (parent support was the first) of whether he meets with overall failure or success in his effectiveness as a student. This correlation was also more significant than academic performance, class size, yearly expenditure per pupil, or level of teacher preparation in school success. As the level of self-esteem increases, so do academic achievement scores—and as self-esteem decreases, so does achievement.

There are other parallel benefits of having a sense of mission. High-self-esteem children are more outgoing, more assured, and develop stronger, more mature friendships. They are more likely to join peer groups who are worthy of their friendship. These students are also more likely to develop good relationships with their teachers and to participate in extracurricular activities—again, making the school experience one that is more enjoyable and helpful in sustaining the ups and downs that accompany meeting the challenge of the learning experience.

○ HOW CHILDREN FIND MEANING

I frequently conduct workshops for young people around the country, and I ask them what brings meaning and purpose to their lives. A typical response came from a young man in a recent workshop with a class of high school seniors. I asked the seniors to identify what they felt the purpose of their lives to be and when they had first discovered that purpose. Young people often confuse *mission* for where they're going to college, where they'll live, or what they're going to do for a job. And while that's misguided (you and I might say that our purpose includes developing a higher spiritual consciousness), it's a good place to start. I usually proceed from that point. Kevin told me he wanted to be a veterinarian. Here's his story:

Kevin

"My mother and I were on our way to my soccer practice one day when I was in the eighth grade. Lying on the grass near a stop sign was a white cat licking its wounds. It looked really hurt. I begged my mother to let me go over to look at the cat. Well, the cat was hurt quite badly, and I managed to persuade my mom to take it to a local animal hospital. The vet cared for the cat, and my mother was left with the bill for a stray animal we didn't know. My mother paid the bill anyway!

"We took the cat home and I put it in my room and shut the door. I sat down and began to cry. Here I was sitting on my bed, stroking this strange cat, and I couldn't understand my feelings. But then I thought that the tears were about what a good feeling it was to have helped this wounded animal. So I got up and went down the street and put up a sign that said, 'If you lost your cat, call this number.'

"As I was walking home, I crossed over to the other side of the street and as I looked down at the sidewalk, I saw a tall mustard plant in full bloom. For some reason, it triggered something. The moment I gazed at the flower, I knew right then that I wanted to be a vet. It was this cat incident that made me realize I was most happy when I was with animals. I realized that I was drawn to other people's pets and was always rescuing dogs and cats and birds and bringing them home. I felt most honorable when I was in a caretaking role with animals. This whole incident just mirrored back in a big way what captured my attention most and what made me feel the most satisfied. I can still see the crack in the sidewalk at the moment that I decided I was going to build a career out of helping animals. I saw myself first in a small practice, then a bigger one, and then in an animal hospital that I had built.

"Well, someone did come for the cat—a guy who lived not more than two blocks away (funny that I had never seen the cat before), and I felt even better that I had helped. But I still have a soft spot in my heart for that cat. And you know, he comes around to visit now and then. I think he's grateful—he knows. I think animals know that we help them. I took a psychology course just to get some insight into my idea. I think being a vet will be a very important way to spend my life. I'm a senior now, and I still have my heart set on being a vet."

I asked Kevin if he had ever changed his mind about that goal. "Absolutely not. Never!" he replied instantly. "I've written so many term papers about the subject, and I work part-time in a pet store, and I've taken the courses I'll need to get into college so that I can do it. No, I'm very sure I'm going to be a vet."

I met Kevin's mother that evening in a program the school sponsored for parents. I was curious to ask about her side of the story and to see if Kevin, in fact, had ever swayed from that goal. "Oh yes," she replied. "When he was a second-semester junior, he didn't know if he wanted to be a large-animal vet, or a small-animal vet! Other than that, I'd say no. But what I remember most from that incident, is that it changed Kevin in many ways. Here was this child, an unmotivated learner, and sometimes reluctant to go to school. Sometimes I had to get mean with him to get him out of bed! He didn't have many friends, and he wasn't all that excited about sports either. But, from that day on, he was on fire, he was so motivated. He studied, he got along well with his teachers, he was more interesting to talk with and to be with, and other kids began inviting him to their homes—it was just the most incredible thing.

From that day on, Kevin had a reason for doing things and taking charge of his life. It was heartwarming. It was wonderful.

"My husband and I have three children, and Kevin was the difficult child. I'm embarrassed to say it, but there were many times that I just didn't like my son all that much, and I felt awful that a mother could feel this way. When Kevin had a purpose, though, he had conviction. I respect and greatly admire my son. Kevin is a wonderful young man."

Kevin's story is not at all uncommon in terms of a major attitudinal shift that's experienced when a child's life takes on meaning. Parents are the initial key. You can best help your child develop a sense of mission by helping him think through the meaning he wants to attach to life. Unfortunately, many children have not been taught the spiritual principles that help us find meaning and provide a living anchor for our lives. What spiritual essence are you providing for your child?

You can help your child examine mission by thinking about those contributions he'll make through his work. Then help him to set meaningful goals so he can work toward them in a systematic way. (Pay close attention to what captures your child's attention, and make a special point to help him examine those interests and turn them into goals.) Help your child answer questions such as:

- Who am I?
- What am I going to do with my life?
- What am I doing when I'm most happy?
- Do friendships really matter?
- What is the purpose of life—is it more than survival? Is it to accrue financial success in the early years so I can re-tire and travel in my later years? Is it to develop loving relationships?
- Is life really a journey and not just a destination?

These are thought-provoking and sometimes painful questions for young people to sort out. Although answering these questions is a very personal journey, it's caring parents who teach their children the importance of thinking through the questions and who help their children find meaningful answers.

○ HOW PARENTS TEACH MEANING: A PERSONAL TALE

You can let your child wander around aimlessly, hoping he will eventually discover answers on his own, or you can help him discover them. Remember, it's generally parents who provide the framework for caring and meaning. In this regard, I think about what provided the initial framework for what I would eventually define as *meaning*.

I learned much about what was meaningful from my dad. I remember the trigger points vividly, and I can still recall the details of what he said some twenty-five years ago—like Kevin, who could describe even the mustard bloom growing in the crack in the sidewalk in detail when he discovered what was most meaningful to him, I remember not only what my dad said, but how he said it, where it was said, and can still describe all of it in great detail:

I grew up on a beautiful farm in Iowa. My parents were the kind of people who were generally described as the "salt of the earth and the backbone of the community." But I was greatly disappointed that fate had dropped me off in the middle of the heartland in a most harsh and cold climate. Like all children, I thought that there had been a great universal mistake and I had been placed in the wrong family and most definitely in the wrong state! I disliked coping with the elements, and the winter nights in Iowa are so freezing cold that you have to make rounds in the middle of the night to see that livestock aren't stranded in a place where they would freeze to death. Newborn animals had to be taken into the barn and sometimes warmed up in order to be kept alive. Winters are *very* cold in Iowa!

I loved my dad as much then as I do now. Incredibly handsome, strong, charismatic and energetic, he was always on the go—it was not uncommon to see him walking with all six of his children trailing behind, trying to keep up. We were in awe of him but, better yet, we honored him. Now I better understand why: There are no inconsistencies in his life. He is an honorable man.

He is also very principled. As a child, I knew how much he loved farming. He was at home working with animals. He felt at one with the earth and took great pride in planting and harvesting the crops. He refused to hunt out of season, even though deer, pheasants, quail, and other game roamed our farmlands in abundance. He refused to use soil additives or feed the animals anything other than natural grains. He taught us why he did this and why we should embrace the same ideals. Today I can appreciate how conscientious he was, because he held those ideals in the mid 50s, long before there was an attempt at universal commitment to earthwide environmental preservation.

Dad was also an impatient man, but not in the middle of the night when he was making rounds. Back then, many years ago, I felt that I was secretly his favorite child (it's quite possible that each of us six children felt that way). Now, that was both good news and bad. The bad news was that I was the one selected by Dad to go with him for these midnight and early morning barnyard checks, and I absolutely detested getting up in the middle of the night, leaving a warm bed to go out into the frosty air. The good news is that Dad was at his best and most lovable during those times. He was most understanding, most patient, most gentle, and I saw a side of him that was to make a compelling difference in my life to this day. He was a model teacher—always focusing on the *whys*, the reasons for doing.

He talked endlessly for the hour or so that it took to make the rounds. He talked about his war experiences and the *whys* of that war: In school, I found history exciting and familiar. He talked about what he gained from his travels and why seeing the world was important: He instilled in me a need and love of traveling; I had worked in or visited over thirty countries by the time I was thirty years old! He talked about the need for and love of learning and why a formal education is important, and talked about the difference between intelligence and wisdom. He wanted me to go beyond my high school degree: He instilled in me the confidence to do so; eventually, I completed a Ph.D. and, later, earned a second doctorate.

He talked about standards and values, developing character, and what it meant in the course of a lifetime: I write and teach on a similar theme. He talked about how to make and evaluate decisions, when to cut your losses and walk away, and when to stick it out, even in the face of adversity. He talked about the concept of *being and becoming,* and not just *having and getting;* I still use those phrases. "Never sell out on your heart," he said. He talked about gut instincts and how to decipher between those and emotions and how to avoid being fooled by others. He said, "Always listen to your instincts, and know that all the answers you'll ever need are within you. Take quiet time alone; be still enough to find the answers within, and then listen to them. Find something you love to do, and then live a life that shows it. Your goals should stem from your values, and then your work will radiate your heart's desire. This will divert you from all silly distractions that will only serve to waste your time—your very life is about time, about how much you can grow in whatever years you are given. Care about people," he said, "and always respect Mother Earth. Wherever you shall live, be sure you can see the trees, the sky, and land."

When I reflect on how my father loves and values his children, I'm genuinely sorry for young people who will never know their fathers in this way—will never see the power of character, ethics, drive, and sensitivity all in one person as I do in mine: my dad. My dad modeled what he talked. I knew he was serious about me because of the way he taught his virtues to me. I knew he thought I was worthy, and he wanted me to see that worth.

Dad's message made sense to me, because I never saw any conflict in the way he lived his life. He had thought about his life and he lived it daily. He bought and paid for several farms over the years (he's as active today as he was then). He married and has loved the same woman for a lifetime. My mother and he, now married for nearly fifty years, are inseparable sweethearts still. They are the greatest lovers I've known. And Dad loves his family. I thought he was overly protective of his six children, but now that I'm a parent, I can see that he was determined that we be caring and responsible adults. He refused to lose us to destructive vices. To this day, five of his children live within a few miles of him, and they themselves have chosen a version of his lifestyle: they are devoted spouses and parents, and agriculture is their chosen work.

There is a twist to all this, and I suspect it's because of his taking me on those midnight rounds. I took a different direction than did the other five children. By the time I was twenty-six I had completed college and traveled around the world. I began a career as an educator, counselor, and university professor and eventually wrote several books for parents and children, to share what I had learned about the importance of developing self-esteem in the childhood years. My messages to my daughter, while altered a bit, are the values that I learned from my father, tempered with my life experiences, of course. They continue to be passed on.

I should tell you a bit about my daughter: She's a tomboy, a beautiful 5'9" athlete who letters in three sports each year, frets over the difference between an A and B, and was just named a finalist for the title of Miss Teen California. But it's not her outward gifts and accomplishments that remind me of my parents. People always tell me that my daughter possesses a great kindness, a light, a special fire deep inside that radiates outward. I think my father's character is still living, in his granddaughter.

The rewards of esteeming their children and being dedicated parents have had a most nourishing effect on the lives of my parents as well. As of this writing, my father is at the Mayo Clinic in Rochester, Minnesota, for a battery of tests, scheduled to take from six to eight days. It is December. Because of the harsh winter, he took a hotel room near the clinic (where he is an outpatient). Because of obligations at home, my mother was able to stay with him for only the first few days. So on Christmas eve, they were apart.

I called first my dad in Rochester from California to say, "Merry Christmas." He sounded down and despondent. I called my mother in Iowa. She was even more down and despondent. "This is the first time your father and I have ever spent the holidays apart," she lamented. "It's just not Christmas without him."

I had fourteen dinner guests arriving, all ready for a festive evening. I turned to cooking, not fully able to get my parents' dilemma off my mind. I called my sister in Iowa. She called my brothers. We conferenced by phone. It was settled: My younger brother would drive the two hours to Rochester to pick up my father and bring him home, without telling my mother.

I called my father to tell him of the plans. "Oh, no," he said. "It's far too dangerous to come out on a night like this!" My brother knocked on his door. He called me from Dad's room after telling him that he had no choice.

Tim and my Dad started for Iowa. We kids kept track of their progress, the journey, and the weather by talking with them on my brother's car phone. By now, all my guests had arrived and had become part of this ordeal. Whenever the phone rang, we put it on the speaker phone so we could all hear the latest! The phone rang, and it was Dad on the car phone: "Bobbie [my nickname], how can I possibly go home without a gift for your mom? It would be the first time in nearly fifty years I didn't get her perfume for Christmas!" We (by that time, my entire dinner party was engineering this plan!) called my sister to get the names of nearby open shopping centers so they could stop for the only gift my dad would consider giving mom: the same brand of perfume he has given her every Christmas.

At 9:52 that evening, my brother and my dad left a little

shopping mall in Rochester for the trip home. At 11:50, they drove up to the farm. My father stood out of sight around the house.

"Mom, I visited Dad today and he said to bring you his laundry," my brother said as he handed my mom the suitcases.

"Oh," she said sadly, "I miss him so much, I think I'll do these now."

Said my father coming out from his hiding, "You won't have time to do them tonight!"

I phoned my mother. "Merry Christmas, Mother!"

"Oh you kids . . ." she said, crying. My guests cheered.

Although I was two thousand miles away from them, that was one of the most special Christmases I've shared with my parents. And, of course, to date, my parents have not been apart on Christmas eve. That's the strength of children who love and honor their parents and, of course, of the commited and marvelous marriage my parents share.

I know you can tell similar stories. But do you? Perhaps you are a single parent or a parent who had a less than idyllic background. You might hesitate to talk about your family, thinking that would not be good role-model behavior. Perhaps your family caused you pain that you have not yet worked through.

Your family life does not have to be television-perfect for you to have drawn strength from it. In nearly every family, there is someone who gives love unselfishly, who cared and taught you the values you have today. Talk about that person with your child. Tell him how you overcame the obstacles to develop your own personality, your own character and morality. In this time of family chaos and impermanence, it is important to talk with your child. Help him to make sense of it all. Show him where they come from, even if your background was painful. You overcame it and developed into a stronger person; tell your child how you managed to do so. Remember that children learn what is meaningful from you. I work with many young people and families where children have little if any sense of mission in their lives. Many people today are void of any spiritual principles, yet it's this understanding that can lead us to living our lives in a purposeful way.

○ IT'S UP TO YOU!

I find that in this time of great and uneasy social change, there are many families that are dysfunctional, many lives torn apart by family hurts and pain, and separation and divorce; many adults busy defining their lives by material success and rewards, or working hours that are not conducive to building the lives of their children. The result is that many children are physically homeless and emotionally bankrupt. If they aren't, they know of other children who are.

It doesn't have to be that way. I believe that one of the greatest gifts you can give your child is the spirit and willingness to go forward in a positive, purposeful, and loving way. Like my father's influence on me, what your child comes to regard as the mission of his life is shaped by you. Paraphrasing a famous line, Jonas Salk reminded me, "Children must have roots and wings: wings to fly away and roots to know where to land."

18 GETTING THERE: HELPING YOUR CHILD SET AND ACHIEVE (WORTHWHILE) GOALS

Another important component of helping your child develop a sense of mission is to help him determine what *is* of purpose and work toward accomplishing it. This means helping him to set and achieve worthwhile goals. Children with goals are vibrant children because they have found something meaningful they want to do. They have a sense of where they are going. A recent Gallup Poll revealed that only 25 percent of all adults feel purposeful in their work, and even fewer feel an overall satisfaction with their life! Those who did express satisfaction said they were working toward two or more goals that were important to them.

A goal is like having a map. It helps you determine the direction in which you should be heading, so you know where to focus your time and energy. When a child gets used to working toward an identified goal, he soon establishes a pattern to behave in a certain way. If your child walks a particular path to school often enough it becomes a habit, and he can follow it without even thinking, knowing that it will lead him to his destination.

Having goals ensures success because efforts are being channeled in a single direction. Best of all, success in one area usually leads to success in another area—and that's the whole idea. Maybe you've seen something similar to this played out:

"My son is a poor student until football season," said Maria. "But Peter's goal to be a part of the team motivates him during the football season into getting passing grades, because he has to maintain certain grades to stay eligible for the team. And when he applies himself, he does get good grades. Unfortunately, when the football season is over, he sets virtually no goals. It's back to being a reluctant student."

O HAVING GOALS GIVES YOUR CHILD'S LIFE MEANING

Does your child set and achieve goals? Whether your child is six or sixteen, you can help him learn the cycle of setting and achieving goals. Goals stem from dreams and desires, and that's where you'll want to start with your child. Below are some questions for you to ponder first.

1. *What are your child's strengths?* What does your child do well? Remember, we're all different. Your child might be good at languages, but his best friend is a powerful athlete and another friend finds math and science easy. Sometimes it takes a while to identify those strengths, but they're there. The more things your child is exposed to (so long as he has some time to explore them), the better his chances are of finding what he's really good at.

   I suggest to parents that every two or three months they read one book to their children, regardless of their ages. Read the biographies of exemplary people. Note how these individuals were ordinary people who possessed character, values, and dedication to attain their goals and that these were their real strengths. Point out that there was usually one particular turning point in their lives. For example, a dancer might have been taken to the ballet by her parents when she was just a child and said, "That's it—that's what I want to be!" Kevin discovered he wanted to be a veterinarian from the experience of seeing a wounded cat and caring for it. The experience triggered for him how good about himself he had felt all the many times he had helped stray or wounded animals and how sympathetic he had felt toward them. Although Kevin and his mother didn't make it to soccer practice that day, taking time out and following Kevin's feelings of caring for the wounded cat had high payoffs.

2. *What captures your child's attention?* A key to helping your child set goals (at least in the beginning) is to center them around what he's good at. What captures his attention? We all do better in those things that interest us. In physical education class, your child might be good at volleyball because he likes it. But how good is he at baseball or square dancing? Have you ever lost all track of time? Have you ever been involved in a project and suddenly found that several hours had passed before you realized it?

   Watch for those times when your child is so absorbed or involved in a project that nothing else seems to matter. He'll be concentrating on that one thing because it is of great interest to him. When he's looking for a book in the library, what does he pick up and read? What informational programs does he watch on television? What class does he really enjoy? What activities does he most enjoy doing? When he feels completely absorbed in something, what is he doing? If you'll take the time to write down these attention grabbers and examine them, you'll have a better composite picture of his interests. Talk with your child about his areas of interest. Is he aware of them too? What are his thoughts for achieving worthwhile goals in those areas?

3. *What does your child feel strongly about?* Help your child identify what he feels strongly about. You'll know you're on the right track when he can list his wants. At first he'll have a lot of different ideas about what he wants, and you'll want to help him select two or three and then get specific: Turn them into a goal. You may find that the goals are broad and general, such as, "I want to get a new bike," or "I want a car," or "I want to be a veterinarian." Help him examine his

goals from every aspect to see which ones are really important and which are not. Say, "Yes, you want to be a part of the soccer team this year, but you don't sound very convincing. How much do you want to be a part of the team? Why is that important to you? What are you doing to make sure you are a part of the team?"

Remember that your child will work harder and with more enthusiasm toward goals that are important to him. If sports seem to be an interest, read him stories of athletes (or steer him toward books about athletes that he can read on his own), or visit with athletes in your town, or subscribe to magazines that highlight the challenges of the "thrill of victory and the agony of defeat." He'll discover that athletes have to practice two, three, or more hours a day, sometimes giving up other interests because being the best at their sport is usually their number-one goal. In other words, achieving a goal requires an intensity of purpose.

4. *What opportunities do you make available to your child?* What you expect of your child becomes an important part of his aspirations. Something as simple as taking your child to a college campus when he's in eighth or ninth grade sets in motion a dream of wanting to go to college. In many cases, it's the very campus he visits that becomes the dream. If he does attend that college, the campus becomes a hallmark for his studies and the career he chooses (and sometimes the person he marries) and usually serves as the location where he will begin a first job and a family. Which opportunities do you create for your child—with him in mind—and which activities are the most convenient for you? Know that you influence by your actions.

The Nine Key Areas for Your Child's Goal-Setting

There are nine key areas that give meaning to our lives. Help your child talk about his goals in each area—why the goals are important; what his plans are for attaining them—and then help him develop a plan to achieve them. You'll find that the time you spend communicating with your child about his goals can be very meaningful. Each of these nine key areas has its place of importance and meaning in your child's life. Helping your child commit to goals in each of them helps him to have a balanced life and to determine what is of purpose for and to him.

1. *Peace of mind.* The search for meaning, spiritual fulfillment.
2. *Personal relationships.* Goals in relationships (with parents, friends, teachers, others).
3. *Learning and education.* What would he like to know more about?
4. *Status and respect.* To which groups does he want to belong? From whom does he want respect?
5. *Leisure time.* Which activities (hobbies, sports, travel) would he like to learn more about or do more of?
6. *Fitness.* Goals for his physical fitness and overall health.
7. *Money needs.* Goals for having enough money to do the things he wants to do.
8. *Work.* What kind of job area is he choosing? What are his goals for productive work and career success?
9. *Others.* Goals that may not fit into the previous categories.

With these areas in mind, you're a bit more prepared to guide your child in setting goals. Below are some guidelines for helping your child bring his goals to fruition.

Six Questions to Direct Goal-Setting

1. *Is it your goal or your child's?* If your child doesn't really want something, it's unlikely he'll make the commitment needed to accomplish it. He'll give up when faced with hard work. He should "own" the goal. If you're trying to convince your child to set goals you would like to see attained, you're going to have to help him see each goal as his own, otherwise he's not going to be very motivated toward achieving them. If you want him to be a good student, that's one thing, but if *he* wants to be a good student, that's another. He's likely to be a

good student because that is his goal, too. He has to have an inner fire, a drive that says, "It's important to *me*."

2. *Is his goal attainable?* Your child has to believe that he can meet his goal, that it is achievable. Note that the goal doesn't have to be an easy one, but there has to be a better than fifty–fifty chance he can meet it.

It also has to be a challenge. There's a saying that goes, "Most people don't aim too high and miss—they aim too low and hit." The same will be true for your child if he sets goals that are yours and not his or if the goal is too easy. If his goal is to get at least a C on his paper and he knows he can do better, what's the challenge? If his goal is to do at least twenty sit-ups and he can already do nineteen with no problem, what's the challenge?

3. *What makes his goal worth achieving?* What are the benefits of the goal? Are they worth the time and effort? When your child's teacher is lecturing and she says, "Now, this next material will not be on the test, but you should know it anyway," what does your child do? Does he pay as much attention as he normally would, or does he exchange a grin with his friends, sit back, and relax—not taking the material seriously because he knows he won't be tested on it and assumes there's little benefit to taking notes and paying attention?

When you are helping your child to set a goal and begin working toward it, take a few minutes to talk about what he's going to get out of accomplishing it—the benefits. Try it yourself first. For example, suppose one of your goals is to be in better physical condition. How many benefits can you think of that will motivate you toward the effort it's going to take? You might feel better physically, develop better body strength, do more activities with greater ease, feel better emotionally, look better, maybe get more positive comments from others who have observed your new health, gain more confidence, and so on. The more reasons you think of for achieving the goal, the stronger will be your desire. And the stronger the desire, the easier it is to reach your goal.

4. *Has your child put his goal in writing?* Have your child write the goal down. When he writes it down, it makes it clear in his mind and keeps him organized. It makes for a plan of attack. Plus, your child can see his progress when he crosses off a written goal. Your child internalizes it when he puts pencil to paper. If it's only in his head, he can easily forget about it. We have hundreds of thousands of thoughts daily; most are forgotten in moments. But those we take the time and effort to focus on matter more.

Suppose that you want to build a house and you hire an architect. He meets with you and says, "I have a lot of great ideas. Here I'm going to put the master bedroom; here I am going to put the Jacuzzi; here I'm going to put the living room . . ." You listen for a while, then say, "I'm having trouble remembering and visualizing all this. May I see your blueprints please?" The architect smiles at you and says, "Blueprints? I never write anything down. I keep it all in my head!" Are you going to let this person build your house? No way! Even if the architect is a genius, no one can work without a blueprint. The same is true for your child's goals. Writing them down provides a blueprint for his efforts.

Post your child's goal where he can see it. Children can get pretty shortsighted. I talk with many children who set a goal and who, one week later, have lost sight of it! Make several copies of your child's goals and post them where he can see them, such as on his mirror, on the refrigerator, and on his notebook.

5. *Are the deadlines realistic?* Teach your child how to break long-term goals into short-term goals. For example, if getting into college is the long-term goal, he'll need to break it down into a series of short-term goals, ranging from doing well in each of his classes to getting the money together for tuition.

Goals and deadlines seem a lot easier to reach when they are broken down into manageable tasks. Help your child set dates for each goal, major and minor. Some dates are predetermined. If he's going to take the SAT college admission exam, for example, he has to adjust to the testing schedule.

But he can still set intermediate deadlines: to have the vocabulary learned by this date, the math by that date, and so on. Having a date written down motivates him and helps him manage the task. It also helps him prioritize where and how he will allocate his time. Then, when he sees he's nearing a deadline, he can push himself just a little harder or know when to plan down-time and playtime. When he does accomplish his goal within the deadline, he feels successful.

Make sure your child doesn't set overly ambitious deadlines. Don't let him aim for making ten new friends this month if he's a very shy person who has trouble making two friends a year. Don't let him plan to take ten seconds off his sprint time if he has not taken off more than one second a semester so far. Don't let him set an A as his goal in math if he's not even getting C's now.

6. *Has a reward been established?* Let's say that your child has set a goal and accomplished it. He did something he set his mind to do and he deserves to be proud of himself and to take the time to feel the satisfaction of having accomplished something. Teach him to do something nice for himself as a reward. Ask him, "What one nice thing will you do for yourself because you have been diligent and hard at work on your goal?" Maybe it's a few days of down-time, or a new item of clothing, or tickets to a special concert. This is a form of praise, and it is best generated by your child for his accomplishments.

Even Young Children Need Goals

Even in first grade children are not too young to learn how to set goals. I teach parents to use what is called a wish list, with which you help your child generate two or three things that are important to achieve. Take a piece of illustration board or blank poster board and suggest that your child draw a picture of each goal on the board. Then hang the board in your child's room as a constant reminder of what she's working toward. Children's goals are both large and small. They can be as important as developing a sense of responsibility by feeding and watering the family pet every day or as seemingly minor as keeping a room clean for two weeks. The importance of goal-setting is to empower your child to look forward to something of purpose—to something that is worth spending time on. In the beginning, it will serve as a way of helping your child learn to be responsible.

You might be surprised at how diligently a young child is willing to work at achieving a goal—if it is important to him. One small child I knew decided that her leisure-time (or funtime) goal was to learn to ride her two-wheeler. She achieved her goal three days later. Before having verbalized it and seen it written down, she hadn't seemed to be able to do so.

Today, many elementary schools invite children from kindergarten up to enter an annual science fair. Parents will probably never find more enthusiastic students for such science projects than their five- to seven-year-olds. If you suggest that they set their learning-and-education goal around a science fair, most young children will avidly comply. With a bit of investigating those things they really want to learn about (an animal . . . the ocean . . . shells or rocks . . . stars . . . why leaves fall in autumn . . . how incense is made—the possibilities are endless), you can watch your child wholeheartedly throw himself into learning. Smaller goals, such as getting to the library and finding children's books on the subject, can be made and met along the way, as your young child becomes familiar with the goal-setting process.

It may take some creative prompting on your part, but it is possible to help your young child become quite adept at goalsetting in each of the nine key areas we've reviewed. Once, a young, single mother I knew made a large night sky on a huge sheet of poster board and then hung it in her children's bedroom. She asked her five- and three-year-olds to do one thing each day that would make God happy. Each of these small spiritual goals meant a star for the night-sky poster in their room. The child worked on meeting this simple goal and placed his own star where he wanted. The point is not that the goals were impressive, but that young children were learning to set and achieve them.

With younger children, the goals have to be modified to take less time to achieve, to allow for more concrete forms of progress being made and, perhaps, to have more visible forms of gratification as a result of their accomplishments. Still, with time and thought, goal-setting can be one of the most enjoyable exercises for nurturing self-esteem in your young child.

○ TURNING OBSTACLES INTO OPPORTUNITIES

Perhaps, it appears that your child has no striking motivation, no drive, or desire to set goals for himself. He may say he doesn't know what he wants or what he's good at. We all know that children can sometimes be experts at giving excuses for why they can't do something. Whether they say, "Goals aren't important," or "I don't know how," or "Someone might make fun of me," or "I might fail," as parents we can help our children find what is of value and inspire them to find the hidden treasures they possess.

A friend of mine illustrates this concept by telling the story of a farmer who got bored with farming and decided to seek his fortune in a gold mine. After selling his farm, he went to Alaska and searched for gold. He was gone many years and had all sorts of adventures. But he never did find gold, and he lived a very poor life, sometimes not having enough food and never having a nice place to live. Finally, exhausted and out of hope, he travelled back to see his former farm, for old times' sake. To his amazement, he found that a mansion stood where the farmhouse had been, and the grounds were beautifully groomed and landscaped.

He knocked on the door. The new owner came out to talk to the former farmer. "What on earth happened here?" asked the bewildered farmer. "You barely had enough money to buy the farm from me, as I remember. How did you get so rich?"

The new owner just smiled. "Actually, it was all due to you.

There were diamonds on this property—acres and acres of diamonds!"

The old farmer scoffed. "Diamonds! I knew every inch of this land, and there were no diamonds here."

The new owner nodded and pulled from his pocket a lump of what looked like coal. "I carry around this small one as a good luck charm. Here is one of the diamonds from this property."

The farmer was amazed. "That's a diamond? I remember seeing a lot of those all over this land. I used to swear at them and kick them because they got in the way when I was plowing. I thought they were lumps of coal! That doesn't look anything like a diamond to me!"

You see, the farmer didn't recognize the diamonds when he saw them. Not all opportunities look like diamonds. In their unpolished form, diamonds look like lumps of coal. Your child has diamonds in his life that he may not recognize right now. For example, if he's able to explain things to classmates so that they frequently ask him for help, that skill, with practice, could make him an exemplary teacher, consultant, or public speaker. When you recognize special traits in your child, do you find ways to help him develop them?

○ THE SIX FACETS OF SELF-ESTEEM: A REVIEW

You may feel overwhelmed by all the information you've assimilated. Fear not, you'll find that taken step-by-step, it will quickly become an integral part of your daily parenting. With so much to digest, now may be a good time for us to review the six elements that build self-esteem.

1. *A sense of physical safety.* A child who feels comfortable at home, at school, and in his everyday environment acts with confidence. He is free to be open to the challenges of childhood and to exercise his normal and healthy curiosity.

2. *A sense of emotional security.* The emotionally trusting child opens up. He knows he won't be put down or ridiculed and becomes trusting and compassionate.

3. *A sense of identity.* A child who knows who he is feels comfortable with himself. He recognizes that he has a role and that he is important.

4. *A sense of belongingness.* A child who feels he belongs learns to relate to others. He develops interpersonal skills that make him more outgoing and friendlier. He develops strong and lasting friendships.

5. *A sense of competence.* A competent child dares to try more, to challenge himself, to reach ever farther. He builds success upon success—in school, at sports, in personal relationships.

6. *A sense of mission.* A purposeful child feels worthy of love. He knows he has a place. He sets goals for himself and derives satisfaction not only from achieving them but also just from working toward them.

In short, a child who embraces these qualities develops a strong sense of self-esteem that makes him happy with who he is. He is open, caring, compassionate, and loving. He is proud of himself and a pleasure to be with. He enriches your life and continues along the path of becoming an emotionally secure, mature, loving adult.

○ IT'S UP TO YOU!

Life needs to make sense. We have to feel there is meaning in life. This need is even stronger in children, who often believe they have little control over their lives. They eat what food is served, go where they are taken by Mom and Dad, and do what the teachers tell them to do. They have to have some part of life they can call their own.

One way to develop this is to have goals. As a parent, you can teach your child the skill of goal-setting. Begin early to show him how to identify what is important to him and develop a plan for accomplishing his goals. Even if the goals are not reached immediately (think of a ten-year-old who wants to be a professional baseball player), knowing what they are and (identifying them) making them seem real helps children feel they are working for a reason. This helps build self-esteem by showing the children that they are vital, worthwhile contributors to the family and to society.

As parents, it's our responsibility to motivate our children in their goal-setting—as they see these goals met, they'll build confidence and demand more of themselves as their self-esteem is nurtured.

19

HOW DO YOU FEEL ABOUT BEING A PARENT?

○ THE IMPORTANCE OF A PARENTING PHILOSOPHY

Your child will need to develop many life skills in order to live a life characterized by meaning. This means you must be willing to help him to be loving and compassionate, to value meaningful work, to nurture and sustain the warmth of friendships, to set and achieve worthwhile goals, and so much more.

How will you choose what you want for your child? How will you prioritize what is worth doing? How will you manage your life, that of your child, and everything else? That's where a philosophy serves you well.

A philosophy articulates what you want from your parenting. It specifies the activities needed for nurturing your child. It defines and clarifies your role, and directs the selection of strategies for nurturing, guiding, and disciplining your child. A philosophy helps you to answer questions and to make decisions from among the many choices you have to make along the way—should you move to a new neighborhood? accept a new position? stop working full time? return to work? and so on.

What Is Your Parenting Philosophy?

What might we do to behave in ways that can shape the experiences of our children so that they might indeed reach their highest level of human potential? I find that when parents haven't thought about this, they struggle with parenting on a day-by-day level. Parenting can easily become routine work, filled with hassles of juggling schedules and meeting the basic and important daily needs of children. You see, *parenting* and *parenthood* are quite different.

Parenting is so much more than *rearing* children. I myself have written a number of books that have largely to do with helping parents manage the strains of parenting and to help children themselves manage the stress and strains of childhood. *Stress in Children* is a book that examines the collective toll of stress in each of the childhood years and delineates what we can do about it. *Helping Your Teenager: A Survival Guide to the Adolescent Years* focuses on understanding the adolescent years and ways to forge communication and bonding that can help to lessen the estrangement that typically both parents and teens feel in these tumultuous years. Books like *Achievement, Happiness, Popularity and Success, A Self-Esteem Book for Young Adults* and *Self-Management Skills for Children* and *Goal Setting Skills for Young Adults* were written for young people themselves, to help them learn how to monitor and manage their day-to-day lives.

From my research and teaching, from my work with parents, young people, educators, and others working with children, and from my own years of parenting, I know how important it is that we think about what we are doing, that we recognize and understand the underlying motivations of our actions—the why we do what we do—if it is to be of meaning. We must know how we will go about guiding and nurturing our children. It can be difficult, if not disastrous, if we don't. Effective parenting begins with having thought deeply about the priority of our children in our life and about our intentions for nurturing and guiding them.

At the heart of all parenting activity is an attitude that governs our actions toward our children and our feelings about parenthood. Each of us has a parenting philosophy already in place, and it's usually pretty obvious to others.

Marlene

Marlene has been rushing around, trying to get errands completed this afternoon. The post office, last on her list, is about to close. She rushes toward the post office, hoping to make it before they close the door. Her three-year-old is running along behind, trying as best he can to keep up. Hungry, tired, and discouraged about ever catching up to his mother, he stumbles and falls to the ground, crying. Marlene yells to him to catch up and when he doesn't, she dashes toward him, grabs him, and slaps him, saying, "Now you have something to cry about!" The child screams and pounds his feet on the sidewalk, refusing to cooperate.

Meanwhile, across town a similar chase is on, but with a different result:

Glenda

Glenda turns to her tired and out-of-sorts three-year-old and says, "Mommy's sorry, Aaron. I'm going much too fast for you, aren't I? Here, let me carry you. We have to get to the post office before it closes. We're almost finished now, and then we can go home, fix lunch, and play." She swings him up into her arms as she dashes off in the direction of the post office. Her reassuring words, kisses, and soothing strokes comfort him. He snuggles into her arms, feeling reassured and safe. She is able to continue her hurried pace in completing her task.

You've no doubt seen these philosophies played out many times over in a number of ways. But notice how the action toward the child is drastically different in each example above. Marlene sees her son as a burden keeping her from doing what she has to do. Her resentment and impatience win out over empathy for what it's like being three years old with short legs and not much interest in errands. Glenda's response, on the other hand, is one of empathy. She's able to understand her child's frustration and work with it in a way that's soothing to her child and enables her to complete her task. Most of all, she preserves the relationship, and her child's self-esteem is intact.

What Is Your Parenting Style?

Like Marlene and Glenda, you, too, already have some kind of philosophy in operation. So does your parenting partner. It shows up in your style in managing your children.

Your **parenting style** reflects how you feel toward children or decisions you've made about being a parent. The way you were reared provides the major influence on your parenting style. Maybe you are bringing up your child the way you were brought up. Possibly the opposite is true: You decided you would never rear your child the way you were reared. You might be reacting against your parents' style, which often swings the pendulum strongly in the opposite direction. The demands of your career, your personality and disposition, the participation of your parenting partner, and your beliefs about children in general all shape your values, ideas, and decisions governing your actions. But are they what you want?

You Choose Your Philosophy

A philosophy, then, is your check-and-balance sheet for your behaviors in rearing your children. Children learn what they live. And they generally live out what they have learned.

You can change your parenting style. You can choose what you want for your child and for yourself. You can decide what you want to bring about for your child and yourself and then create it. The first step is clarifying what's going on now.

- What is your philosophy?
- How did you formulate it?
- Was it deliberate?
- Did it seem to just emerge?
- Is it based mostly on what your spouse wants?
- Is it based on the expectations that your mother imposes?
- Is it based on your career demands?
- Is it based on how you were reared (your parents' philosophy)?
- Is it based on how your friends choose to rear their children?
- How is it working?
- Is it what you want?

The next step is to think about what you really do want. Think about your values. What are the highest values you hold for your child? What would you like them to be? These are important questions to think through. Unfortunately, some parents don't spend enough time clarifying their belief system that governs specific actions that lead to effective and purposeful outcomes in guiding and disciplining their children. But they should: A philosophy helps us translate love and caring into action.

○ THE BENEFITS OF HAVING A PARENTING PHILOSOPHY

Below are some of the benefits of consciously choosing a philosophy of parenting. The idea is that you see the value of carefully thinking through and evaluating a philosophy that will guide your actions toward your child, enable you to be more satisfied and effective in your role as a parent, and allow you to stay in your role as protector and parent to your child. (Remember, if your current parenting actions aren't what you want, you can change them.) The following list is just a beginning, and you will probably want to add to it.

- With a philosophy, I understand why I do the things I do; I recognize the underlying motivations that make me act the way I do.
- With a philosophy, I can look at ideas about parenting that are reactive and influenced by my childhood and determine which values I really want to impart and which ones I want to change.
- I direct myself to think about what is important to me, such as the love and respect of my child, and this guides my actions.
- I become more aware of my strengths, of how much I have to offer a child, of how much I have to share, and this gives me courage and confidence to pull through the tough and challenging times.
- I set goals for myself as a parent and have a concrete objective to work toward. This helps me change what I don't like about my parenting and to set new standards to work toward.
- I become more clear about what I really want for my child and what I'm actually giving him.
- I become more aware of my own repressed but natural resentments about parenting, such as the lack of freedom and the sacrifices, and I am able to acknowledge these in a healthy manner.

You Can Change Your Parenting Style

By its very nature, parenting is a series of learning-by-doing experiences. Yet, floundering in the dark or winging it, hoping you'll accidentally say and do the right thing is not very beneficial. Think about it: Would you go on an interview without being prepared, without first knowing what skills were needed for doing the job, what you wanted from the position and the company, and what you could offer? Probably not. Yet many parents are struggling with the remains of negative emotional baggage and are in need of coming to terms with their own past childhood pains. Still hurting, these very adults make little time to deal with the real needs of family members. The feelings of emotional neglect build. Symptoms surface whenever stress and pressure mount. Many families are managed on the basis of crises, moods, quick fixes, and instant gratification, rather than on sound principles. Parents and children become cynical, critical, or silent, or they start yelling and overreacting, or they refuse to deal with it all, and leave. Parents and children alike are leaving their families. Separation and divorce rates are very high, as is the number of youth runaways.

Designing Your Parenting Philosophy

After you've taken the time to think through these philosophical questions, think about what you want for yourself and for your children. Design your own parenting philosophy. Start by writing down all the things you believe about your ideals for your child and those things that you would like to bring about through your parenting. Do this for each of your children. Call this your This-I-Believe paper. My original working paper for my daughter was designed years ago, when I first began a serious quest for putting into practice the beliefs I held about parenting. This paper gave way to a second and a third draft, each one further clarifying my involvement in her life. My first draft is presented below to give you an idea of how to begin.

THIS I BELIEVE

I have but one year each to see my daughter be one, two, three, four, five, six, seven, eight, nine, ten, eleven, twelve, thirteen, fourteen, fifteen, sixteen, seventeen, and eighteen years old. I very much want to know her at each of these ages.

I want so much for her to respect, love, and really care about me. I want to do the right things in bringing about these conditions.

I don't have all the answers to parenting my daughter. Her needs keep changing. Although my parents showed me what love and caring were about, I need to keep talking to others about what they have learned, and I need to keep reading. Because she is so important to me, I don't want to say what I hear some parents say when their children leave home: "I wish I had . . ."

I want always to be asking "How is my daughter faring—at home, at school, with friends, with me?"

I want her to experience me and my love and caring. I want to form a most special and rich relationship together. I want our bonding to last all of my lifetime and hers.

I will take the time to create and sustain our relationship.

I will examine the nature of my lifestyle on her, and I am prepared to change it if it means protecting and preserving her well-being.

I want her to be happy.

I want her to be healthy. I will emphasize nutrition. I will care for her when she is ill.

I promise to keep her safe. I will not harm her physically. I will not allow others to harm her. I will see that she is in environments that value safety.

I will strive to place her in surroundings where others value their children as I do her.

I will foster her self-esteem: I will not belittle her or swear at her. I will not be emotionally abusive to her. I will help her to believe in herself and to develop a healthy sense of respect for others.

I will strive to develop her talents and interests by exposing her to activities that she's interested in (riding horses, gymnastics, sports). I will try not to impose my interests on her for my own selfish reasons.

I will help her learn self-control and self-discipline.

I will always present her father in a positive light as a loving and caring father, and I will not sacrifice her or the importance of her father to her, regardless of our relationship throughout our lifetime.

I want her to know my parents and the richness of their love, as well as other family members—my brothers and sisters and their children. I will work toward keeping those bonds, no matter where I may choose to live in the world.

I will postpone certain elements of my career if need be, especially in her early and teen years. I will examine if my work roles are having a seriously adverse effect on her or our relationship. Through it all, I will design my work around what is productive and of value to me. I will share the joy of purposefulness with her, that she will come to know me and my joys.

When I was growing up, I thought that my mother was the most beautiful woman I knew. I remember how proud I felt when she would come to school to pick me up or I went with her anywhere. It was a wonderful feeling that I'd like my daughter to feel. I want her to be proud of my appearance. I will stay fit and in good health for me and for her, that I might model the importance of physical fitness, health, and female beauty.

Based on the series of statements above, I created the first draft of my philosophy:

MY PHILOSOPHY

Because I love and value my daughter, I will be an active and nourishing part of her life. I will protect her from physical harm and emotional hurt, and I will strive to keep my lifestyle, work, marriage, and health in harmony with my needs and hers. I hold her as a priority in my life. She will be an important factor in the decisions I make.

After you have completed your This-I-Believe working paper, design your philosophy statement. Encourage your parenting partner to complete one, too. Frame your philosophy and put it on your desk beside the projects that have a tendency to consume your life. Post a copy in the area where you get dressed each morning to remind yourself how important it is that you use your parenting energies wisely. Over the course of a lifetime, your years of active parenting are very brief.

What Is Your Family's Mission?

Just as each parent has a philosophy governing his or her parenting activities, healthy families have a guiding philosophy, too. It's called a **mission statement.** This statement acts as a family unit's guiding star. Just as we plan to be successful in our businesses and in our work roles, we can plan to be successful in our family life. The capacity to enjoy our families seems to come more easily to some than others. Sometimes parents have a difficult time learning to leave a messy desk at work or a kitchen in disarray in order to relax and enjoy one another or their children. They feel a moral obligation to be a good provider or a perfect housekeeper that precludes their closing the door and going for a walk in the park or around the block together. Yet time taken to play and relax pays off in ways clean desks and shiny floors never can. Our mates or our children will not be as they are now ever again. If we don't take the time to enjoy our families, we've lost an opportunity forever. Healthy families know this and give play- and leisure time high priority.

Having a successful family life is not just a question of finances. Money does not ensure that parents will care for their children's physical or emotional needs, or spend time with their children, or teach them the skills they need to grow and prosper in a healthy and purposeful way.

Fundamentally, your mission statement becomes your Constitution by which you measure everything else in your life. Writing a mission statement takes deep introspection. Writing and reviewing it forces you to think through your priorities and to align your behavior with your beliefs so that you're not being driven by everything that happens to you but, rather, by what you're trying to do. Write one, and then review it every six months as you and your family grow and change.

The mission statement should include this credo: "In our family, we value each person, and each person has a right to be respected and listened to." Think about the importance of this statement and how it would govern your actions and the actions of each family member. A mission statement is also helpful in getting both parenting partners to examine not only their individual parenting philosophies, but also in seeing how their philosophies are similar and different, how they complement or detract from each other, and what both partners want for their children and their family life.

Parenting can be the most rewarding of our lifetime experiences. By thinking about what we want for our children, we will also come to know parenthood as the joyous experience that it can be. What is your family mission statement, and how does it govern your family life?

○ THE JOY OF BEING A PARENT

Though parenting seems to be focused on doing and giving continually to our children, we get much in return. Through our children we will come to know ourselves in a way we never thought possible. This insight alone brings into focus the meaning of our personal journeys through time, alters our feelings of aloneness, and completes our own unfinished cycle of childhood.

As we introduce our children to each new phase of maturation and help them develop a set of attitudes and skills to surmount the challenges they will encounter along the way, we discover just how much we have grown and changed. And we learn much about ourselves along the way. We find that teaching our children the ways of the world is a learning experience for us too. I know this has been true for me.

What I Learned from Parenting

In helping my daughter learn and grow, she has taught me. Parenting has taught me the meaning of

- *Love.* By loving my daughter, I tapped into a reservoir and found there a well of unending love. I didn't know I could love so much.
- *Joy.* As a result of my efforts, I see my daughter prosper as a healthy, intelligent, and compassionate person.
- *Happiness.* By giving and sharing myself with her, I've experienced the deepest level of happiness.
- *Empathy.* In seeking to understand my child, I have had to put myself in her place. Sometimes my heart will ache as I watch her struggle with a lesson or a consequence. I learned the meaning of unconditional caring.
- *Patience.* Even with my guidance, Jennifer experiences the world through her own eyes, in her own time, at her own pace. Some things you just can't hurry.
- *Endurance.* I discovered unsuspected strength within myself. In meeting her needs, I had to care for her when I myself was sick or had other impending responsibilities. In the face of unforeseen illness and accidents, I had to make tough decisions on my own. As a single parent, I was challenged to be totally responsible for supporting both of us and affording our ideals with style. I learned that I could.
- *Listening.* I learned to listen not only to her voice but also to her feelings and subtle behavior to hear what she was saying, rather than what I would prefer to hear (many times these were different).
- *Responsibility.* Because she's so precious to me, I learned that I can accept the duties and obligations of being a parent and that I can be depended upon to fulfill them. She can count on me: I will not sell out on her.

• My *child*. By listening and observing, I discovered what she needed from me, and learned that sometimes it was different from what I had expected.

Being a parent has taught me how fragile human life is.   Although this feeling began with my pregnancy, as soon as my child was born I felt at a very deep level that her life was mine to protect and that I was committed to it at all costs. I knew that protecting this human life would be the most compelling of all experiences. Such feelings opened up a door to feel for and about those whose lives are in jeopardy anywhere in the world, such as by starvation or war.

Being a parent has taught me empathy for other parents.   I think that parenting connects parents everywhere. Once I sympathized with the mothers of sick, crying, injured, or missing children. Now I feel with them. Parenthood has made me realize that other mothers have felt the same joys, pains, and traumas that I have felt. Sharing in this sisterhood is a very bonding feeling.

Being a parent has taught me how to set priorities.   After I accepted that my days were not going to get suddenly longer simply to accommodate me, I resigned myself that my deep-seated desire for perfection had to go. Some things must be done; others are a matter of choice: Will I call an old friend, or will I make time to work out? People who calm me, stimulate and motivate me or inspire or encourage me are important. People who drain me, confuse me, drag me down, or depress me are not.

Parenthood has taught me efficiency.   Before I had my daughter, setbacks made me disappointed, and confrontations sped up my heart rate. All the energy that used to be spent on tension and anxiety is now channeled into getting the work done efficiently. Other people appreciate it too. Other people don't want those around who are always stressed out. They want people around who are performing their work with efficiency and style.

I've learned to be consistent and assertive. Communicating what I want with clarity and sufficient detail is required. When my daughter was small, I learned that if children don't share their toys, they don't have any friends. If they don't go to bed by eight, they'll be difficult and grouchy the next day. Cause and effect is just as valid for teens and adults. I sometimes worry about being thought of as bossy or demanding. But when you're in the position of having other people depend on you—at home or at work—thinking with clarity and being consistent and assertive are essential.

Parenthood has taught me a lot about the nature of adults. Basically, adults have the same needs and desires as children; we just express ourselves more subtly. I've learned that it's futile to argue or try to reason with a toddler or teen in a tantrum; you wait until he's calmed down. An adult needs to be treated the same way. I've learned that independent types of all ages who run off to cry alone don't really want to be alone; they just want to speak their piece and be reassured in private, without a crowd.

When you associate with children, you can see in the grown-ups you know all the same types: the clown, the show-off, the prima donna, the kid who puts other kids down to build himself up, all of them just a little bit scared of something. When seen this way it makes adults easier to understand.

Parenthood has taught me that I can take charge of my life. When you're in charge, you learn quickly from your mistakes and feel your accomplishments. You can accomplish what you want, and when things go awry, you just start over again. By having learned to control my surroundings, I've learned to control myself. I have learned self-discipline.

Parenthood brought me from childhood into adulthood. Being a parent changed my view of the world, of life, and of humanity. Through my experience of parenting, I learned that because I was constantly on call to model effective behavior, I was to become a better, wiser, and more loving person than I might otherwise have been. And, of course, I also learned what I was not but wished I were.

○ IN CONCLUSION: IT'S UP TO YOU!

I want to leave you with a few words of hope and encouragement—and a challenge: You can function at the survival level or at a creative, positive, and joyful level. Choosing the positive and joyful path makes the journey a rewarding one for us and for the children we have brought into our lives. I believe beyond doubt that the parent–child relationship is the most important, meaningful, and memorable relationship of the human experience.

Make your children a priority, be a parent, nourish a sense of order and structure, and of course, love them.

I wish you joy and rewards.

HELP ORGANIZATIONS

Many organizations, some with toll-free 800 phone numbers, provide helpful information, among them:

Drugs Hotlines
1-800-COCAINE (toll-free): This is the National Drug Abuse Hotline, a confidential, drug abuse treatment, referral (including local referral), and information service. Provides help for drug abusers and other concerned individuals.

National Institute on Drug Abuse: P.O. Box 2305, Rockville, MD 20852. Telephone same as above.

Alcohol
Alcoholics Anonymous: General Service Board, New York, NY 10016

Alcoholics Anonymous is an international fellowship of men and women who share the common problem of alcoholism. Family members of alcoholics can receive help through groups associated with Alcoholics Anonymous, mainly Al-Anon and Al-Ateen. Al-Ateen, Al-Anon Family Group Headquarters, P.O. Box 182, New York, NY 10159-0182. Local Al-Ateen chapters are listed in some telephone directories, or contact a local Al-Anon group for more information.

National Clearinghouse for Alcohol Information (NCAI): P.O. Box 2345, Rockville, MD 20852, (301) 468-2600.

NCAI is a service of the National Institute of Alcohol Abuse and Alcoholism. The clearinghouse collects worldwide information on studies and programs pertaining to prevention, training, treatment, and research aspects of alcohol abuse and alcoholism and shares this knowledge with interested professionals as well as with the general public.

Family Stress
Check the telephone directory or contact the United Way organization in your

area for the Family Services Agency nearest you. These organizations offer a variety of counseling services.

National Child Abuse Hotline: toll-free (800) 422-4453. The National Child Abuse Hotline handles crisis calls and provides information and referrals to every county in the United States. The hotline is manned by professionals holding Master's or Ph.D. degrees in psychology. The hotline, a program of Childhelp USA in Woodland Hills, California, also provides literature about child abuse prevention.

Stepfamily Association of America: 28 Allegheny Avenue, Suite 1037, Baltimore, MD 21204; (301) 823-7570. The national Stepfamily Association provides information about local chapters and issues a newsletter. Local chapters offer classes, workshops, and support groups for blended families. Some classes, workshops, and services are free.

Crisis Centers
Hotline: Crisis counseling and information available twenty-four hours a day, seven days a week: (800) 352-0386 in California; (800) 421-6353 elsewhere.

Youth Runaway

National Runaway Switchboard: (800) 621-4000. For the name of a runaway or teen crisis shelter in your area, write: National Youth Work Alliance, 1346 Connecticut Ave., N.W., Washington DC 20036

Suicide Prevention
Almost every state has one or more suicide hotlines and suicide prevention centers. Check with your local phone operator for the hotline number in your area.

Family Support
Big Brothers/Big Sisters of America: 230 N. 13th St., Philadelphia, PA 19107; (215) 567-2748. Families under stress and single parents can find extra support and occasional respite from parenting responsibilities through this program. Under the direction of professionally trained staff, volunteers support families by working with children in need of additional attention and friendship. Call the national office or the local agency listed in the telephone book.

Family Service America (FSA): 11700 W. Lake Park Dr., Park Place, Milwaukee, WI 53224. FSA is a membership organization of agencies that deals with family problems serving more than a thousand communities throughout the United States and Canada. Member agencies serve families and individuals through counseling, advocacy, and family life education.

National Coalition Against Domestic Violence: 2401 Virginia Ave., N.W., Suite 305, Washington, DC 20037, (202) 293-8860. The coalition is a membership organization composed of independently operated shelters for battered women and their families as well as individuals. To locate a shelter in your area, contact the coalition in Washington, DC.

Parents Anonymous (P.A.): P.A. is a self-help program for parents under stress and for abused children. There are no fees, and no one is required to reveal his or her name. Group members support and encourage each other in searching out positive alternatives to the abusive behavior in their lives. To locate a P.A. in your area, call toll-free: out of California (800) 421-0353; in California (800) 352-0386.

Adults Molested As Children United (AMACU): P.O. Box 952, San Jose, CA 95108, (408) 280-5055. Parents United developed AMACU, a self-help program for adults who were sexually abused as children. Members work through weekly therapy groups to resolve the problems and conflicts that the sexual abuse has caused in their lives. To find a local AMACU group, or for referrals to local sexual abuse treatment specialists, contact the office in San Jose.

The National Center for Missing and Exploited Children: 1835 K Street, N.W., Suite 700, Washington, DC 20006, (202) 634-9821. The center assists families, citizens' groups, law enforcement agencies, and governmental institutions. The center also has a toll-free number for reporting information that could lead to the location and recovery of a missing child. The number is (800) 843-5678.

SUGGESTED READING

Ackoff, Russell. *The Art of Problem Solving.* New York: John Wiley and Sons, 1978.

Anderson, Eugene; Tedman, George; and Rogers, Charlotte. *Self-Esteem for Tots to Teens.* New York: Meadowbrook/Simon and Schuster, 1984.

Anglund, Joan Walsh. *A Friend Is Someone Who Likes You.* New York: Hartcourt and Brace, 1985.

Axline, Virginia M. *Dibs: In Search of Self.* New York: Ballantine, 1967.

Barksdale, Lilburn S. *Essays on Self-Esteem.* Idyllwild, CA: The Barksdale Foundation, 1977.

Baron, Jason D. *Kids and Drugs.* New York: Putnam, 1983.

Bedley, Gene. *The ABCDs of Discipline.* Irvine, CA: People-Wise Publications, 1979.

Bennett, William. *Schools without Drugs.* Washington, D.C.: U.S. Department of Education, 1989.

Bergstrom, Carol. *Losing Your Best Friend: Losing Friendship.* New York: Human Science Press, 1984.

Berne, Eric, MD. *What Do You Say After You Say Hello?* New York: Grove Press, 1971.

Berne, Patricia and Savary, Louis. *Building Self-Esteem in Children.* New York: Continuum, 1989.

Bessell, Harold and Kelly, Thomas, Jr. *The Parent Book.* Rolling Hills Estate, CA: Jalmar Press, 1977.

Bingham, Mindy; Edmondson, Judy; and Stryker, Sandy. *Choices: A Teen Man's Journal for Self-Awareness and Personal Planning.* El Toro, CA: Mission Publications, 1985.

Blume, Judy. *Are You There, God? It's Me, Margaret.* New York: Dell, 1970.

———. *Then Again, Maybe I Won't.* New York: Dell, 1971.

Booraem, Curtis: Flowers, John; and Schwartz, Bernard. *Help Your Children Be Self-Confident.* Englewood Cliffs, NJ: Prentice-Hall, 1978.

Borba, Michelle. *Esteem Builders.* Rolling Hills Estate, CA: Jalmar Press, 1989.

Bradley, Ben. *Where Do I Belong? A Kid's Guide to Stepfamilies*. Reading, MA: Addison-Wesley, 1982.

Branden, Nathaniel. *Psychology of Self-Esteem*. Los Angeles: Bantam, Nash, 1969.

———. *What Is Self-Esteem?* Asker, Norway: First International Conference on Self-Esteem, August 1990.

Briggs, Dorothy Corkille. *Celebrate Yourself.* Garden City, NY: Doubleday, 1977.

———. *Your Child's Self-Esteem*. New York: Dolphin, Doubleday, 1975.

Brookover, William. *Self-Concept of Ability and School Achievement*. East Lansing, MI: Office of Research and Public Information, Michigan State University, 1965.

Buntman, Peter H. *How to Live with Your Teenager*. New York: Ballantine, 1979.

Buscaglia, Leo. *Living, Loving and Learning*. Thorofare, NJ: Charles B. Slack, 1982.

———. *Love.* Thorofare, NJ: Charles B. Slack, 1972.

Cetron, Marvin. *Schools of the Future.* New York: McGraw Hill, 1985.

"Children Having Children: Teen Pregnancy in America." *Time.* December 9, 1985. pp. 78–90.

Clems, Harris and Bean, Reynold. *Self-Esteem: The Key to Your Child's Well-Being.* New York: Putnam, 1981.

Coopersmith, Stanley. *The Antecedents of Self-Esteem.* San Francisco: W. H. Freeman, 1967.

Cretcher, Dorothy. *Steering Clear.* Minneapolis: Winston, 1982.

Crockenberg, Susan and Soby, Barbara. "Self-Esteem and Teenage Pregnancy," *The Social Importance of Self-Esteem*. Berkeley: U.C. Press, 1989.

Crow, Lester and Crow, Alice. *How to Study.* New York: Collier, 1980.

Curran, Dolores. *Traits of a Healthy Family.* Minneapolis: Winston, 1983.

Danziger, Paula. *The Cat Ate My Gymsuit.* New York: Dell, 1973.

Davitz, Lois and Joe. *How to Live Almost Happily with Your Teenagers.* Minneapolis: Winston, 1982.

"Do You Know What Your Children Are Listening To?" *U.S. News & World Report.* October 28, 1985.

Dobson, James. *Preparing for Adolescence.* Santa Ana, CA: Vision House, 1978.

Dodson, Dr. Fitzhugh. *How to Discipline with Love.* New York: Rawson Associates, 1977.

Dreikurs, Rudolf, MD. *Children: The Challenge.* New York: Hawthorn, 1964.

Drew, Naomi. *Learning the Skills of Peacemaking.* Rolling Hills Estate, CA: Jalmar Press, 1987.

Dyer, Wayne. *What Do You Really Want for Your Children?* New York: William Morrow, 1985.

Earle, Janice. *Female Dropouts: A New Perspective.* Alexandria, VA: National Association of State Boards of Education, 1987.

Elkind, David. *All Grown Up and No Place to Go.* Reading, MA: Addison-Wesley, 1984.

"Family Fitness: A Complete Exercise Program for Ages Six to Sixty-Plus." *Reader's Digest* (Special Report). 1987. p. 2–12.

Feingold, Norman S. and Miller, Nora Reno. *Emerging Careers: New Occupations for the Year 2000 and Beyond.* Maryland: Garrett Park Press, 1989.

Fensterheim, Herbert. *Don't Say Yes When You Want to Say No.* New York: Dell, 1975.

Fox, Lynn and Lavin-Weaver, F. *Unlocking Doors to Self-Esteem.* Rolling Hills Estate, CA: Jalmar Press, 1983.

Freed, Alvin. *TA for Tots.* Rolling Hills Estate, CA: Jalmar Press, 1976.

Freed, Alvin and Freed, Margaret. *TA for Kids.* Rolling Hills Estate, CA: Jalmar Press, 1977.

Fromm, Erich. *The Art of Loving.* New York: Bantam, 1963.

Fugitt, Eva D. *He Hit Me Back First!* Rolling Hills Estate, CA: Jalmar Press, 1983.

Gardner, James E. *The Turbulent Teens.* Los Angeles: Sorrento Press, 1983.

Gardner, Richard. *The Boys and Girls Book about Stepfamilies.* New York: Bantam, 1982.

Getzoff, Ann and McClenahan, Carolyn. *StepKids: A Survival Guide for Teenagers in Stepfamilies.* New York: Walker, 1984.

Ginott, Haim. *Teacher and Child.* New York: Avon, 1972.

Glasser, William. *Schools without Failure.* New York: Harper and Row, 1969.

Gomes-Schwartz, B. "Child Sexual Abuse: The Initial Effects." *Library of Social Research,* Vol. 179, 1990.

Gordon, Thomas. *Parent Effectiveness Training.* New York: Peter H. Wyden, 1974.

Greenberg, Polly. *I Know I'm Myself Because . . .* New York: Human Science Press, 1988.

Harris, Thomas A., M.D. *I'm OK—You're OK.* New York: Avon, 1967.

"Has Rock Gone Too Far?" *People* magazine. September 16, 1985. pp. 47–53.

Haynes-Klassen. *Learning to Live, Learning to Love.* Rolling Hills Estate, CA: Jalmar Press, 1985.

Holly, William. "Self-Esteem: Does It Contribute to Students' Academic Success?" Oregon School Study Council, University of Oregon, 1987.

Holt, John. *How Children Learn.* New York: Delta, 1967.

Hyde, Margaret O. *Parents Divided, Parents Multiplied.* Louisville, KY: Westminster/John Knox Press, 1989.

James, Muriel and Jongeward, Dorothy. *Born to Win.* Menlo Park, CA: Addison-Wesley, 1971.

Jampolsky, Gerald G., M.D. *Teach Only Love.* New York: Bantam, 1983.

Johnson, David W. and Johnson, Roger T. *Learning Together and Alone: Cooperative, Competitive and Individualistic Learning,* 4th ed. Englewood Cliffs, NJ: Prentice-Hall, 1987.

Kalb, Jonah and Viscott, David, M.D. *What Every Kid Should Know.* Boston: Houghton Mifflin, 1974.

Kaufman, Roger. *Identifying and Solving Problems: A System Approach.* San Diego: University Associates, 1989.

Keegan, Andrew. "Positive Self-Image—A Cornerstone of Success," *Guidepost.* February 19, 1987.

Kehegan, V. Alex. *SAGE: Self-Awareness Growth Experiences.* Rolling Hills Estates, CA: Jalmar Press, 1989.

Keirsey, David and Bates, Marilyn. *Please Understand Me.* Del Mar, CA: Prometheus Nemesis, 1978.

"Kids and Cocaine: An Epidemic Strikes Middle America." *Newsweek.* March 17, 1986. pp 58–63.

Kirst, Michael. *Conditions of Children in California.* Policy Analysis for California Education (PACE). California: U.C. Berkeley, 1990.

Knight, Michael E.; Graham, Terry Lynne; Juliano, Rose A.; Miksza, Susan Robichaud; Tonnies, Pamela G. *Teaching Children to Love Themselves.* Englewood Cliffs, NJ: Prentice-Hall, 1982.

Kohen-Raz, Reuven. *The Child from Nine to Thirteen.* Chicago: Aldine Adterton, 1971.

Kohlberg, Lawrence and Gilligan, C. *"The Adolescent as Philosopher: The Discovery of Self in a Postconventional World,"* Daedalus 100 (4), 1971.

Kreidler, William. *Creative Conflict Resolution: More Than Two Hundred Activities for Keeping Peace in the Classroom.* Glenview, IL: Scott, Foresman, 1984.

Lansky, Doug and Dorfman, Aaron. *How to Survive High School with Minimal Brain Damage.* Minneapolis: Meadowbrook, 1989.

Lewis, David and Greene, James. *Thinking Better.* New York: Rawson, Wade, 1982.

Lorayne, Harry and Lucas, Jerry. *The Memory Book.* New York: Stein and Day, 1974.

Kuczen, Barbara. *Childhood Stress.* New York: Delacorte Press, 1982.

Maslow, Abraham. *Toward a Psychology of Being.* New York: D. Van Nostrand, 1962.

McCabe, Margaret E. *The Public High School in the Year 2010: A National Delphi Study.* Dissertation. La Verne, CA: University of La Verne, 1983.

McCabe, Margaret E. and Rhoades, Jacqueline. *How to Say What You Mean.* California: ITA Publications, 1985.

McCullough, Charles and Mann, Robert. *Managing Your Anxiety.* Los Angeles: Tarcher/St. Martin's Press, 1985.

Miller, Gordon Porter and Oskam, Bob. *Teaching Your Child to Make Decisions.* New York: Harper & Row, 1984.

Montessori, Maria. *The Discovery of the Child.* Notre Dame, IN: Fides, 1967.

Naisbitt, John. *Megatrends.* New York: Warner, 1982.

Newman, Mildred and Berkowitz, Bernard. *How to Be Your Own Best Friend.* New York: Random House, 1973.

Neufeld, John. *Lisa, Bright and Dark.* New York: S.G. Phillips, 1969.

Palmer, Pat. *Liking Myself.* San Luis Obispo, CA: Impact, 1977.

————. *The Mouse, the Monster, and Me.* San Luis Obispo, CA: Impact, 1977.

Peale, Norman Vincent. *You Can If You Think You Can.* Pawling, NY: Foundation for Christian Living, 1974.

Pelletier, Kenneth. *Mind as Healer, Mind as Slayer.* New York: Delacorte Press, 1977.

Postman, Neil. *The Disappearance of Childhood.* New York: Delacorte Press, 1982.

Richards, Arlene Kramer and William, Irene. *Boy Friends, Girl Friends, Just Friends.* New York: Atheneum, 1979.

Samples, Bob. *Openmind/Wholemind.* Rolling Hills Estate, CA: Jalmar Press, 1987.

Sanderson, Jim. *How to Raise Your Kids to Stand on Their Own Two Feet.* Congdon and Weed, 1978.

Satir, Virginia. *Peoplemaking.* Palo Alto, CA: Science and Behavior Books, 1972.

Schuller, Robert Charles. *Self-Esteem: The New Reformation.* Waco, TX: Word Books, 1982.

Schriner, Christian. *Feel Better Now.* Rolling Hills Estate, CA: Jalmar Press, 1990.

Sexton, Thomas G. and Poling, Donald R. *Can Intelligence Be Taught?* Bloomingdale, IN: Phi Delta Kappa Educational Foundation, 1973.

Sheehy, Gail. *Pathfinders.* New York: Morrow, 1981.

Sheinkin, David. *Food, Mind and Mood.* New York: Warner, 1980.

Shles, Larry. *Aliens in My Nest.* Rolling Hills Estate, CA: Jalmar Press, 1988.

————. *Do I Have to Go to School Today?* Rolling Hills Estate, CA: Jalmar Press, 1989.

————. *Hugs and Shrugs.* Rolling Hills Estate, CA: Jalmar Press, 1987.

————. *Hoots and Toots and Hairy Brutes.* Rolling Hills Estate, CA: Jalmar Press, 1989.

————. *Moths and Mothers/Feathers and Fathers.* Rolling Hills Estate, CA: Jalmar Press, 1989.

Silberstein, William. *Helping Your Child Grow Slim.* New York: Simon and Schuster, 1982.

Simpson, Bert K. *Becoming Aware of Values.* La Mesa, CA: Pennant Press, 1973.

Skager, Rodney. *Prevention of Drug and Alcohol Abuse.* Sacramento: California Attorney General's Office, 1988.

Skoguland, Elizabeth R. *To Anger With Love.* New York: Harper and Row, 1977.

Smith, Manuel J. *When I Say No I Feel Guilty.* New York: Bantam, 1975.

Stainback, William and Stainback, Susan. *How to Help Your Child Succeed in School.* Minneapolis: Meadowbrook, 1988.

Steffenhagen, R. A. and Burns, Jeff D. *The Social Dynamics of Self-Esteem.* New York: Praeger, 1987.

Steiner, Claude. *Original Warm Fuzzy Tale.* Rolling Hills Estate, CA: Jalmar Press, 1977.

"Teenage Fathers." *Psychology Today.* December, 1985, pp. 66–70.

Viscott, David, M.D. *The Language of Feelings.* New York: Pocket Books, 1976.

Vitale, Barbara M. *Free Flight.* Rolling Hills Estate, CA: Jalmar Press, 1986.

———. *Unicorns Are Real.* Rolling Hills Estate, CA: Jalmar Press, 1982.

Wahlross, Sven. *Family Communication.* New York: Macmillan, 1974.

Warren, Neil Clark. *Make Anger Your Ally.* Garden City, NY: Doubleday, 1983.

Wassmer, Arthur C. *Making Contact.* New York: Dial Press, 1978.

Whitely, John. *Moral Character Development of College Students.* Irvine, CA: U.C. Irvine, 1980.

Wilson, John. "Motivation, Modeling, and Altruism." *Journal of Personality and Social Psychology,* Vol. 34, December 1976.

Winn, Marie. *Children Without Childhood.* New York: Pantheon, 1981.

Winter, Arthur, M.D., and Winter, Ruth. *Build Your Brain Power.* New York: St. Martin's Press, 1986.

Wright, Esther. *Good Morning Class—I Love You!* Rolling Hills Estate, CA: Jalmar Press, 1989.

Wyckoff, Jerry and Unell, Barbara. *Discipline without Shouting or Spanking.* Minneapolis: Meadowbrook, 1988.

Young, Elaine. *I Am a Blade of Grass.* Rolling Hills Estate, CA: Jalmar Press, 1989.

Youngs, Bettie B. *Friendship Is Forever, Isn't It?* San Diego: Learning Tools, 1990.

———. *Goal Setting Skills for Young People.* San Diego: Learning Tools, 1989.

———. *Helping Your Teenager Deal with Stress.* Low Angeles: Tarcher/St. Martin's Press, 1986.

———. *Problem Solving Skills for Children.* San Diego: Learning Tools, 1989.

———. *Stress in Children: How to Recognize, Avoid and Overcome It.* New York: Avon, 1985.

———. *A Stress Management Guide for Young People.* San Diego: Learning Tools, 1988.

Youngs, Bettie B., and Tracy, B. *Achievement, Happiness, Popularity and Success.* San Diego: Learning Tools, 1988.

INDEX

About the Author

BETTIE B. YOUNGS, Ph.D., Ed.D., is an international lecturer, author, counselor, and consultant. Her work has spanned more than sixty countries for more than two decades, earning her a reputation as a respected authority in the field of personal and professional effectiveness. She is the author of fourteen books, which have been translated into sixteen languages, as well as a number of audiocassette programs.